CAMDEN COUNTY
NEW JERSEY
MARRIAGES

Records Filed in the Office of the
County Clerk

Alphabetically Arranged by
H. STANLEY CRAIG

H. STANLEY CRAIG, *Publisher*
MERCHANTVILLE, N. J.

Southern Historical Press, Inc.
Greenville, South Carolina

This volume was reproduced from
An 1932 edition located in the
Publisher's private Library
Greenville, South Carolina

All rights reserved. No part of this publication may be reproduced,
stored in a retrieval system, transmitted in any form, posted
on to the web in any form or by any means without
the prior written permission of the publisher.

Please direct all correspondence and orders to:

www.southernhistoricalpress.com
or
SOUTHERN HISTORICAL PRESS, Inc.
PO Box 1267
375 West Broad Street
Greenville, SC   29601
southernhistoricalpress@gmail.com

Originally published: Merchantville, NJ, 1932
Copyright 1932 by H. Stanley Craig
ISBN #0-89308-303-8
All rights Reserved.
Printed in the United States of America

CAMDEN COUNTY MARRIAGES

BOOK A

Abel, Thomas—Sarah Homan, 6-18-1854.
Aborn, Henry—Elizabeth Roller, 1-17-1848.
Achuff, J. Newton, New York—Maria Roop, Germantown, Pa., 4-10-1864.
Ackerman, Clinton M.—Mary C. Shick, 1-29-1863.
Ackley, Charles—Rachel Madkiff, 6-3-1846.
  Henry—Sallie A. Wilkins, 9-20-1864.
Adams, George—Deborah Perce, 2-20-1864.
  John—Anna Shreve, 12-31-1854.
  Mark A., Jr.—Hannah Ireland, both Atlantic co., 11-4-1854.
  Richard—Rebecca L. Brown, 1-5-1853.
  Thomas—Hannah Hutton, Newcastle, Del., 8-22-1854.
  William—Eliza J. Jones, 5-21-1851.
  William H., Sussex co., Del.—Sarah Dialogue (d. Adam), 12-17-1856.
Albertson, Thomas H.—Mary Jane Brown, 1-10-1847.
Aldrich, Wm.—Rachel M. Cox, 4-22-1847.
Alenbart, Charles—Ann Gray, 10-11-1845.
Allen, Burret W—Elizabeth Thorn, 12-23-1844.
  Isaac—Sarah Williams, 3-22-1846.
  John B.—Sarah A. Wilson, both Trenton, 7-24-1853.
  Kimsey C.—Susan Ruth Ann Biswick, 10-23-1858.
  Samuel D.—Julia A. Parker, 9-13-1844.
Allibone, Thomas R.—Margaret Smith, both Philadelphia, 2-1-1866.

CAMDEN COUNTY MARRIAGES—BOOK A

Allington, Israel W.—Sarah Besser, 2-7-1848.
Allnutt, James—Catharine Dolton, 5-12-1852.
Amon, Joseph H.—Mary H. Stow, 1-8-1852.
Anderson Charles F.—Georgianna Hamilton, 6-30-1864.
  George W.—Theressa Tate, 8-10-1862.
  John—Mary Anneny, 9-30-1854.
  John W.—Sarah M. Stratton, 2-1-1855.
  John W. T.—Elizabeth Brown, 7-24-1865.
  Paul, Glassboro—Rachel Watson, 4-29-1866.
  Samuel C.—Amelia Broadwater, 8-27-1854.
  William—Mary Elizabetn Harvey, 8-4-1861.
  William R.—Mary Ellinor Bats, 11-27-1865.
Andrews, John—Elizabeth Cassady, 6-15-1850.
Aneson, John H.—Mary Mouton, 11-16-1850.
Angelow, John C.—Hannah H. Jaggers, 3-6-1865.
Anindale, Merrick—Catharine Martin, Trenton, 4-27-1864.
Archer, Benjamin F.—Mary Sloan, 7-6-1865.
Ard, Edward—Mary Garety, 3-29-1852.
Armstrong, Charles F.—Margaret Smith 1-1-1852.
  Isaac—Susan Ann Cox, 12-23-1858.
Arndt, Ralph S.—Sarah W. King, 2-12-1856.
Arnold, John C.—Amanda Richman, 12-26-1863.
Arthur, David—Sarah Ann Mann, Woodbury, 11-27-1845.
Ash, Samuel K.—Martha Jane Munshover, 6-6-1863.
Ashley, A. G. M.—Caroline Haas, 7-26-1865.
Atkinson, Amasa—Kate Parker, Philadelphia, 12-27-1855.
  Moses D.—Mary R. Lashley, 3-9-1854.
Augustus, Peter Theodore—Sarah Victoria Brown, 2-19-1860.
Auld, James—Jane Moore, 7-26-1844.
Austin, John C.—Margaret Lee, 3-23-1865.
Ayres, Charles S.—Tabitha H. Braker, 11-16-1856.
  Ephraim S.—Priscilla S. Lock, 4-5-1860.
  George H.—Matilda H. Marshall, 8-4-1855.
Bacon, Smith—Jane W Hires, 12-8-1858.
Badaley, Joseph—Ann Givens, both Turnerville, 7-5-1853.
Bailey, John W.—Sarah Elizabeth Lemons, 9-2-1862.

Baird, James F.—Susan Witheat, 7-8-1863.
Baker, Ellis—Jane Ann Smith, 2-18-1845.
  John—Jane A. Madciff, 8-13-1862.
  William V.—Elizabeth Risley, 10-23-1851.
Bakley, John—Mrs. Rebecca Petit, 8-8-1844.
Banard, Frances—Ann Elizabeth Williams, 4-29-1862.
Benks, Nathan C.—Margaret Risley, 12-9-1862.
Bankson, Mark—Rebecca Brown (colored), 3-1-1845.
Barbaht, Edward—Elizabeth B. Denny, 5-24-1847.
Bareford, Mark—Sarah Hooper, 11-16-1858.
Barnet, Edward—Elizabeth Bennett, 12-20-1864.
Barr, Robert P.—Ann Warner, 3-24-1851.
Barret, Chas. M.—Mary Ann Knight, both Glou. co., 3-31-1857
  Daniel P.—Maria Craig, 12-20-1851.
  James—Ann Webb, 11-2-1847.
  Joseph H.—Louisa Beetle, 5-20-1854.
  Samuel—Frances Ann Anderson, 9-12-1854.
Barryman, George—Eliza Ann Wilson, 1-24-1852.
  John—Bridget VanWiggin, 10-26-1853.
Barth, Nicholas—Elizabeth Bozorth, 7-10-1859.
Batcheler, Benjamin—Ann Toy, 12-10-1856.
Bateman Theophilus—Ann Alkire, Nov., 1844.
Bates, Hiram—Amy Tucker, 6-20-1858.
  John—Annie E. Bates, 10-9-1864.
  John R.—Hannah Stafford, 12-2-1867.
  Joseph E.—Ann Eliza Smith, 3-6-1846.
  Micajah—Emeline Bodine, 5-5-1858.
  Thomas P.—Anna Silver, 7-14-1866.
Batten, Albert—Elizabeth Curtis, 2-8-1862.
  Washington G.—Elizabeth Cheesman, 2-6-1851.
  William—Caroline H. Arnold, Clarksboro, 1-14-1850.
Batts, George—Sarah Berry, 10-9-1847.
  John—Sarah Bishop, 8-22-1847.
Beaston, Samuel—Matilda Knowlton, 3-18-1856.
Bebe, Lenard—Mary Dare, 12-27-1845.
Bechtell, William H.—Keziah H. Pancoast, 5-13-1852.
Beck, Alexander—Elizabeth Whiteside, 12-22-1847.

    John R.—Emma C. Wicks, 8-22-1859.
Becket, Adolphus—Abigail Bozorth, 7-31-1846.
Beckett, Benj. F.—Hannah A. Grace, Dennisville, 7-3-1862.
    Harry C.—Elizabeth M. Beckett, 5-11-1865.
    Lewis—Elizabeth Fisher, 6-20-1848.
    Reeve R.—Elizabeth Ann Hewitt, both Gloucester co., 2-6-1862.
Beckley, Marmaduke—Sarah Risley, 1-5-1845.
Beebe, Charles—Sarah Cambridge, 1-5-1866.
    Ephraim, Salem—Mary Collins, Millville, 1-2-1865.
    Lewis—Emma Cossaboon, 6-27-1853.
Beechey, Alfred, Philadelphia—Sophia C. Tice, Williamstown, 9-26-1858.
Beetle, James—Sarah B. Endslow, 1-14-1858.
    William B.—Mary Jane Higgins, 6-25-1861.
Bell, Thomas—Sarah Porch, 5-4-1849.
Belson, William—Mary G. Bloom, 9-6-1844.
Bender, Henry S.—Cecelia Browning, 9-24-1845.
    John—Elizabeth Gregory, 8-22-1844.
    Robert S.—Jane McCowan, 11-4-1855.
Bendler, Joseph—Elizabeth Beckley, 6-13-1844.
Bennet, Calhoun—Mary M. Williams, 1-2-1851.
    Charles—Martha Owen, 8-7-1852.
Bennett, Charles—Keziah Bennett, 3-1-1846.
    Henry R.—Margaret Camp, 9-4-1856.
    Joel H.—Rebecca M. Wells, 1-25-1866.
    William—Whilhelmina Steubear, both Philadelphia, 1-1-1866.
Berkenstock, John T.—Louisa R. Reutykeing, 5-20-1855.
Berry, Andrew—Lewizer Jones, 7-5-1845.
    James M., Philadelphia—Sarah A. Hickman, 11-26-1845.
    Joseph, Sr.—Phebe Ann Moore, 4-9-1853.
    Thomas—Martha Ann Hewitt, 7-18-1844.
    William A.—Rebecca A. Craver, 3-18-1852.
Berryman, Charles H.—Sarah Queen, 4-29-1863.
    John M. P. (s. Charles and Susan A.)—Mary A. Christy (d. Benjamin F. and Lydia), 5-19-1866.

Betchey, David L.—Mary Hullings, 7-20-1856.
Betts, Achilles—Eleanor Stocup, 1-20-1850.
Biber, Philip A.—Anna F. Bozarth, 7-19-1846.
Biddle, Charles—Mary Duffle, 12-8-1845.
  Thomas Lemuel—Susan Seeds, 8-24-1865.
Bideeman, Thomas—Hannah Ann Plum, 12-13-1855.
Binsall, Henry S.—Deborah A. Brown, 4-16-1854.
Bird, Elisha P.—Martha J. Neiplin, 10-7-1863.
  Nathaniel J.—Jane Pierpont, 9-12-1853.
Bishop, Albert—Annie McCormick, both Philadelphia, 7-20-1863.
  Charles—Mary C. Corson, 7-20-1850.
  Charles E.—Mary E. Cordon, 7-30-1850.
  James—Mary J. Cobb, 4-15-1853.
  Theodore—Harriet Davis, 1-16-1845.
Bittle, George C.—Sarah C. Bishop, 6-15-1862.
Blake, James—Ellen Jones (colored), 4-19-1845.
Blaker, Adam, Philadelphia—Emma Jess, 8-7-1858.
Blakesly, Joel—Ann Turner, 5-22-1847.
Bleakley, Micage—Catharine Bendler, 9-24-1850.
Bodine, Daniel—Elizabeth Paff, 12-31-1851.
  John—Emeline Kellum, 5-3-1861.
  John F.—Martha Swope, 9-14-1844.
Boggs, Isaac—Sarah Gilmore, 3-10-1854.
Bogue, Charles—Deborah Williams, 6-10-1858.
Boiles, John C.—Mary Ann Woodington, 3-15-1858.
Bois, Nathan, Philadelphia—Mary Adams, Atlantic co., 12-27-1846.
Bolt, Morris L. H., Philadelphia—Marietta H. Loring, Gloucester co , 1-1-1847.
Boone, Edward A.—Margaret Griffee, 8-2-1837.
Booth, John P.—Sidney Mary Parry, 7-3-1853.
Bottomley, Thomas—Catharine Barrett, 1-1-1854.
Bourguin, Gordon M.—Kate Radcliffe, 6-8-1863.
Bowditch, George—Laura Holmes, 5-20-1852.
Bowen, Joseph—Matilda Fortner, 10-4-1850.
Boyd, David—Ellen Belles, 11-26-1856.

8 CAMDEN COUNTY MARRIAGES—BOOK A

Bezorth, Thomas—Mary Ann Orr, 8-9-1853.
  William—Sarah Burdsall, 6-30-1847.
  William—Ann Eliza Risley, 1-16-1851.
Bradbury, Ralph, Philadelphia—Caroline Lodge (d. Fleetwood and Mary), 3-1-1855.
Braddock, George E.—Eliza E. Cheesman, 5-19-1844.
Bradford, Francis—Mary Ann McMahon, 12-16-1855.
Bradshaw, Claudius—Eliza Jane Marks, 12-25-1858; also recorded as 1-30-1859.
Bradway, Thomas D.—Sallie E. Miller, Salem, 3-28-1860.
Brady, Joseph—Mary Ann Logan, 11-24-1859.
Brage, Andrew—Ann Moss, 4-14-1855.
Brayne, David, Salem co.—Mary Cowperthwaite, 5-2-1852.
Brennsholtz, Jacob—Priscilla Dennis, 10-27-1860.
Brewster, Joel—Rebecca Williams, 12-25-1859.
Breyer, Lawrence—Margaret Frick, 6-10-1855.
Brick, Samuel F.—Caroline R. Clark, 4-6-1848.
Bright, Elias, Pennsville—Lydia W. Hutchinson, 8-7-1865.
Broadwater, Robert James—Mary Elizabeth McCloud, 6-16-1853.
Brock, Charles—Sarah M. Glenn, both Trenton, 6-25-1853.
Brockington, John H.—Mary Amanda Fish, 8-3-1862.
Broome, Jonathan, New York—Emma D. Mulford, 2-15-1859.
Brown, Caleb—Rachel Williamson, 3-6-1852.
  Charles—Elizabeth Shinn, 7-8-1845.
  Charles—Hepziba Barton, 8-15-1850.
  Charles, Swedesboro—Sarah J. Powell, 7-27-1865.
  Clayton—Sallie L. Kates, 1-31-1864.
  George—Frances Carey, 9-13-1864.
  George H.—Anna Shields, 9-9-1854.
  Henry—Rachel Calloway, 12-24-1857.
  Henry L.—Sarah J. Bennett, 7-5-1856.
  John—Margaret Smith (colored), 3-20-1847.
  John—Hester Ann Holcombe, Washington twp., 12-18-1852.
  John, Plainfield—Hannah E. R. Francis, Newark, 5-6-1861.
  John P.—Margaret M. Scott, 12-5-1858.

CAMDEN COUNTY MARRIAGES—BOOK A 9

Brown, John S., Burlington—Hannah Ann Horner, 3-18-1850.
  Joseph—Matilda Fortner, 10-4-1850.
  Peter V.—Julia Stoops, 8-22-1858.
  Richard—Sarah Mall, 11-29-1845
  Samuel—Hannah Draper, 7-1-1855.
  Thomas P.—Mary Bachelor, 8-19-1851.
  Tites A.—Elizabeth Anna Bella Henry, 8-4-1859.
  Valentine—Maria A. Bender, 9-26-1858.
  William H.—Hannah Ann Taylor, both Elsinborough, 9-20-1854.
Browning, Edward—Ketura Johnson, 9-2-1858.
  Eli (s. John and Elizabeth)—Sarah Ann Marshall (d. Robert and Sarah), 6-1-1848.
  Joshua P.—Rebecca Browning, 6-25-1857.
  William R. (s. John and Ann)—Mary Burrough (d. Reuben and Mary), 4-27-1848.
Bronson, V. W.—Lydia A. C. Shepard, 9-25-1859.
Brunshultz, Andrew Davis—Catherine Aides, 3-26-1855.
Bryant, Isaac, Jr.—Sarah Sedman (wid.), 3-11-1847.
Buck, David—Ruth Brown, 12-24-1855.
Budd, John—Sarah G. Sayres, 11-17-1845.
  Joshua—Mary E. Smith, 3-31-1863.
Burdsall, Joseph—Mary Ann Wilkins, 10-10-1849.
  Samuel, Jr.—Isabella Tilton, 9-16-1855.
Burk, Thomas—Lydia Reynolds, 3-28-1845.
Burkett, John—Sarah F. Roseman, 9-6-1866.
Burns, James, Burlington co.—Mary Moon, 8-10-1852.
Burr, Mamre G.—Elizabeth Frances Ha.vey, 12-7-1854.
  Samuel E.—Moorestown—Sarah E. Richardson, 11-5-1858.
Burrough Benjamin, Philadelphia—Elizabeth Ireland, 11-6-1845.
  James (s. Reuben and Mary)—Elizabeth L. Pine (d. Daniel and Margaret), 2-28-1850.
Bury, Joseph—Agnes A. Chew, 1-1-1857.
Busby, John—Abigail Emeline Holmes, both Essex co., 2-4-1852.

CAMDEN COUNTY MARRIAGES—BOOK A

Butcher, Morris, Burlington—Sarah Morris, 9-21-1846.
  William A.—Amanda Hatfield, 2-8-1865.
Butler, Jacob—Hannah Maria Young, 7-6-1850.
  Peter C.—Rebecca Wood, 2-10-1865.
Button, John—Mary Ann Ross, 1-1-1848.
Byard, Ezekiel—Sarah M. Stokeley, 6-12-1862.
Byrnes, John, Moorestown—Sallie M. Reed, 12-25-1863.
  Peter—Catharine Walsh, 3-4-1851.
Cade, Thomas J.—Beulah Giberson, 7-3-1854.
Cain, Ziba—Margaret Cook, 5-11-1854.
Calloway, Philip P.—Naomi Watson, 7-19-1862.
Calvert, James—Martha Hemming, 4-7-1851.
  Thomas—Mary Jane Holmes, 7-1-1855.
Campbell, Neal—Jane Wilson, 9-23-1855.
  Walter C.—Rebecca Haines, 1-28-1850.
Cann, Davis—Christiana Savorns, 7-28-1854.
Cannon, James—Matilda Ann Smith, 5-20-1858.
Carels, Edmond—Abbie Cook, 7-22-1866.
Carhart, Samuel, Jr., Philadelphia—Mary A. Wood, Mullica Hill 1-1-1852.
Carman, Henry H.—Catharine S. Hill, 12-25-1849.
Carney, William—Caroline Kelley, Burlington co., 9-2-1854.
Carpenter, George W., Jr.—Elizabeth C. Vanhorn, 10-7-1862.
Carslo, Samuel—Hannah Mulford, 10-1-1859.
Carter, Benjamin F., Woodbury—Elizabeth M. Reeves, 10-26-1854.
  Carney—Elizabeth Falkenburgh, 9-9-1854.
  Charles S.—Martha Andrews, Washington twp., 11-18-1852.
  George W.—Mrs. Sarah Ann Hugg, 9-30-1855.
  Jesse—Isabella Conagam, 1-15-1846.
  Thomas J.—Mary J. Elwell, Philadelphia, 7-12-1855.
Cathcart, Benjamin—Mary C. Vansciver, 3-12-1856.
  Samuel, Philadelphia—Mary A. Wood, Mullica Hill, 1-1-1852.
Cattell, Theodore—Caroline A. Mapes, 1-17-1864.
  William S. (s. John)—Mary McClure, 1-14-1858.

Challiss, Joseph—Emeline Kay, 10-26-1848.
Chamberlain, George W.—Hannah A. Webb, 7-25-1863.
 James—Abigail Forley, Philadelphia, 8-4-1861
Champion, Edward—Elizabeth Hickman, both Atlantic co., 9-20-1850.
 John—Cordelia M. Arnett, both Pittstown, 9-2-1865.
Chance, Isaac—Sarah Muncey, 3-8-1862.
Chapman, Joseph (s. John and Mary)—Sarah P. Hannah (d. John and Rebecca), 4-28-1853.
Cheesman, Cornelius—Mary Ann White, 10-2-1851.
 John—Ellen M. Tarkington, both Turnerville, 8-19-1865.
 Thomas J. (s Wm. and Hester)—Mary Barnes (d. William and Mary), 2-13-1864.
Chester, Samuel A.—Hester Ann Adams, 7-9-1864.
Chew, Alexander (s. John and Mary Olive)—Sarah Porch (d. Ralph and Ann), 11-2-1849.
 Aquilla D.—Amanda M. Duval, 8-12-1854.
 Edward—Mary McFarland, both Gloucester co., 1-2-1851.
 Elwood, Gloucester co.—Mary G. Keen, 9-21-1850.
 George W.—Charlotte S. Quicksell, 9-28-1856.
 Job, Gloucester co.—Caroline Z. Gant, 11-9-1865.
 Leonard—Mary C. Lock, both Gloucester co., 10-3-1850.
 Montraville— Annie C. Taylor, 9-17-1858.
 Robert—Joanna Bishop, 7-7-1858.
 Theodore—Sarah McFarland, 8-8-1850.
Chiney, Luther C.—Margaret Ann Rodman, 6-25-1847.
Chopalet, Stephen— Catharine Duffy, 3-1-1853.
Clair, William S.—Elizabeth Ann Toy, 12-25-1853.
Clark, Elisha—Ann Tice, 12-3-1857.
 James F.—Elizabeth Barrett, 2-21-1857.
 John S. (s. Elisha and Bathsheba)—Eunice Gillard (d. George and Elizabeth), 7-19-1851.
 William—Eliza Harrison, 11-7-1850.
Clavey, John—Eliza Phillips, 7-3-1853.
Clennas, Samuel—Martha Lewis, both Lancaster co., Pa. 10-1-1857.
 Clevenger, John—Roxanna Mapes, 7-22-1854.

CAMDEN COUNTY MARRIAGES—BOOK A

Clift—Powell—Catharine Clewell, 6-15-1847.
Clifton, James N.—Cecelia W. Mideleton, 9-1-1855.
Cline, Micajah—Elizabeth String, 8-6-1854.
  Silas—Hannah Jones, 2-20-1864.
  William—Mary Ann Andrews, 1-21-1850.
Clopper, George H.—Charlotte T. Beany, 6-2-1859.
Cloud, Charles—Amy Pine, 10-26-1844.
Coates, Benjamin M.—Louisa Carey, 4-26-1863.
Dobb, Francis B.—Sarah Catherine Robertson, 6-15-1862.
Cochran, George, Trenton—Margaret Meally, 8-30-1847.
Colby, Joseph—Mary A. Britten, 1-22-1853.
Cole, Reuben—Eliza R. Ellis, 9-4-1865.
  William J.—Mary Ann Hickman, 3-5-1853.
Coles, Charles B. (s. Charles and Rachel)—Mary M. Colson (d. Jonathan and Hannah P.), Gloucester co., 8-6-1865.
  Joseph M. (s. Samuel and Mary Ann)—Harriet Bateman (d. Stephen and Maria), 1-29-1851.
  Thomas (s. Samuel and Mary Ann)—Sarah A. Gilbert (d. Achilles and Hannah), 12-11-1849.
Collett, Charles F.—Elizabeth Farmington, 9-5-1862.
  George H.—Mary Huffsey, 8-8-1844.
Collier, William—Annie Hyde, both Philadelphia, 3-8-1865.
Collins, E. Bentley—Sallie A. Edwards, 3-4-1865.
  William—Elizabeth Leese, 4-3-1861.
Conklin, William H.—Lydia Ann Jones, 12-23-1857.
Conley, Benjamin—Elizabeth Lewallen, 2-10-1865.
  James—Hannah Clark, 10-22-1855.
  Joseph—Caroline Duffield, both Philadelphia, 11-16-1864.
Conlin, Dennis, Deptford—Louisa Batten, Barnsboro, 8-6-1853.
Conly—Daniel Brian (s. Oliver and Phebe)—Mary Miller (d. Isaac and Rachel), 10-5-1856.
Connelly, Andrew—Mary Feeny, Cranberry, 1-1-1860.
  Dominic—Rachel P. Horne, 8-4-1849.
Conner, Joseph Givens—Josephine Estelow, both Philadelphia, 9-7-1865.
  Orlando, Philadelphia—Josephine Hopkins, 10-7-1861.

Conohan, Hugh—Bathsheba T. Tucker, 11-4-1853.
Conover, John—Caroline Hoffman, 1-3-1855.
   Joseph—Elizabeth Craver, 5-15-1852.
Conrow, George W.—Catharine O. Barrett, 3-22-1854.
   Samuel J —Phebe Barrett, 4-21-1853.
Cook, John—Amelia Munser, 8-17-1866.
   Joseph—Eliza Ann Watson, 11-7-1847.
   William H.—Jane Barker, 5-11-1845.
Cooley, Maximilian—Mercy Lanning, 1-20-1845.
Cooper, Alexander—Hannah C. Cooper, 5-7-1845.
   Edward H., Clarksboro—Martha A. Batten, Berkley, 12-22-1864.
   Edward Waterman—Priscilla Ann Bendler, Washington twp., 10-26-1852.
   John L —Jane C. Lukens, Philadelphia, 9-8-1852.
   Joseph—Jane Mess, 12-19-1854.
   Richard S.—Elizabeth P. Dermott, 10-31-1861.
   Robert—Caroline Bradley, 2-7-1852.
   Samuel P.—Mary Jane Plum, 12-13-1847.
   Thomas F. C. (s. Joshua and Mary), Philadelphia—Ellen Horn (d. Henry and Ann, 9-6-1860.
Coopley, Wm.—Lucretia Whitehead, 11-25-1854.
Copperthwaite, Lafayette—Gerusha Rodgers, 2-28-1847.
Cordery, Enoch, Absecum—Ann E. Willis, Monmouth co., 1-5-1846.
Corsen, Edward S.—Emaline Fifer, 4-21-1854.
   Isaac—Rebecca B. Higbee, 6-25-1854.
   James C.—Mary Ellen Shinn, 6-26-1862.
Countryman, John—Cline Hamilton, both Burlington co., 5-10-1854.
Coutts, George W.—Margaret Williams, 12-24-1855.
Cowan, Borough M.—Mary Josephine Williams, 9-11-1854.
   Edward L,—Fannie A. Callery, 3-12-1863.
   John —Rebecca A. Leslie, 9-3-1863.
   Morton—Elizabeth Watts, 4-19-1852.
Cowperthwaite, Joseph—Hannah Ann Fish, 10-22-1854.
   Samuel S. E.—Ann Eliza Lavinia Winner, 2-4-1848.

Cox—Charles S.—Matilda M. Mullin, 8-5-1862.
   Edward—Caroline Shane, 10-24-1854.
   Henry B.—Sarah A. Ross, 7-1-1857.
   Jonathan—Ruth Cossaboon, 1-31-1846.
   Samuel—Mary L. Peters, 12-12-1844.
   William—Margaret Powell, 1-19-1844.
Craig, Peter—Margaretta King (colored), both Evesham, 4-24-1851.
Craighton, Thomas—Mariah Jones, both Gloucester co., 11-26-1847.
Cramer, Ezra W.—Frances Crane, both Manahawkin, 9-7-1849.
Crammer, Charles—Charlotte C. Middleton, 6-21-1854.
Craver, David—Mary Brown 8-24-1862.
   Joseph—Beulah Cassaday, 5-20-1852.
Crim, William T.—Susan Summers, 5-10-1863.
Crist, George (s. Michael and Louisa)—Louisa Clanagan, both Williamstown, 6-5-1849.
Croft—Thomas F.—Ann Castle, both Philadelphia, 10-10-1847.
Crolle, Thomas—Elizabeth Emmet, 8-13-1844.
Croshaw, Elwood—Sarah A. Gauntt, 3-3-1859.
Crossley, John—Barbara Tomlinson, 2-17-1857.
Culp, John—Agnes I. Griffins, 7-14-1855.
Curtis—James—Ellen Steward, 5-24-1863.
   Joseph—Mary Brasington, 12-24-1851.
Curts, Charles W.—Maria Helzels, 2-12-1854.
Curry, Edward—Sarah Neal, 1-26-1860.
Daker, John M.—Sarah Libant, both Williamstown, 4-11-1846.
Dale, Charles—Elizabeth McGlindy, 6-27-1851.
Daniel, Robert—Adaline Ford (colored), 3-24-1864.
Dare, Edward—Rebecca Cade, 3-14-1864.
Davidson, George H.—Qhuma Shoemaker, both Gloucester co., 1-11-1866.
Davis, Enlose—Rebecca Urven, 3-19-1844.
   Hamilton S.—Elizabeth Porch, both Franklinville, 1-30-1847.

CAMDEN COUNTY MARRIAGES—BOOK A   15

Davis, Isaac—Lydia Ann Thomas (colored),12-29-1859.
  Nathan—Jane Walker, 6-15-1861.
  Perry—Rachel Bouras, 12-26-1861.
  Richard—Susan Sickler, 2-4-1863.
  Samuel—Betsy Jane Hix, 2-14-1850.
  Samuel—Sarah Ann Borton, both Medford, 7-29-1852.
  Samuel—Mary Ann Vanderslice, 9-9-1858.
  Samuel F.—Sarah A. Sickler, 1-4-1866.
  Thomas—Josephine E Hall, 3-13-1861.
  Thomas Murat (s. Thomas and Sarah), Philadelphia—Harriet Sooy (d. Joab and Catherine), 4-8-1858.
Day, Elwell—Catharine Ann Thorn, 1-1-1845.
  George W.—Sarah Simpson, 4-8-1855.
Dayton, James L.—Rebecca H. Doyle, 7-24-1854,
Deets, George H.—Rachel J. Goff, 6-5-1854.
  William—Catharine Hartman, 4-13-1847.
Dehart, Samuel P.—Nellie Sickler, 8-11-1864.
Demster, William H.—Anna R Murphy, 6-4-1864.
Denfer, John—Mrs. Sarah Denfer, 7-30-1861.
Denken, James—Annie Mitchell, 9-1-1861.
Dennis, David G.—Catharine D. Nichols, Recorded 4-1-1852.
  William S.—Priscilla Hamilton, 8-17-1851.
Dent, John—Eliza Barrett, 1-18-1855.
Derby, Charles C.—Susan Naylor, 10-29-1857.
Devinney, M. E.—Emma S. Jackson, 1-29-1865.
  Solomon R. (s. Michael and Ann), Mays Landing—Sarah R. Phifer (d. Jonathan and Margaret), Lumberton, 9-1-1860.
Dewalt, Samuel—Elizabeth Cowan, 9-6-1851.
D'Hart, John—Hannah Ann Cox, 9-30-1844.
Dickson, Henry—Sarah Mullica, 4-1-1856.
  John—Mary Rebecca Wilson, 4-5-1860.
Diggs, William H.—Mary Ann Severson, 2-14-1856.
  Wm. H., Philadelphia—Mary Evans, 10-27-1858.
Dilks, Gearge C.—Deborah Starn, both Gloucester co., 9-21-1865.
  Presmul, Carpenters Landing—Mrs. Ann Park, 8-9-1863.

Dilks, Thomas J.—Emma L. Crain, both Gloucester co., 11-4-1862.
Dimbick, Benjamin—Hannah Phifer, 8-22-1855.
Dixon, Jesse—Theodocia Ann Hillman, 10-16-1845.
  John T.—Rebecca Soder, 8-29-1863.
  Philip—Deborah Hendrickson, 11-30-1856.
Dodd, Jacob, Burlington co.—Louisa Starn, 11-2-1851.
Donly, Wm. W.—Mary E. Goforth, 4-14-1864.
Donnelly, John—Lucinda Evans, 6-12-1864.
Dougherty, Edward N.—Rachel Ann Venable, 12-7-1847.
  John—Elizabeth Wetsall, 5-24-1850.
Doughten, James—Sarah Peak, 1-14-1847.
Doughton, Wm. S., Westville—Abigail R. Clement, 10-12-1845.
Doughty, David—Emma Margaret Hawkins, 9-24-1853.
  Isaac C.—Rebecca Conover, 6-25-1857.
  John—Mary Getsinger, 2-12-1846.
Dover, James L.—Matilda Highgate, both Philadelphia, 10-1-1846.
Dowell, James M. Caroline Yohe, 5-15-1850.
Down, Thomas W.—Lyde Ann Reel, 2-16-1861.
Drigour, Eli—Rebecca Williams, 6-1-1859.
Duffield, Joseph—Mary Dill, 1-2-1847.
Duncan, Benjamin—Eliza Matlack, 9-27-1849.
Dunham, James E.—Melesa Husted, both Salem, 3-11-1854.
Dunlap, Hamilton (s. Alex and Lillie Ann)—Mercy Ann Williams (d. Wm. and Ann), 2-2-1861.
Durham, Benjamin—Sarah Woodland, 10-22-1846.
  John—Julia Ann Wilson, 12-18-1854.
Earl, Walter—Mary Norcross, 4-6-1854.
Earley, William—Mary Ann Pearson, 7-25-1846.
Earling, Daniel—Sarah Indicott, 3-9-1848.
Earnest, Charles—Ellen Hodgson, Philadelphia, 12-10-1861.
Eastlack, George C.—Adeline Barber, Gloucester co., 12-18-1856.
  George W.—Deborah F McCulley, Gloucester co., 9-3-1862.

Eayre, Franklin, Mt. Holly—Rebecca Daim, Moorestown, 1-2-1855.
Edgly, Jacob—Alice Gaunt, 5-15-1851.
Edwards, Clayton—Elizabeth Ivins 10-28-1861.
  Daniel W.—Ann Louise Mayberry, 2-14-1849.
  Somner, St. Louis, Mo.—Mary E. Fenton, 2-12-1866.
Elberson, Thomas—Mrs. Phebe L. Headly, 3-23-1848.
Eldridge, John—Adaline Meckey, 3-21-1853.
  Joseph S.—Ella M. Reed, 12-25-1852.
  Thomas—Sarah Ford, 3-20-1845.
Elfreth, Jeremiah—Harriet Shaw, 7-6-1864.
Ellis, John H.—Sarah S. Sooy, 11-19-1846.
  Joseph I.—Sarah A. Haines, both Burlington co., 4-8-1852.
  Jeseph R.—Julianna Armstrong, 4-12-1860.
  Thomas Y.—Sarah Ann Armstrong, 11-17-1864.
  William—Sarah Thornly, both Germantown, 9-9-1854.
Elwell, Isaac, Pittsgrove—Rachel DuBois, 10-7-1865.
  William S.—Ellen Amelia Tice, 1-28-1848.
Emery, Chas. H.—Mary ———,* 12-18-1856.
  Robert—Isabella Cramer, 10-27-1865.
Emmitt, John—Isabel Cossaboon, 11-14-1855.
Engle, William—Mary Ann Clevenger, 5-10-1853.
English, Samuel—Jane Calvert, 2-27-1850.
  Samuel—Ann Prescott, 4-11-1850
Entwistle, John—Catharine Monks, both Philadelphia, 10-23-1857.
Estrada, Carlos Diegueda, Puerto Principe, Cuba—Fannie A. McCurdy (d. John W.), 10-30-1856,
Etchels, Joshua, Chester, Pa.—Elizabeth C. Briant, 9-13-1865.
Etlene, George—Mary Parker, 11-7-1861.
Evans, Edward—Anna Tice, 1-9-1851.
  John—Mary McIlhone, 7-31-1851.
  Samuel J.—Hannah R. Scott, 10-29-1863.

*Illegible.

Evans, William Henry, Burlington co.—Sarah E. Lloyd, 5-21-1863.
Ewan, John W.—Mary Ann Ivins, 10-1-1861.
Ewen, Jonathan, Burlington co.—Josephine Hutter, Atlantic co., 3-13-1858.
Eyles, William H.—Mary E. Shaw, 7-14-1865.
Fakey, Michael—Catharine McHugh, 11-19-1855.
Fanning, William Henry—Ann Solter, 8-21-1852.
Farrow, Eli—Priscilla Lenard, 6-2-1844.
Feltman, Mathias—Elizabeth Shep, 11-22-1856.
Felton, Henry P.—Amanda S. Davis, 8-30-1858.
Fenner, George W., Wilmington—Rebec Bonsal, 9-13-1856.
    Samuel J.—Margaret A. Dobleman, 11-28-1859.
Ferrell, William H.—Elizabeth A. Chew, 12-8-1863.
Fifer, Thomas—Martha Ann Wells, both Medford, 8-1-1852.
Filhower, Henry—Margaret Cithgart, 8-19-1855.
Findley, George W.—Susan B. Jones, Philadelphia—8-30-1846.
Firth, Isaac—Mrs. Sarah S. Moore, 8-9-1851.
Fish, Albert—Emeline Hubbs, 9-28-1854.
    Charles P.—Elizabeth Budd, 2-15-1863.
    Hiram—Elmira Collins, 1-6-1858.
Fisher, Abraham S.—Mary Cobb, both Milford, 9-19-1846.
    Benjamin S., Dr.—Rebecca E. Vanicomb, both Marlton, 9-25-1845.
    Edward—Emma Boone, 12-25-1855.
    George (s. John), White Creek, N. Y.—Elmira Westcoat (d. John), 7-1-1863.
    John—Anna C. Russel, 5-1-1862.
Fitzmyer, John—Jacobin Ray, 6-19-1852.
Fitzpatrick, Joseph—Mary Ann Donnold, 2-28-1856.
Fletcher, Thomas R.—Susanna S. Sudraff, 5-22-1864.
    Flore, Peter—Massa Carl, 6-2-1849.
Force, Edward V.—Celinda S. Bell, 12-2-1861.
    Edward V.—Selinda S. Bell, 8-27-1863.
    Jacob—Rebecca Cheesman, both Gloucester co., 1-22-1846.
    William, New York—Mrs. Elizabeth Richards, 5-29-1855.

CAMDEN COUNTY MARRIAGES—BOOK A 19

Ford, Benjamin—Sarah Eldridge, Swedesboro, 8-20-1845.
  Samuel (s. Samuel), Emma I. Gaunt (d. Reuben), 2-9-1864.
Fortiner, Samuel M.—Mary H. Cooper, Washington twp., 11-10-1845.
Foster, Mark, Atlantic co.—Jennie Cline, 3-21-1864.
  Thomas, Jr.—Prudence Elliott, Philadelphia, 10-24-1855.
Foul, Henry D.—Rachel Carman, 6-23-1844.
Fowler, Elwood—Frances Bates, 9-3-1846.
  Joseph F.—Eatteth Fox, 9-22-1858.
Fox, Adam—Susan Leeds, 4-5-1850.
  Daniel—Sarah Myrase, 12-9-1844.
  Joseph B.—Elizabeth A. Cheesman, 12-22-1859.
  Peter—Alice Powers, 12-8-1845.
Frances, Thomas—Catharine J. Fenner, 6-5-1853.
Franck, John L.—Josephine Impson, 11-4-1865.
Francois, Charles—Elizabeth Burrows, both Philadelphia, 5-21-1859.
Frankish, Daniel D.—Hannah Spencer, 7-22-1855.
Franklin, Joseph W.—Elizabeth Fowler, Woodbury, 2-16-1855.
Fraser, John B.—Emma Louisa Kennedy, 7-15-1862.
Fredericks, William— Cecelia Snyder, 9-8-1853.
Freeman, James—Amanda M. Bates, 11-30-1857.
French, Charles B., Philadelphia—Sarah Longcahe, 7-9-1846.
Fry, William Henry—Sophia Amelia Delamore, both England, 10-11-1854.
Gage, John—Sarah Rowley, both Philadelphia, 7-1-1860.
Gaites, Elisha—Ann Mann, 10-11-1845.
Gale, Budd Daniel—Lydia Ann Haines, 12-24-1857.
Galbraith, James—Elizabeth Jones, 5-22-1847.
Gallager, John F.—Susan Watson, both Gloucester co., 2-26-1863.
Gandy, Hope W., Cape May co.—Mary Williams, Weymouth, 11-29-1851.
Ganges, John—Elizabeth Hoagland, 5-19-1862.
Gardner, John, Burlington co.—Amelia Parvain, 11-14-1853.

CAMDEN COUNTY MARRIAGES—BOOK A

Garrett, Charles, Salem co.—Esther Ann Lewallen, 3-17-1858.
Garrity, Edward—Sarah Clark, 10-19-1855.
Garton, William C., Philadelphia, Elenor S. Remley, 9-25-1845.
Garwood, John—Melena Ann Kirby, 11-19-1863.
Gaskill, DeWitt Clinton, California—Anne C. Everett, 12-20-1859.
  George B —Catharine Patterson, 4-3-1862.
  Henry C.—Ann S. Hay, 1-1-1852.
  Joseph—Anna C. Angeroth, 6-12-1865.
  Samuel B., Bridgeport—Deborah Hurff, Center Square, 10-14-1858.
Gaul, James, Moorestown—Mariah Charles, 12-6-1851.
Gaunt, Jesse—Hannah M. Casperson, Gloucester co., 7-5-1853.
Genett, Henry—Annie B. Martin, 12-10-1858.
Gessler, John—Caroline Miller, 2-16-1863.
Gibbs, Joseph—Hannah Stibbs, 1-23-1864.
Giberson, Jacob E.—Emily C. Woodrow, 9-2-1866.
Gibson, Jacob—Sarah A. Stetzer, 11-14-1861.
  John H.—Virginia Meyers, both Mt. Holly, 5-23-1864.
Gilmore, Thomas—Mary Bishop, 4-29-1847.
Gilbert, Thomas A.—Martha Cox, 4-25-1858.
Ginlerd, Wm.—Elizabeth Berryman, 5-20-1854.
Girard, James—Sarah E. King, 2-27-1853.
Githens, Hosea H.—Jane Edwards, 8-12-1860.
  Samuel—Rachel Clement, 8-4-1846.
  Thomas—Ella F. Clark, 9-8-1864.
Givens, William, Deptford—Elizabeth Barryman, 8-30-1854.
Givin Nathaniel—Elizabeth Kaltley 12-2-1853.
Gifford, Daniel—Temperance Foster, both Millville, 3-10-1866.
  Imlay—Margaret Stokely, 11-27-1847.
Gleason, Wm.—Ellen Ivins, 7-18-1857.
Glover, Benj. B.—Esther Z. Bell, 9-19-1859.
  Chalkley—Sarah Branson, 12-24-1846.

CAMDEN COUNTY MARRIAGES—BOOK A 21

Glover, Fdward H., Philadelphia—Maria Eliz. Halaron, 12-23-1857
Goldenberg, David G. W.—Henrietta Hendrickson, both Burlington co., 8-21-1861.
Goodwin, Edward—Mary Ann Shute, 3-26-1851.
Gordon, Charles H.—Mrs. Elizabeth Smith, 3-5-1848.
  Charles W.—Eliza Smith, 4-23-1863.
  David A.—Mary B. Stanger, Malaga, 9-1-1856.
  Samuel R.—Rebecca Vansant, 4-11-1864.
  William—Mary Ann Schwaal, 8-17-1859.
  William H., Wilmington—Rachel R. Moody, Philadelphia, 5-10-1846.
Goren, Sinnickson—Amy J. Porch, both Gloucester co., 3-29-1851.
Gormand, Edmond P.—Catharine Spidol, 6-15-1847.
Graham, Samuel W.—Georgianna McCormick. Recorded 5-12-1857.
  William T. (s. Sarah), Virginia—Angeline Strickland, 1-1-1856
Granger, Niles, Philadelphia—Isabella Adams, 11-7-1850.
  William—Mary Eliza Oakford, 9-29-1863.
Grant, Saml.—Turnerville, Mary LeCroy, Swedesboro, 2-19-1863.
Greeley, William—Hannah Ivins, 7-2-1851.
Green, George—Frances Bland, 11-17-1855.
  John—Mrs. Nancy Warrington, 2-7-1848.
Griffin, James—Sarah Ann Boyle, 5-25-1854.
Grigg, Horace H.—H. Virginia Hanistead (d. James and Mary Ann), 4-24-1855.
Groff, Nathan—Adelia Andrews, Cumberland co., 10-25-1857.
Groves, Jacob G.—Sarah C. Wills, 1-1-1863.
  John—Eliza Neill, 8-17-1861.
  John—Priscilla Ann Shaw, 3-31-1863.
  Joseph—Elizabeth Bailey, 5-12-1854.
  William—Mary D. Marple, 5-11-1864.
Guinder, Charles—Mary Leady, both Philadelphia, 1-24-1858.
Gurlkey, William—Mary Elizabeth Price, 7-4-1854.

CAMDEN COUNTY MARRIAGES—BOOK A

Guy, Thomas, Bristol, Pa.—Harriet Stackhouse, 6-28-1865.
Hackett, Josiah S., Salem—Ruth S. Ross, 1-1-1860.
Hagell, Philip—Elizabeth Keen, 3-18-1855.
Hagerman, Samuel—Louisa Macpherson, 4-1-1856.
Haig, Peter—Lydia Ireton, 10-31-1852.
Haines, Alexander—Elizabeth Peabock, both Burlington co., 9-1-1844.
  Benjamin—Abigail Steidler, 8-16-1856.
  George H.—Caroline Farnham, 1-2-1865.
  James B.—Elizabeth Cheesman, 3-22-1846.
  Josiah—Hannah Middleton, 12-31-1846.
  Samuel W.—Elizabeth T. Ayres, 2-5-1857.
  Thomas—Phebe Bishop, 12-5-1859.
Hall, Richard, Maryland—Amanda Carels, 1-3-1859.
Hallett, Nathan W.—Mrs. Mary A. Goddard, both Lake, 1-8-1863.
Hamill, Alexander—Susan C. Stetser, 4-19-1852.
  Samuel H., Harrisburg, Pa.—Kate Carmany, Lebanon, Pa., 8-10-1865.
Hammel, Charles S —Mary J. Tucker, 3-9-1851.
Hammell, Charles S.—Henrietta Dunn, Pennsylvania, 1-5-1860.
  Horace, (s. Moses), Moorestown—Emma Erskin Cox (d. Jona. and Mary C.), 11-24-1864.
  Simeon—Louisa Williams, New York, 12-6-1862.
  S———*—Mary Pendergrass, 1-5-1856.
Hammick Henry—Sarah Hopkins, 12-7-1844.
Hammond, Thomas R.—Sarah Emily Church, 5-9-1859.
Hand, William—Eliza McFiners, 8-20-1855.
Hankins, John—Elizabeth Wescoat, 7-3-1852.
  John—Mary Fidelia Cowles, 11-14-1860.
Hanson, William—Abby P. Hanson, 4-15-1852.
Harbert, Wm. H. Pedricktown—Mary A. Bartholomew Philadelphia, 8-3-1865.
Harmon, Conrad—Christianna Frank, 12-17-1854.

---

*Illegible.

CAMDEN COUNTY MARRIAGES—BOOK A 23

Harper, Charles—Abigail Peas. 10-4-1851.
Harricks, John—Jane Richards, Wilmington, Del., 9-15-1849.
Harrington, John—Rebecca Smith, 6-7-1863.
Harris, Isaac—Hannah E. Thomas, 10-2-1845.
 Joseph—Susan Ann Owen, 8-7-1852.
 Joseph—Margaret Jones, both Burlington co., 10-5-1854.
 Samuel—Louisa H. Budd, 10-27-1847.
 William Shakespeare, New York City—Sarah Lacy, 12-28-1852.
Harrison, George—Mary Brown, 9-25-1845.
Hart, John W.—Alice H. Doughty, 6-15-1854.
Hartman, Alexander, Monmouth co.—Sarah A. Vanderbilt, Atlantic co., 3-14-1854.
 Jacob—Barbara Angels, 9-27-1854.
 William Lock—Hannah Ann Mills, 10-28-1862.
Harvey, Alexander—Delie Fagan, Newark, 8-6-1865.
 John—Margaret Sap, 5-11-1853.
 Thomas—Elizabeth Henry, both Philadelphia, 4-15-1865.
Hatcher, Edward—Christiana, Dekalb, 2-2-1854.
Hawes, George—Maria Hull, 11-16-1850.
Hay, Charles—Mary H. Lippincott, 12-19-1844.
 John—Mary R. Lummis, 1-15-1865.
Hayes, Charles—Rebecca Suster, 12-16-1858.
 Robert G.—Alice G. Pepper, 11-29-1862.
Hayman, Robert, England—Mary Campbel, Ireland, 9-6-1853.
Heath, F. S.—Josephine K. Waithman, 5-19-1864
Heaton, Clayton C.—Anna F. Floyd, 8-28-1864.
Hedger, Justice, Cincinnati, O.—Mary Ann Cheesman, 9-30-1846.
Henderson, Benjamin—Emma H. Marple, 5-3-1863.
 Charles B.—Charlotte Bate, 7-5-1851.
Hendrickson, Joseph—Mary S. Rowan, 2-9-1854.
 Joseph F.—Keziah H. Jones, 3-26-1853.
Hennick, Mike—Anna Englebreak, 1-21-1855.
Henry, Charles—Christena Heesley, 7-16-1857.
Heppard, Matthew—Eliza Budd, 4-20-1859.
Hermage, Charles—Emma F. Hill, 6-8-1857.

CAMDEN COUNTY MARRIAGES—BOOK A

Heritage, Josiah F.—Mrs. Jane G. Stanger, both Glassboro, 3-8-1866.
  Thomas—Theresa W. Sears, 4-27-1848.
  William E.—Harriet McFarland, both Gloucester co., 3-14-1850.
Hersh, Joseph—Mary Wentworth, 9-9-1847.
Hewitt, John—Hannah DeHart, 12-18-1847.
  Jordan—Theodotia Ann Bowers, 10-26-1850
Hewlings, Albert—Martha Norcross, 12-2-1855.
  John—Sarah Ann Hinchman, 19-5-1851.
  Josiah—Abigail Ann Dilks, 8-7-1851.
Hews, Thomas—Ann Eliza Hackney, 4-18-1844.
Hibs, George F.—Marian B. Wallace (d. John and Susan), 11-19-1857.
Hidkman, Andrew M.—Mary Sturges, 3-25-1855.
Hicks, John—Lilah Davis, 4-9-1963.
  William—Rebecca Schreger, 4-16-1846.
Higenbotham, Joseph F.—Emma Kaffer, Burlington co., 10-24-1864.
Higgins, John D. (s. Seldon and Polly)—Eleanor Davis (d. Benj. and Eleanor), 12-30-1858.
Hilard, Philip—Sarah E. Dawson, 2-11-1858.
Hill, Samuel B.—Jerusha Bates, 11-29-1846.
Hillman, Joseph P.—Sallie Fenton, 5-12-1858.
Hillyer, Nathan—Amanda Vanhart, 4-28-1853.
Hinchman, Isaac—Priscilla Middleton, 11-29-1846.
  Meritt—Sarah Sarchet, 3-1-1859.
Hineline, Wm. S.—Lizzie Pechman, 9-28-1863.
Holl, George—Emma Plimlott, 12-24-1865.
  John—Mary Eliz. Ayres, 8-21-1859.
  Louis F.—Meminia Tenner, 5-25-1865.
Hollis, Charles J (s. Chas. and Angelind), Philadelphia—Emma W. Wood (d. Isaac and Eliza), 10-29-1860.
Hollingshead, George B.—Rebecca S. Jinnett, 5-14-1846.
  Thomas—Mary Garwood, 3-28-1856.
Holsten, William H. Fislerville—Martha W. Husted, 6-19-1865.

Holt, James—Susannah, 6-11-1851.
Holton, Clarence E.—Jennie M. Lewis, 3-31-1873.
Hooten, John—Mary Messick, 9-25-1851.
Horn, John—Bessie Cream, both Philadelphia, 5-2-1863.
Horne, Isaac—Sarah Smith, 12-21-1849.
Horneff, George—Emma Cairoli, 1-25-1866.
Horner, John—Ella Fenton, 4-27-1865.
   Martin—Martha Ann Hinchman, 12-6-1854.
   Thomas A.—Elizabeth Peak, 4-14-1846.
Horsfull, Charles H , Capt.—Amy W. Brooks, 8-1-1862.
Hothouse, John (s. John and Margaret)—Grace Carson (d. Robert and Jane), 11-20-1860.
Hougeras (or Fougeras) R. J.—Sallie Metzger, both Philadelphia, 3-17-1864.
House, Jacob—Sarah Ann Shimp, both Allowaystown, 9-6-1860.
Houseman, Frederick—Katharine Frederica Klein, 1-1-1856.
Howard, James—Elizabeth Williams, 8-26-1852.
   James H. Patience Ross, 4-3-1864.
Howell, Allen—Sarah C. Davis, 12-16-1845.
Hoyd, James—Rachel W. Lovett, 2-14-1859.
Hudson, Charles—Keziah Sickler, 5-4-1850.
Hudsworth, Edward, Philadelphia—Caroline Ingram, 7-22-1865.
Hughes, Enos—Anna Suters, both Atlantic co., 10-24-1850.
   William—Rachel Day, 4-27-1847.
Hulfish, Charles, Bordentown, Anna Creaty, 3-5-1866.
Hulings, Samuel—Sarah Porce, 9-24-1850.
Hults, Curts—Charlotte H. Williams, 3-27-1851.
Humphries, Richard S.—Eveline C. Fetters, 2-10-1841.
Hunt, Samuel—Margaret M. Farrow, 5-18-1845.
Hunter, Charles—Elizabeth Stevens, 4-8-1852.
   Edward—Hannah B. Severns, 10-5-1854.
   Emanuel—Ann Severns, 11-4-1852.
   Thomas M.—Ann Cambray, 3-3-1854.
   William, Philadelphia,—Sarah Buck, 9-17-1853.
Huntsinger, John—Sarah A. Simmerman, 2-21-1863.

Huntsman, George W.—Jane McEwen, 9-10-1854.
Hurff, George—Alice Farrow, both Washington twp., 12-22-1852.
  Joseph—Sophia Turner, 11-1-1863.
Hurley, Franklin—Sallie E. Monroe, 1-1-1866.
Husler, William—Julia Boyle, 1-5-1855.
Husted, William C.—Mary A. Wheaton, both Swedesboro, 6-10-1854.
Hyde, Richard—Lizzie Bellon, 1-2-1864.
  Thomas—Louisa Blair, 9-13-1864.
Hyder, John—Isabel McCann, 3-23-1854.
Ildark, William—Mary Jane Bennett, both Burlington co., 1-7-1854.
Inglen, Alfred—Mary A. Newton, both Burlington co., 5-18-1851.
Inman, Jos.—Catharine Lamar, 1-2-1858.
Ireland, William—Mrs. Millicent Porch, Williamstown, 3-14-1859.
Irwin, Edwin—Rachel Hughes, both Philadelphia, 7-13-1845.
Isenberger, Paul—Louisa Scover (wid.), 7-15-1865.
Ivins, Isaac—Harriet Newell Jones, 12-23-1851.
Jackson, James—Rachel Askins, 5-24-1863.
  John—Mary Boyer (colored), 2-16-1859.
  Joseph—Ellen Emary, 11-13-1845.
  Warner—Sarah King, 10-6-1862.
  William A.—Annie Eliza Wells, both Moorestown, 7-22-1863
Jacobs, Isaac—Rebecca Sanders both Reading, Pa. 1-4-1855.
Jaggard, James J.—Martha S. Cattell, 8-20-1862.
Jaggers, David L.—Susanna D. Shaw, 8-18-1856.
  Isaac F.—Margaret Southard, 10-26-1854.
James, Charles H.—Phebe A. Combs, both Philadelphia, 6-11-1854.
  Edward L.—Sarah A. Beckworth, 8-3-1862.
  Thomas W.—Isabella Hunt—11-4-1858.
Jeffers, William N.—Louisa Robinson, Philadelphia, 7-3-1847.
Jeffries, Joseph—Elizabeth Dill, 3-4-1846.

CAMDEN COUNTY MARRIAGES—BOOK A 27

Jennings, Charles—Hannah Hewitt, 1-2-1854.
  George—Amanda Jane Kesler, 8-3-1845.
Jess, Bowers—Lydia Hogan, 8-20-1860.
  Charles—Matilda L. Patterson, 9-6-1857.
  Ira B.—Maria E. Ford, 10-12-1854.
  Lorenzo—Mary R. Harris, 11-5-1860.
Jewell, Charles H.—Elizabeth Hamilton, 8-5-1854.
Jobs, James, Bordentown—Sarah Paden, 10-1-1862.
Johnson, Alexander—Esther J. Epley, 8-26-1863.
  Alfred—Henrietta Barnes, 4-25-1861.
  Edward S.—Hannah Primrose, Delanco, 5-26-1864.
  Eli W.—Anna E. Carson, both Gloucester co., 2-14-1861.
  George W.—Elizabeth M. West, 5-28-1856.
  Hugh—Margaretta Huston, both Kensington, 10-18-1867.
  John—Bathsheba Roads, 6-16-1846.
  John—Martha A. Sturgis, 1-4-1864.
  Thomas—Rachel Jones, 5-23-1846.
  Thomas—Abigail Ann Banister, 12-20-1847.
  Thomas—Mary I. Williams, 10-20-1860.
  William W. Salem co.—Emma M. Wilson, 4-20-1865.
  William B. W.—Anna E. R. Johnson, Burlington co., 10-26-1854.
Joice, James—Margaretta D. Abbott, 1-5-1847.
Jones, Anthony—Eliza Ann Cramer, 9-14-1850.
  Edmund, Franklinville—Harriet S. Wilson, Repaupo, 2-16-1860.
  Edward F.—Sarah Farrow, 12-24-1860.
  Ephraim S., Bridgeton—Rebecca Sharp, 3-5-1859.
  Frederick B.—Mary E. Farrow, 6-7-1860.
  Isaac, Washington twp.—Martha Bozorth, 7-13-1852.
  James—Louisa Flocher, 1-9-1863.
  Joseph—Mary Ann Trays, 8-1-1852.
  Lloyd—Sallie E. Andrews, both Tuckerton, 3-20-1866.
  Owen R.—Mary F. Ross, 11-15-1855.
  Richard (s. Richard and Sarah)—Harriet G. Middleton (d. Wm. and Mary), 2-12-1851.
Joseph, John—Hannah Bates, 8-24-1853.

Jones, Samuel—Betsey Dowton, 6-15-1850; also recorded as 7-15-1850.
  Tobias W.—Isabella Hunt, 11-4-1857.
Jordan, Alexander H.—Hannah C. Hay, 1-2-1852.
  Jacob H., Philadelphia—Martha M. Harrison, 11-7-1865.
  John P.—Emaline Horner, 11-17-1862.
  Joseph C,—Mary Clarke, 9-19-1859.
Kaighn, Alfred—Cornelia S. Johnson, 11-10-1859.
  W. L.—Lizzie V. Pimlotte, 1-1-1865.
Kattze, George—Rebecca Didifield, 2-19-1848.
Kay, John, Marlton—Rachel L. Edwards, 9-10-1846.
  William—Elizabeth Dockerty, 8-16-1858.
Keen, William—Elizabeth Elder, 9-18-1855.
Keesby, John—Eliza Ann Lefevour, 12-12-1854.
Kellum, Benjamin—Emeline Ware, 6-5-1845.
  Edward—Barbary Ann Southard, 5-26-1855.
Kelly, John E.—Isabella Cole, 8-6-1864.
  Joseph—Rebecca Winer, 6-20-1844.
  William—Elizabeth Taylor, 1-12-1864.
Kemble, Joseph L.—Eliza Ann Haines, both Burlington co., 10-2-1851.
  Levi—Martha McNelly, 9-12-1854.
Kendle, James—Elizabeth Banes, 2-28-1859.
Kennedy George W., New York City—Elizabeth Hulling, Bridgeton, 7-29-1858.
  Henry P.—Mary Jane Harris, 8-23-1862.
Kenworthy, John J.—Emma Finney, 11-15-1864.
Kerlin, William, Philadelphia—Mary D. Butterworth (d. Edward I.), 1-5-1854.
Kershaw, James—Sarah Bailey, both Millville, 2-20-1863.
Keyser, Christopher—Mary Schuar, 2-18-1855.
Kiffcart, Gilbert—Mrs. Mary McNeal, 2-5-1848.
Killey, David—Sophia T. Thorn, both Bordentown, 2-14-1859.
Kindle, Jacob—Elizabeth Banes, both Williamstown, 2-28-1859.
King, Cornelius—Elizabath C. Foster, 2-2-1853.

CAMDEN COUNTY MARRIAGES—BOOK A 29

King, George Henry—Margaret Shenoskea, 9-30-1854.
  Lewis—Caroline Parkhouse, 7-28-1851.
  William B.—Laura J. Parker, both Trenton, 7-18-1853.
Kirby, Wm. Cooper, Swedesboro—Anna A. Ford, 1-27-1859.
Kirkbride, Jonathan—Frances A. Fortner, 2-2-1857.
Kline, David M., Morris co.—Lydia H. Roberson, Hunterdon co, 10-19-1846.
  Thomas B. R (s. Micajah)—Arabella Friell (d. James), 1-2-1864.
Knatt, Benjamin—Charlotte Woods, both England, 1-18-1864.
Knauff, John Philip—Bertha Stehr; recorded 10-10-1851.
Knight, Joseph—Sarah L. Sharp, 3-29-1852.
Knisell, Joseph, Deptford—Mary Amanda Jones, 8-4-1853.
Knotts, Wm. W—Hannah A. Wiltsey, 10-26-1847.
Knox, Wm. H., Philadelphia—Sarah Somers, 4-14-1856.
Koch, Conrad—Phebe Jain Nail, 11-12-1851.
Korhn, Joseph—Phebe Sutton, 10-26-1851.
Kraft, George—Anna M. Flowers, 8-9-1865.
Kunder, Franklin—Anna Elizabeth Gratz, 1-7-1860.
Lacony, John—Hannah Ann Bryan, 10-23-1844.
Lafferty, John—Eunice Thomas, 11-18-1849.
  Robert (s. Hugh and Agnes), Philadelphia—Sarah Howarth (d John and Lydia Ann), 5-10-1860.
  William—Mary Phifer, both Atlantic co., 1-21-1852; also recorded as 1-31-1852.
Lake, Henry—Nancy Ann Ageson, 9-7-1845.
Lamb, Thomas—Huldah Smith, 2-1-1851.
Lane, William H.—Aramella S. Baker, 2-28-1850.
Lashley, John—Ruth H. Hampton, both Gloucester co., 4-5-1851
Latchman, William—Abigail F. Turner, both Gloucester co., 11-23-1850.
Latham, William L.—Frances A. Outhout, 12-25-1864.
Laurence, Dana—Caroline Lewis, 1-5-1852.
Lazarus, Israel—Sarah Moody, both Philadelphia, 4-19-1846.
Leatherburg, Ezra, Fieldsboro—Lizzie Farmer, 4-25-1865.

CAMDEN COUNTY MARRIAGES—BOOK A

Leas, Joel—Caroline Rix, 10-18-1882.
Lee, George, Jr.—Susanna Pearce, 8-14-1844.
  Thomas—Martha Jane Nickles, 1-3-1858.
Leech, Joseph. Trenton—Mary E. Mintle, 9-15-1865.
Leees, Charles H.—Lydia Coolas, 1-25-1853.
Leek, Theodore, Trenton—Anna B. Nichols, 6-11-1865.
Leonard, Dayton—Sarah Steelman, 9-17-1846.
  Jacob—Phebe Young, 8-6-1853.
Letts, Riley, Beverly—Martha A. Heulings, Philadelphia, 3-5-1865.
Lettz, James M.—Martha A. Brown, 5-1-1856.
Levett, Richard F.—Sarah Wright, Salem, 3-25-1852.
Levis, Joseph L., Philadelphia—Mrs. Susanna C. Kirkbride (nee Budd), 7-10-1865.
Lewallen, Samuel H.—Rebecca A. Jones, 3-28-1861.
Lewis, Henry W. (s. Asher and Elizabeth)—Emily L. Bulson (d. Gilbert and Pamelia, 11-22-1860.
  James—Ann Pedrick, 3-29-1853.
  William—Elizabeth Janes, both Chester, Pa., 8-17-1859.
Ley, John—Elizabeth Thomas, 7-17-1854.
Librant, Mark—Rachel Garren, 1-22-1848.
Light, Franklin, Capt.—Sarah Matlack, Gloucester co., 7-8-1858.
Lilly, James D.—Anna Maria Bennet, 7-17-1852.
Lindell, William W., Louisville, Ky.—Mary A. Smith, 11-5-1857.
Lindsey, Charles F.—Rebecca Ellis, both Mt. Holly, 5-3-1865.
Linton, Benjamin—Hannah R. W. ———, 7-26-1860.
Lippincott, Charles— Lydian Tomlin, 11-25-1858.
  Charles D.—Hannah F. Duball, 11-16-1865.
  Charles W—Sarah A. Martin, 1-17-1858.
  Ellis—Rebecca J. Boen, 2-15-1851.
  Isaac—Elizabeth Matlack, 12-26-1844.
  Noah E.—Lizzie Horner, both Burlington, 3-2-1865.
Lisher, Norman—Mrs. Elizabeth Ireland, Philadelphia, 3-25-1861.

Little, James—Sarah Oliver, 12-5-1854.
Livermore, Jonas—Ann H. McElroy, 5-8-1855.
Livzey, Jesse S.—Rosanna Izard, 3-19-1848.
Lock, David—Elizabeth Jane Nail, 5-3-1852.
Locke, James D.—Mattie Dorsey, 3-2-1865.
Lockerm, Elisha—Ellen Oney, 12-23-1858.
Lodge, Fleetwood, Jr.—Sarah Barnett, 5-7-1855.
Long, John—Mary Doughty, 9-24-1853.
  Joseph S.—Elizabeth M. Whitecar, 9-20-1850.
  William—Mary Whitecar, 9-7-1850.
  Wiliam C., Carpenters Landing—**Isabella Clark, Barnsboro**, 4-5-1865.
  William T.—Margaret E. White, 8-12-1862.
Longacre Henry (s. John and Mary)—**Ruth Williams** (d. John and Ruth), 1-31-1861.
Longmire Charles—Emma E. Kulp, both **Germantown**, 1-2-1865.
Lord, Bartholomew—Bridget Higgins, 3-11-1854.
  David E., (s. David and Hannah)—Lena Smith, 5-22-1866.
Loyd, Branson—Deborah Wiltsey, 6-14-1845.
Loynd, Thomas—Elizabeth Smith, 7-4-1863.
Luee, Thomas—Mary Eliza Peterson, 5-29-1864.
Ludlam, Alexander—Susanna Roth, 6-2-1845.
Luellen, Richard B.—Amy Allen, 12-1-1853.
Luis, John—Barbara Schmick Lindmann, 7-7-1860.
Luff, Samuel—Mary Ellen Stack, Bucks co., **Pa.**, 11-4-1852.
Lummis, Samuel—Sallie A. Earley, 8-31-1862.
Lutger, William—Anna Lane, 12-11-1851.
Macalister, William, New York City—**Abigail Ann Shute**, 12-24-1861.
Madden, Francis L.—Margaret Williams, 10-20-1851.
  William—Ruthanna Kurbow, both Pennsylvania, 12-25-1858.
Magnin, Jerome—Amelia LaBlotier, 6-25-1866.
Maguire, James—Mary Iszard, 3-1-1852; also recorded as 3-6-1852.
  Wm. I.—Mary A. C. Roberson, 3-17-1859.

Malny, William S. (s. Thomas and Ruth A.)—Mary E. Davis (d. Benjamin), 1-6-1856.
Mapes, Mark H.—Anna King, Burlington co., 5-7-1866.
Marche, John—Emma France, both Philadelphia, 7-14-1864.
Marcy, Alexander, Dr.—Hannah Mecray, Cape May, 8-24-1861.
Marien, Alfred Cezar—Sarah Hogson 11-26-1863.
Marley, Robert—Frances Schofield, 9-28-1861.
Marmbeck, Leabine—S. V. A. Smith, 9-3-1865.
Marple, Wiliam B.—Lydia Ann Curtis, 2-16-1854.
Marshall, Charles—Hannah Moore, 2-11-1866.
  Davis G. W.—Henrietta Hendrickson, 8-21-1861.
  Isaac Cooper—Mary Anne Sparks, 3-24-1859.
  Jeremiah—Maria Monroe, 11-18-1846.
  Joseph G.—Tamson Sharp, 10-25-1854.
  Joseph W.—Sarah Agnew, Nicetown, Pa., 9-28-1863.
  J. Wesley—Clara Moore, 8-6-1854.
  Robert—Sarah E. Johnson, 3-2-1858.
  Thomas J.—Anna Perkins, 5-21-1855.
  William—Jane Blair, 2-9-1858.
  William D.—Rebecca M. Gregg, 10-25-1863.
Marter, Henry H.—Maria Vandegrift, Pennsylvania, 12-25-1865.
Martin Caleb—Eliza Jane McFarland, 11-9-1844.
  Elmer—Mary Culp, 8-23-1856.
  Samuel—Nancy Ann Aggerson, 3-1-1853,
  William—Isabella Hustin, 9-18-1846.
Mason, Phineas E.—Rejoinia Lock, 9-5-1851.
  Thomas—Marian Duglas, 7-24-1845.
  William H.—Hannah Lippincott both Vincentown, 11-13-1845.
Mathews, Franklin (s. James M. and Mary), Berks co., Pa.—Anne E. Ulmer (d. Joseph and Anna Brook), 4-7-1875.
Mathis, Josephus C. S.—Mary J. Shourds, 2-2-1854.
Matlack, James B.—Charlotte Huston, 8-13-1863.
  Reuben B.—Ann Fox, 9-27-1852.

CAMDEN COUNTY MARRIAGES—BOOK A 33

Matlack, Wm. H.—Sarah Rebecca P. Hale, 12-22-1859.
Matlock, John W—Sarah Jane Repsher, 11-1-1851.
  Joseph—Elizabeth Marshall, 12-25-1844.
Mattson, James—Elizabeth Hendrickson, 4-11-1846.
Maurer, Charles—Caroline Drehr, both Philadelphia, 7-30-1865.
Maxwell, Henry S., Philadelphia—Elizabeth N. Quicksall 5-26-1859.
May, Charles—Ellen Moore, 6-1-1845.
Mayers, Joel—Sarah Kennedy, 8-1-1858.
Mayhew, Isaac—Mrs. Judith Somers, 5-26-1852.
Mayne, Armand Victor, Philadelphia—Emily Ivers, 12-2-1858.
Mays, Henry, Philadelphia—Margaret V. Anderson, 7-3-1855.
McAdoo, Robert—Hessey Berryman, 4-2-1856.
McAlless, Francis—Isabella McCreedy, 9-3-1845.
McCalmouth, Peter—Rebecca B. Wiley, 1-5-1854.
McCandless, David—Jane Bisby, both Philadelphia, 6-11-1855.
McClain, John G.—Rachel Miller, 4-27-1864.
McClenand, James—Elizabeth Vare, both Gloucester co., 1-18-1862.
McClure, John—Mrs. Ellen Jaggard, 12-21-1847.
McColester, Edward—Elizabeth Adams, 5-3-1847.
McCullough, George, Philadelphia—Jane Middleton, 12-18 1854.
McDermott, Francis—Emma H. Shute, 12-31-1853.
McElhaney, John—Martha Wells, 1-1-1846.
McFarlan, William, Mansfield, Conn.—Jane Short, 1-30-1854.
McGregor, Alexander—Margaret McDonald, 9-15-1855.
McKeever, John—Emma Rebecca Hazleton, both Burlington, 7-6-1854.
McKeighan, Daniel—Mary Olden, 6-11-1844.
McKillip, James—Mrs. Mary Afra Palmer, both Williamstown, 11-20-1858.
McKinney, James—Mary Ann Stow, 6-12-1859.

CAMDEN COUNTY MARRIAGES—BOOK A

McLaughlin, Richard—Sarah Herah, 5-6-1861.
  William—Mary Hurley, 12-21-1850.
McMann, John—Mary E. Anderson, 3-24-1864.
McName, Noclaus, Philadelphia—Martha Dunning, 11-14-1852.
McNeill, John— Heyl, A. E. (d. Harry C.), 4-27-1858.
McQuestion, James (s. James and Ellen)—Ann Tweed (d. John and Barbara), both Washington twp., 12-21-1849.
McVayne, Harry—Martha Henry, both Washington twp., 8-11-1852.
McWharton, Geo. B.—Lydia R. Moore, 12-22-1859.
Mead, Harvey—Susette Wilke, Philadelphia, 6-20-1856.
Measey, William—Hannah Elizabeth Bird, 4-17-1853.
Meeley, George, Jr., Swedesboro—Rhoda Pancoast, Woodstown, 9-24-1865.
Mercer, Robert P., Wilmington, Del.—Emma Merrikew, 3-16-1865.
Merryweather, Thomas—Deborah Warrington (d. John), 7-9-1858.
Mickle, Lewis S., Salem co.—Matilda C. Carter, Gloucester co., 10-19-1865.
Middlemiss, George—Elizabeth Merrin, 6-29-1863.
Middleton, Amos—Sarah Jane DeLacour, 2-28-1844.
  George H. (s. Wm. and Elizabeth), Pittsgrove—Mary Folwell Iredell (d Joshua and Rebecca), Salem, 2-14-1856.
  John B.—Mary Hempstead, 6-7-1854.
  Joseph—Mary L. Sheetz, 10-30-1865.
  Wm. C.—Deborah Pierce, 3-29-1859.
Millard, Abram—Mary Freeman, 3-31-1847.
Millburn, Jacob—Mary Butterworth, 6-25-1850.
Miller, Daniel J.—Catharine Ireland, 5-11-1850.
  Edwin F.—Josephine O'Donnell, 10-10-1859.
  Jacob, Philadelphia—Catharine Otway Diverty, 11-21-1860.
  Thomas—Elizabeth Gull, 7-19-1856.
Millette, William—Jane Hill, both Philadelphia, 12-9-1846.
Mills, Benoni—Amanda Lavinia Stiles, 1-18-1851.

CAMDEN COUNTY MARRIAGES—BOOK A 35

Mills, William, England—Elizabeth Cottington, Philadelphia, 12-14-1862.
Minks. William—Sarah Ann Steelman, 7-4-1844.
Mitchell. Benjamin—Jessie Henderson, 1-16-1854.
Mogey, Alexander—Jane Torp, 4-10-1845.
Moore, Andrew J —Rachel Hews, 3-23-1851.
  David G.—Hope F. Glover, 11-13-1860.
  Elmer—Mary E. Shields, 7-11-1852.
  James W.—Anna R. Mullica, 9-12-1864.
  Richard, Baltimore, Md.—Sharlotta Sulliven, 9-28-1859.
Morroe, Ira—Ann Carman, 1-19-1857.
  Joseph—Sarah G. Stiles, 9-27-1846.
Morgan, Eli B.—Altha Huston, Stroudsburg, Pa., 7-21-1883.
  George—Alice Harris, 9-12-1852.
  Isaac—Sarah Snuffin, 8-10-1850.
  Lewis—Rebecca Ann Beckett, 1-15-1852.
  Randal E, Washington twp.—Mary Josephine Willard, 1-10-1847.
  Richard—Hannah Garwood, 1-1-1846.
Morrice, William H.—Eliza Rutter, 4-21-1853.
Morris, Charles O. (s. Wm. L. and Caroline), Jersey City, — Rebecca Roe (d. David and Rebecca), 4-27-1858.
  John Harned—Eunice Clark Steen, Philadelphia, 3-13-1858.
Morse, George R.—Mary E. Shoemaker, 12-11-1851.
Morton, Noah H.—Helen D. Stroop, 9-11-1864.
Moseby, Thomas—Martha Roe, both Philadelphia, 4-12-1853.
Moss, William—Eliza Quinn, 9-19-1858.
Mott, Daniel—Hannah Wilson, 11-25-1845.
Muer, John—Anna Stehr, 4-27-1852.
Mulford, Thomas W.—Caroline Cole, 11-10-1847.
Mullener, John S.—Beulah A. Lock, 9-11-1853.
Mullica, William—Martha Bates, 8-21-1853.
Mulligan, Charles T., Philadelphia—Emily H. Booz, 5-18-1864.
Mullin, Joseph—Amy Bates, 7-4-1844.
Mulliner, Nathan T.—Hannah A. Shute, 9-28-1854.
Munter, August—Margaret Kelley, 2-16-1841.

Murphy, Daniel—Ann Eliza Flick, 2-3-1864.
  James W.—Charity Suran, 8-6-1851.
  Samuel—Susannah Soloman 1844.
  Stephen R.—Amanda S. Carpenter, 8-22-1863.
Murray, Hugh F.—Mary E. Bell, 5-6-1855.
Myand, John— Mary Elizabeth Scott, 12-14-1859.
Myres, William F.—Caroline C. McCalla, 10-22-1844.
Nack, Jacob—Sarah Monroe, both Medford, 5-13-1860.
Nail, Amos—Charity Edwards, 8-16-1855.
Naulty, Henry P , Philadelphia—Sarah Francisco, 8-5-1855.
Nedleberger, Joseph—Caroline Wensley, 8-4-1852.
Neiland, Francis—Anna Bamford, Philadelphia, 11-24-1857.
Neipling, Lewis W.—Jane M. Pratt, 1-17-1865.
Nemus, Anthony—Esther Ann Snow, 5-24-1862.
Newell, George T., Burlington co — Elizabeth S. Lucas, 12-13-1855.
Newkirk, Joseph—Lydia Newkirk, both Salem co., 12-8-1850.
Newman, David—Elizabeth Donalds, 12-7-1844.
Neville Hamilton—Violet Wilson, 11-16-1857.
Newton, Isaac—Jane VanSciver, 12-15-1845.
Nichols, David L.—Mary M. Black, 1-5-1851.
  Enoch C.—Josephine Ray, 9-16-1864.
  Peter—Rebecca Bowen, 6-6-1838.
  William—Sarah Thompson, 6-8-1862.
Nicholson, Gabriel—Mary Jane Day, 3-8-1852.
  John J.—Sarah E. Marchant 1-16-1866.
  William C.—Tamson R. Hurff, both Washington twp., 4-27-1854.
Nixon, John—Margaret Johnson (d. Wm. and Margaret), 4-20-1857.
Noble, Edward—Eliza Siness, 6-12-1853.
  James—Mary Ann Rulty, 5-21-1854.
Norcross, Isaiah, Glassboro—Ann H. Hart, 3-30-1866.
North, Aaron—Mary L. Leeds, 5-15-1845.
  James L.—Susanna Peters, 2-28-1852.
  John—Emeline Peters, 11-22-1851.
  Joshua T.—Martha C. Nicholson, 3-8-1855.

CAMDEN COUNTY MARRIAGES—BOOK A 37

North, Samuel—Elizabeth Ellis, 9-4-1845.
Nutt, Benjamin—Catharine Coleman, 1-12-1852.
Nutton, B. Y., Kittaning, Pa.—Sophie Rellly, 1-2-1865.
O'Donnall, George M.—Hannah Kunitz, 10-1-1860.
O'Grady, Mark—Ann Callahan, 2-11-1856.
Okey, Henry, Lewiston, Del.—Harriet Laws. 1-22-1858.
Olden, Benjamin Mary Jane Warden, 8-3-1846.
Oltwein, Henry—Catharine Gulick, 9-22-1858.
Ong, Benjamin T.—Emeline S. Dirmitt. 1-9-1857.
Osborn, Daniel B.—Mary Louisa Chadwick, 5-30-1858.
Osgood, William—Mary T. Burrough, 7-31-1844.
Packer, Edward S., Woodbury—Edith Polk, Philadelphia, 3-2-1859.
Parker, Howard—Hannah McCulloy, 9-20-1845.
 Isaac—Sarah Ann Pierce, 12-4-1851.
 James—Mary Ann Stow, 6-12-1859.
 William—Mary Shute, 12-20-1850.
 William H.—Mary Ann Davis (colored), 9-15-1855.
Parks. James—Sallie F. Dehart, 6-15-1862.
 James—Caroline Wynocker, 4-4-1864.
 Josiah H.—Lydia R. Josline, 2-22-1848.
 Lorenzo F.—Anne Maria Powell, 3-3-1851.
 Nehemiah—Mary W. Snyder, 5-21-1864.
Parr, Edward K.—Letitia Johnson, both Bordentown, 10-5-1864.
Parsons, James A.—Anna B. Johnson, 6-12-1859.
 Richard W.—Mary A. McIlwee, 10-26-1871.
Patterson, Charles—Rebecca Statt, 10-9-1859.
 Jacob M., Woodbury—Clementina F. Lloyd, Trenton, 11-7-1854.
 James C.—Isabella Kincaid, 3-25-1858.
 Joseph—Martha McTay, 2-17-1853.
Patton, Walter E.—Anna A. Gregory, 6-6-1854.
Paul, John—Hannah Woodruff. 1-13-1845.
 Samuel, Jr.—Ellen Eliza Broomfield, 5-1-1855.
 William—Sarah Jane Leach, 9-9-1852.
Payden, John—Mary Jane Braman, 11-10-1853.

Payne, Robert—Elizabeth Groft. 4-1-1847.
Peacock, John H.— Rachel Foster both Burlington, 10-2-1853.
Pease. Henry H.—Beulah H. Shinn. 12-15-1858.
Pedgree, George— Hannah Cox, 12-21-1854.
Pemlott, James H.—Rosanna Sloan, 6-27-1854.
Pendleton. Edwin S.—Rosena S. Kean, 9-6-1850.
Penn, James—Sarah Rewbart, 6-5-1852
  William—Margaret Mullica, 11-27-1853.
Pennock, Levi W.— Sarah Ann Minkler, both Pennsylvania, 7-13-1853.
Peragen, Isaac—Ellender Evans, 1-2-1862.
Perkins, Isaiah—Tamer Fisher, 2-12-1863.
  Jesse S.—Mrs. Rachel Tait. 12-25-1855.
Peters, Henry—Sarah Jane Batten. 9-30-1865.
  James F.—Canam H. Cook, 12-23-1849.
  John—Elizabeth Stetser, 10-19-1851.
  John, Jr.—Wilemina Bessee. 9-19-1840.
Peterson, Ezekiel S.—Catharine Dyer, 10-27-1847.
Petherbridge, Richard W., Rev., Pennington—Jane T. McFee, 9-28-1853.
Pettit, John M.—Mary E. Loch, 8-15-1853.
Pheiffer, George W.—Jane A. Bofel, 8-27-1865.
Phifer, John—Isabella S. Hunt, 6-12-1853.
Phillips, James M.—Mary Davy, 2-6-1854.
  John W.—Sarah J Hancock, both Rising Sun, Md., 7-15-1865.
  Thomas—Mary Davis, 1-26-1863.
Pierce, Edward—Elizabeth Denthort, Philadelphia, 1-9-1855.
  Ellis—Elizabeth G. Gibbs, 10-11-1846.
Pierson, Charles T —Sophronia D. Phinney, 5-21-1853.
  Daniel, Jr.—Sarah W. Morgan, 3-4-1848.
  Maurice B.—Elizabeth A. Chew, 11-3-1858.
Pinchin, Alfred, Philadelphia—Sarah M. Wilkins, 9-2-1844.
Pine, John J.—Abigail Buckley, 8-14-1862.
Pinkerton, Wm.—Martha A. Cross, 3-23-1848.
Pinyard, Silvester—Elizabeth Warfield, 3-12-1850.
Pitts, Sheppard— Elizabeth Deputy, 2-13-1862.

CAMDEN COUNTY MARRIAGES—BOOK A 39

Platt, Francis (s. John and Susannah)—Mary Ann Henry d. Thomas and Mary), 6-3-1860.
  William H.—Mrs. Emily Cooper, 10-9-1862.
Plews, Henry (s. John and Mary Ann), Philadelphia,—Ruth Maria McClain (d. James and Isabella), 9-19-1860.
Plum, John S.—Caroline K. Pine, 2-15-1853.
  Joseph C.—Phebe Ann Bate, 12-23-1847.
  Joshua H.—Elizabeth Bittle, 1-2-1857.
  Richard C.—Matilda Ann Fish, 9-13-1847.
  William—Catharine Myres, 2-15-1844.
  William—Rebecca Jane Lippincott, 5-10-1854.
Polk, Elijah C.—Annie M. Moore, 5-27-1885.
  John—Elizabeth Semm, 5-10-1863.
Pond, Anderson—Adah Bowen, 1-17-1847.
  Andrew—Margaret Cook, 6-9-1860.
Porch, Robert S.—Deborah Ann Seran, both Gloucester co., 4-3-1851.
Porter, Joseph C.—Sarah K. Doughten, 5-1-1845.
  William Collins—Sarah Josephine French, 6-28-1850.
Powell, Arthur—Rachel Day, 10-3-1852.
  Charles—Lydia Ann Russell, 2-20-1853.
  John—Mary Davis, 8-18-1858.
  Thomas—Hannah McEnany, 1-29-1859.
  William—Hannah Williams, 12-21-1853.
Pratt, John Jr.—Mary N. Turner, 2-19-1863.
  Rufus N.—Frances E. Giddings, 2-13-1853.
  Samuel—Lydia Ann Wilson, 9-3-1854; also recorded as 12-3-1854.
Price, Andrew Jackson—Elizabeth Fulton, 5-21-1854.
  Howard—Mary Jane Robinson, 3-7-1863.
  Jacob C.—Sarah Smith, 12-15-1845.
  Job—Elizabeth Severns, Westfield, 7-13-1862.
  Samuel G., Capt. (s. Samuel and Mary), Bordentown—Sarah M. Babcock (d. Hesta), 2-19-1855.
Prosser, Joseph—Emeline B. Cook, 2-22-1855.
Purnell, Edward—Alice Becket, 4-3-1845.
Quackerbush, George—Eliza Ann Evans, 5-6-1846.

Quesel, Jeremiah—Hannah McCarty, 5-8-1854.
Quick, John, Jr.—Annie M. Griffin, 4-4-1858.
Quimby, Levi—Sarah Stetser, 8-6-1856.
Quinn, Richard—Sarah Stewart, 4-4-1866.
Rafine, Gideon T.—Sarah J. Andrews, 5-13-1847.
Ramsey, Emmor H.—Rebecca E. Moore, 7-26-1865.
   William G.—Caroline Aldsworth, both Philadelphia, 10-16-
Read, James—Caroline Williams, 9-22-1862.
   John S.—Harriet Key, 12-2-1857.
   William B.—Maria Stetser, 3-21-1859.
Reatty, Joseph H., Mt. Holly—Annie S. Hugg, 11-22-1854.
Redfield, William H., (wid.), Westville (s. Blan and Rebecca) —Ellen W. Jennings (d. Richard and Eliza) Woodbury, 9-9-1866.
Reding, Wilson, Delaware—Caroline Batten, 9-27-1864.
Redman, Charles P. (s. Thomas and Elizabeth)—Mary Ann Albertson (d Josiah and Abigail), 10-14-1853.
Reed, Josiah M.—Sallie A. Williams, 4-5-1866.
Reeve, Augustus (s. Wm. F. and Mary W.), Allowaystown —Rebecca Wood (d. Isaac and Elizabeth), 6-6-1862.
   James D.—Hester Ann Bozorth, 7-2-1846.
Rheubert, Thomas—Eliza H. Cossaboon, 9-8-1856.
Rhoads, Manning F., Chester co., Pa.—Harriet Powell, Cumberland co., 2-2-1858.
   William M., Chester, Pa.—Margaretta Cook, 3-2-1858.
Richards, Launcelet—Sarah Somers Treen, 6-5-1847.
Richardson, Joseph, Beverly—Amelia Strock, 3-27-1864.
Richman, Abraham—Rebecca Ann Horner, 11-28-1846.
   Adam H., Malaga—Lydia Becket, Hardingville, 1-25-1865.
   Calvin G., Hurffville—Lucy A. Upham, Millville, 7-3-1862.
   George B.—Anna Maria Gaunt, 5-25-1845.
Rightz Frederick—Mary Ann Earley, 6-19-1845.
Riley, Andrew—Barbary Watson, 11-19-1855.
   Josiah—Mary J. Wiser, both Sharpto wn, 4-6-1864.
   Peter—Amelia Bodine, 1-24-1847.
   William W.—Eliza Heaton, 2-28-1859.
Ringland, John—Sallie Davenport, Philadelphia, 7-31-1855.

Riley, Caleb M.—Eliza P. Cox, 12-18-1851.
Risley, Isaac—Mary Durr, both Mt. Holly, 10-22-1853.
  John L., Great Egg Harbor—Sarah Jane Cornish, 5-16-1862.
Roath, Joseph H.—Hannah Lee, Mays Landing, 3-21-1862.
Roberts, Azael—Mary E. Ross, 5-5-1844.
  Francis—Susannah Tilman, 3-6-1844.
  Josiah A., Columbia, Pa.—Ella C. Fisler, 12-13-1854.
  Joshua W., Nashville, Tenn.—Anna G. Simmons, 10-15-1863.
Robertson, Ephraim T.—Catharine Ocelia Grinvault, 2-4-1856.
Robinson, Herbert C., Newark, Del.—Martha N. Taylor, 1-5-1860.
  John G —Rebecca Wilmot, 8-15-1865.
  Joseph—Sarah Clayton, both Chester co., Pa., 8-27-1857.
  William—Emily Northrope, 6-26-1862
  William H.—Elizabeth Hoffinger, 1-1-1859.
Rogers, Charles H. (s. Minor and Elizabeth)—Elizabeth Adams (d. George and Martha), 10-4-1863.
  Edwin—Elizabeth M. Glinn, 1-14-1858.
  Eli E., Bridgeton—Anna M. Ewing, 12-10-1861.
  John B., Philadelphia—Sarah Shermer, 2-6-1859.
  Samuel B.—Sarah Wentzel, both Montgomery co., Pa., 8-6-1852.
  Thomas—Martha Ann Buzby, 2-6-1848.
  William J.—Sarah Williams, 10-18-1851.
Roller, Frederick—Elizabeth Shiver, 9-10-1853.
  George, Sr.—Priscilla Smith, 4-5-1853.
  George—Mary Hemmelwright, 3-23-1848.
  Jacob—Sarah Speas, 7-10-1852.
Rose, Edmund R.—Anna Todd, 6-5-1864.
Rosenfelt, Lewis—Adley Chambers, 4-25-1859.
Ross, George F.—Mary Smith, 11-8-1846.
  William—Angelina Hopkins, New Egypt, 9-30-1855.
Roston, William—Margaret McFerill, both Gloucester co. 12-31-1851.

Rothwell, James—Susanna Ellis, 8-12-1852.
Rowand, Albert T.—Mary R. M. Christy, Philadelphia, 12-15-1859.
Rowland, Thompson—Amelia Freeman, Philadelphia, 5-20-1852.
Rudderow, Samuel S.—Sarah Chambers, 12-25-1851.
Ruderow, Levi C.—Sarah J. Christian, 4-6-1854.
Rudrow, Isaac A.—Ann Hooper, 11-14-1862.
Rulon, Elwood (s. Moses)—Mary R. Palmer (d. Abraham and Eliza), 2-23-1865.
  Jesse C., Capt.—Martha B. Burdsall, both Waretown, Ocean co., 6-12-1866.
Rusby, John, Franklin, Essex co.—Abigail Holmes, Bloomfield, Essex co., 2-4-1852.
Rusley, Pollas—Phebe Smith, 8-7-1853.
Russell, James R.—Hannah Righter, 12-17-1854.
  William—Mariah Laton, 10-12-1863.
Ryan, William H.—Maria L. Sheldon, 10-25-1854.
Sabers, Benjamin—Martha Matilda Whittle, 9-14-1845.
Sack, Ezekiel—Mary W. Cloud, 12-16-1858.
Sadler, John—Mary Hankerson, 12-19-1861.
Sage, Elijah—Mary Ann Horner, 8-4-1844.
Sahanker, Henry—Elizabeth Zimmerman, 6-16-1853.
Sammonds, Henry—Eliza Black, 11-27-1862.
Sands, Edward—Hannah Pleasant, 10-22-1859.
  John, Maryland—Jannetta Scott, Pennsylvania, 8-24-1858.
Sarish, Stephen, Dorcas Wright, 4-15-1854.
Saunders, Samuel—Ann Eliza Fort, 4-2-1851.
Sautell, Henry—Caroline Beagary, both Philadelphia, 5-5-1847.
Savage, William Y., Toronto, Can.—Adelia J. Mulholland, 12-21-1860.
Savarine, Levi—Harriet Boyer. Recorded 8-21-1863.
Sawn, Joseph P.—Hannah M. Manus, 11-20-1852.
Sawyer, David E.—Eliza J. Simpers, Greensboro Ind., 4-21-1864.
Sayers, Samuel—Rachel Collins, 8-24-1856.

CAMDEN COUNTY MARRIAGES—BOOK A   43

Scattergood, Samuel Philadelphia—Mary Hunsinger, 1-18-1860.
Schake, Auguste—Mary Gallagher, 3-8-1852.
Schellinger, Charles Cox, Cape Island—Mary Ellen Reeves (d. J H. and Eleanor), Unionville, 11-12-1864.
Schooley, Samuel G.—Clarissa Lippincott, both Moorestown, 2-26-1862.
  William—Rachel Ruderow, 2-28-1856.
Schreiner, Richard, Philadelphia—Catharine Horner, 9-8-1864.
Schubert, John—Emeline Cline, 7-5-1858.
Schwaab, Joseph A.—Sarah Jane Brown, 7-19-1858.
Scott, George W.—Elizabeth C. Muncey, 5-21-1859.
  Thomas R., Deptford—Caroline Elizabeth Cooper, 12-20-1855.
Scovel, James M. (s. Silvester and Hannah)—Mary Mulford (d. Isaac and Rachel), 5-21-1859.
Seaver, Joseph L.—Phebe H. Wilson. both Vincentown, 6-29-1844.
Seeds, Albert, Bridgeboro—Margaret Lynch, Philadelphia, 6-21-1865.
Severman, Thomas H.—Anna M. Stevensou, 9-18-1852.
Severns, Edward—Margaret Horner, both Westfield, 5-26-1862.
Shafer, Samuel—Lenora Sharp, 4-14-1864.
  John—Elizabeth Robinson, 9-17-1865.
Shaffer, Henry—Elizabeth Crispin, 11-26-1846.
Shain, John—Bell Jane Powell, 5-31-1851.
Shallcross, Lewis—Anne Jones, 9-2-1859.
Shameley, James—Julian Travis, 12-9-1865.
Sharp, Charles F.—Priscilla R. Batten, 10-21-1854.
  Frederick—Mary Ann Clement, 10-13-1845.
  Horace M.—Keziah A. Warrington, 3-8-1859.
  Jacob G.—Mary E. Lake, 9-28-1865.
  James—Harriet Booth, 7-1-1853.
  Jesse W.—Mary Ann Smith, 8-7-1851.
  John, Philadelphia—Elizabeth Hoare, 3-1-1855.

CAMDEN COUNTY MARRIAGES—BOOK A

Sharp, Levi P.—Hannah Horner, 1-9-1852.
  Thomas B.—Mary Stafford, 7-20-1862.
  Thomas T.—Catharine A. Smith, 7-12-1854.
  William—Annie McClay, 9-3-1863.
Sharpless, Ellis, Philadelphia—Elizabeth Bruner, 8-8-1855.
Shaw, Hudson L.—Amanda M. Hires, 1-14-1854.
  John Boothroyd—Sarah Ann Stokes, both Philadelphia, 5-28-1856.
  Timothy—Annie H. Stevens, 2-26-1856.
  William A. (s. Joseph and Susan). Philadelphia—Mary Matilda Cole (d. Jesse and Keziah), 3-19-1863.
Shea, John—Mary Ann Queen, 4-25-1852.
Sheldon, Charles W.—Sarah W. Prickett, 4-26-1854.
  Lemuel D.—Abbey North, 9-5-1846.
  Noah W.—Judith C. Smith, Great Egg Harbor, 11-29-1851.
Shepherd, Isaac—Martha A. Parks, 9-8-1847.
  John—Martha Bankhead, 10-4-1855.
Sherwin, Quincey A.—Ann P. Cooper, 2-26-1852.
Shields, Christopher J.—Margaret E. Brown, 5-11-1856.
  Thomas G. (s. Thomas and Sophia)—Margaret Stine (d. John and Eliza), 4-21-1856.
  William—Mary Ann Barton (colored), 12-29-1863.
Shillingforth, James—Lydia Gibbs, 3-22-1846.
Shimp, David—Annie H. Crispin, both Allowaystown, 10-31-1860.
Shinn, Caleb—Rachel Swain, both Chesterfield, 7-18-1854.
  Charles Henry—Hannah M. Shires, 4-21-1856.
  James L.—Mary L. Hancock, both Burlington co., 10-28-1852.
  Jos. H.—Mary C. Sullivan, 10-1-1857.
  Levi—Eliza F. Shick, 8-26-1831.
Shive, Adolph Rushton, Rev.—Elizabeth Eldridge, 10-21-1860.
Shivers, Bowman Hendry—Anna E. Moore, 11-25-1863.
  John—Mary Ann Hillman, 4-8-1847.
  Josiah—Maria Ann Donnelly, 7-22-1858.
Shockley, John, Philadelphia—Adeline Carney, 9-6-1864.

Shone, Cornelius P.—Catharine H. Kindel, 12-15-1863.
   Thomas J.—Sarah Jane Pine, 1-6-1853.
Short, Benjamin—Mary L. Adams, Atlantic co., 10-11-1855.
Shreve, Malon—Harriet N. Chew, 11-29-1849.
Shuman, Jacob—Sarah Ann Jones, 3-2-1847.
Shute, Henry—Beulah A. Green, 12-25-1862.
Sibbett, John A., Hurffville—Ann E. North, 1-25-1866.
Sickler, Benjamin F.—Mary Elizabeth Gardner, 1-4-1866.
   John—Jane E. Sharp, Washington twp., 7-5-1858.
   Joshua B.—Jennie Whitmore, Middleboro, Mass., 8-11-1864.
   Josiah—Mary Ann North, 8-31-1845.
Siegfried, James—Catharine Maria Marche, 2-7-1852.
Silpath, John—Catharine Smith, 3-28-1848.
Silver, John D.—Louisa D. Campbell, 11-24-1859.
   Joshua D.—Rachel H. Mounce, 1-25-1860.
Simcox, John B.—Jane Welden, 9-7-1855.
Simmons, Isaac—Angeline Burroughs, 8-8-1865.
   Stephen—Rebecca Gibson, 12-5-1844.
Simons, Edward, Pennsylvania—Anna L. Megonigal, 5-26-1865.
Simpson, James E.—Sarah J. Evans, 5-19-1863.
Sims, George, Mary Jane Allen, 11-4-1857.
Sine, Jacob—Catharine Hall, 12-24-1853.
Siness, Robert—Margaret Clifford, 4-9-1854.
Sinkings, Charles—Charlotte P. Bird, 6-5-1862.
Skadger, John—Lydia Ann Ingle, 9-16-1852.
Smallwood, Jacob I.—Sarah McDonough, 4-10-1856.
   Joseph T.—Sarah Donhough, 4-10-1856.
Smith, Charles, Philadelphia—Sallie Brock, 9-18-1865.
   Elisha—Lidda Ann Bennett, 5-28-1848.
   Ephraim L.—Caroline Smyth, 12-27-1845.
   Frederic—Rosa Berner, Philadelphia, 11-13-1852.
   German, Martinsburg, Va.—Hannah L. Hewlings, 5-24-1864.
   Henry B., Sussex co.—Catharine H. Blow, Hunterdon co., 3-29-1864.

Smith, John—Martha C. Sparks, 10-25-1845.
  John—Charlotte Wells, 5-23-1846.
  John—Eliza Ann Day, 1-13-1847.
  John, Jr.—Elizabeth Hewlings (d. Lewis and Elizabeth), 4-10-1855.
  Messer—Mary Lorrance, 1-1-1848.
  Richard F.—Jane F. Frazer, 12-22-1864.
  Richardson A.—Elizabeth Coleman, 2-15-1860.
  Samuel—Mary Craig, 6-21-1851.
  William—Behsel Duro, June 1857.
Snow, Jeremiah Garrison—Mary Ann McNichols, 9-25-1860.
  William H.—Millisan K. Hankins, 8-18-1864.
Snuffen, John—Mahala P. Budd, 11-12-1846.
Snyder, Benjamin F.—Susannah Gray, both Gloucester co., 10-18-1861.
  George Henry—Mary Ann Anderson, 4-20-1856.
  John F.—Catharine Ann Rose, 11-21-1852.
Solk, Joseph—Harriet Harris (colored), 1-16-1860.
Somers, George—Elizabeth Baraba, 10-31-1847.
  Jesse S.—Deborah J. Bowen, both Egg Harbor, 3-4-1853.
  Robert—Josephine Pierce, Philadelphia, 7-28-1861.
Sommers, Henry—Mary Corcoran, both Philadelphia, 12-20-1862.
Sorden, Aaron—Anna E. Cline, 12-20-1846.
Southard, David M.—Ann E. Bond, 2-4-1858.
Sowber, Hepolety—Angelina C. Gant, 12-20-1846.
Sparks, Charles A., Philadelphia—Amelia Ross, 11-11-1852.
  David H.—Caroline M. Jones, 9-15-1854.
  Joseph—Sarah Gifford, 3-17-1847.
  Robert—Beulah Stow, 5-20-1854.
Spear, Chas. A., New York—Helen Cooper, at the American Legation, Berne, Switzerland, 7-23-1873.
Speers, Jacob—Barbarett Gros, 9-23-1850.
Spencer, James—Joanna Scott, 12-1-1863.
Springer, Samuel—Rachel Magee, 10-19-1844.
Sprowl, David C.—Rebecca A. Gifford, 6-25-1864.
Stack, Albert Edward—Kate Magdalene Hartner, 1-3-1885.

CAMDEN COUNTY MARRIAGES—BOOK A 47

Stackhouse, Benjamin, Medford— Elizabeth Plum, 1-27-1859.
   Edward H.—Abigail Venable, both Burlington co., 7-11-1844.
Stadem, Daniel—Alice Hokum, 9-10-1854.
Stafford, Joseph C.—Sarah Ann Bowen, 12-10-1846.
Stanger, Andrew J.—Sarah Ann Murphy, 6-5-1852.
   John—Ann W. Bishop, 12-18-1845.
   John—Rosanna Izard, 3-19-1848.
   Solomon—Lydia B. Shute, 2-2-1860.
Starn, Isaac W.—Sarah M. Parker, 8-30-1857.
   Joseph H.—Mary Hinchman, 12-26-1855.
Starr, Moses—Eliza B. Smith, 5-24-1855.
Steer, Martin—Elizabeth Brice, 4-3-1852.
Steinmetz, Savillion A.—Emma A. Brewer, 4-23-1861.
Stephenson, Isaac—Amy I. Heritage, 11-27-1862.
   Samuel M.—Mary J. Gibson, both Gloucester co., 2-27-1864.
Stetser, John M.—Cetharine Blacke, 12-23-1865.
Steverson, Charles—Sarah Gray, 4-17-1856.
   John P.—Fannie E. Reeves, 8-6-1861.
   Richard B. (s. Isaac and Sarah)—Hannah A. Johnson (d. Joseph and Eliza), both Deptford, 4-7-1849.
Stewart, Andrew—Margaret Smith, both Bucks co., Pa., 4-25-1862.
   Andrew J.—Maria W. Ross, 12-25-1854.
   Henry—Sarah Smallwood, 5-17-1854.
Stiles, Reuben C.—Tolitha H. Stiles, 9-17-1861.
   Saml. R.—Sarah A. Harris, 8-16-1862.
   William—Mary B. Hatch, 12-1-1863.
Stillwell, Francis P.—Harriet G. Fennemore, 10-2-1863.
   James O.—Georgian Cornelia Hoffman, 9-9-1847.
   Samuel A.—Susanna A. Clayton, 12-3-1854.
Stokes, Joseph J.—Hannah B. Matlack, 7-18-1852.
   Spencer—Caroline A. Gilkey, 9-5-1852.
Stone, Isaac P.—Mrs. Mary E. Russell Stone, 3-16-1852.
   Joshua P.—Elizabeth W. Marshall, 12-5-1858.
   Richard F.—Mary E. Thompson, 3-20-1859.

CAMDEN COUNTY MARRIAGES—BOOK A

Stone, Robert—Mary Wany, 7-19-1858.
  Samuel— Rebecca Ann Blakley, 12-18-1851.
Story, George, Bordentown—Sarah Steward, Woodstown, 9-2-1846.
  John—Rebecca H. Fish, 3-11-1846.
Stott, Charles, Washington, D. C.—Lillias Young, 7-7-1846.
Stow, Edward—Sarah Loyd, 3-2-1854.
  Jacob—Mary Newton, 9-8-1820.
  John C.—Sarah Bate, 1-11-1865.
  Joseph I.—Martha Matilda Smith, 8-21-1845.
  Stone Harris—Jennie Eliza Cox, 11-18-1844.
  William H.—Henrietta Shane, 3-1-1863.
Stozar, Elias—Jane Dixon, 9-15-1857.
Strang, Peter D., Glassboro—Hannah Thomas, Bethel, 8-20-1862.
Stratton, William R.—Mary E. Fisher, 9-21-1854.
Strickland, John S.—Elizabeth L. Griffin, 6-15-1847.
Strong, Cornelius W., Glassboro—Sarah Jane Sharp, 6-5-1858.
Stroop, Nathan M.—Elizabeth H. Smith, 9-27-1864.
Stull, William—Eliza Shinn, 12-17-1861.
Sturgest, John—Mary Hamilton, 1-23-1859.
Sturgis, Charles C.—Elizabeth S. Cooper, 10-9-1864.
Subers, Joseph E.—Elizabeth Voutier, 4-16-1857.
Sugden, William H.—Lidie Corels, 7-12-1865.
Sullivan, Dennis—Fannie Parnell, 8-6-1865.
  John M.—Elizabeth Fennimore, 4-17-1862.
Sutten, John Boteth—Mary Jane Jennings, both Gloucester co., 12-16-1852.
Sweeten, Gideon W.—Margaret Blelterman, 6-11-1863.
  John—Mattie A. Gaskill, 8-29-1863.
  William J.—Elizabeth A. Cowan, 10-9-1865.
Swiles, George L.—Elizabeth Knisel, 1-26-1858.
Tanier, Joseph—Mary Coates, 5-7-1865.
Tanner, George W.—Josephine A. Hannold, 5-22-1864.
  Milo Eugene—Ann S. Bruner, Wheeling, Va., 1-17-1852.
Taylor, John F.—Sarah E. Kirchenbower, 8-15-1866.

CAMDEN COUNTY MARRIAGES—BOOK A

Taylor, Marmaduke B.—Agnes C. Crain, 9-3-1861.
Test, Goldsou—Tamsen F. Maul, 2-24-1863.
Teuch, Frederick—Lydia Ann Venel, 8-22-1853.
Thackray, Isaac I.—Susan Ann Davis, Philadelphia, 4-23-1854.
Thomas, Benjamin—Isabella Smith, 11-20-1846.
  Edward F.—Margaretta Lyttle, 10-24-1844.
  George—Mary Jane Henry, 12-18-1861.
  James—Hannah Bowen, 11-24-1846.
  John W.—Sarah Ann Chew, 6-25-1850.
  Samuel—Mrs. Elizabeth Bryan Fisher, 4-11-1852.
  Stephen—Louisa Mosely, 3-6-1856.
  William—Mary Sermon, 5-3-1863.
Thompsan, James—Elizabeth White, 7-4-1857.
  James William, Jr., Philadelphia—Laura N. Troth, 10-7-1862.
  John—Hannah A. Ellis, 3-28-1865.
  John R.—Ann Elizabeth Laughlin, 8-2-1860.
Thorn, Charles H.—Caroline Dorsey, 4-16-1846.
  Joseph—Elizabeth Johnston, 3-7-1847.
  Josiah S.—Caroline Hines, 8-10-1852.
  Richard—Sarah Farnum, 8-25-1853.
Thornley, Hiram—Harriet Bayron (d. Samuel), both natives of Lincolnshire, Eng., 2-18-1857.
Thornton, John—Eveline Shreeve, 9-21-1853.
Tomlinson, Charles W. (s. Isaac and Sarah W.)—Roxanna Warrick (d. Edward and Priscilla), 1-17-1884.
Tice, Benjamin—Abigail Tarpine, 6-7-1845.
  Clayton B.—Catharine Eldridge, both Williamstown, 6-17-1858.
  John—Elizabeth J. Hamen, 1-28-1855.
  John R —Rebecca Campbell, 10-2-1853.
  Samuel—Anne Pine, 2-20-1845.
Tilman, Isaac—Lucy Sanman, 7-29-1852.
Tinker, Henry—Mary Giberson, 2-20-1860.
Todd, Michael—Zebiah Pearson, 11-1-1855.
Tomlin, Joseph W.—Sarah Thompson, 12-7-1864.

CAMDEN COUNTY MARRIAGES—BOOK A

Tothwell, James W. Ella Shealey, 4-28-1858.
Townsend, Vandoren—Patience Stafford, 9-28-1862.
Toy, Earle H.—Adeline Hoy, Baltimore, 8-13-1851.
   Samuel A.—Catharine R. Lynd, 8-31-1844.
Treskler, Jacob A.—Christiana Amelia Johns, 6-22-1857.
Tripler, Jacob L., Philadelphia—Louisa Horner, 2-10-1859.
Tucker, Ephraim H.—Elizabeth M. Middleton, 3-7-1854.
Turner, Benjamin F.—Angeline Hughes, 11-4-1865.
   Charles—Mary A. Shaw, 1-18-1865.
   David, Georgia—Emma Burgess 8-6-1865.
   Eugene—Anna S. Baner, Wheeling, Va., 1-17-1852.
   Samuel H.--Mary Cook, 10-25-1865
Turnley, Charles William—Martha Ann Collings, 7-3-1855.
Tush, William—Charlotte Horn, 11-26-1846.
Tuttle, Samuel—Beaula Moore, 8-7-1845.
Tweed, William—Rebecca McIlvaine, 9-1-1845.
Tyes, William—Keziah Page, 5-2-1861.
Tyler, John V.—Achsah W. Tucker, 2-12-1854.
   Samuel—Leweasa Bozorth, 4-8-1867.
Tyling, John, Philadelphia—Mary Emons, 10-18-1861.
Uhler, Levi—Keziah Decatur, 5-20-1854,
Vance, William H—Caroline Peck, 7-3-1851.
Vanclief, James—Margaret Nelson, 12-2-1865.
Vandegrift, Edward, Burlington co.—Hannah Ann Chew, 9-27-1852.
Vandergrift, Abram (s. Isaac and Sarah)—Sarah C. Burrough (d. David and Elizabeth), 5-4-1865.
Vandeveer, Cornelius (wid.), (s. Peter and Mary)—Sarah M. Vandeveer (d. Cornelius and Mary), 2-1-1858.
Vandevere, William—Rebecca Roselle, both Philadelphia, 6-5-1861.
VanDuxter, William (s. Joseph and Mary)—Eliza Jane Jones (d. John and Jane), 10-6-1851.
Vaneman, Jacob—Matilda M. Brown, 10-2-1859.
Vanhart, Charles S.—Hannah Miskelly, 9-8-1860.
Vanhorn, Wm. W.—Mary Ann Restine, 10-27-1855.
Vanmeter, Isaac W., Cumberland co.—Mary Mowers, 2-24-1866.

Vanmeter, Robert—Matilda Newkirk, both Upper Pittsgrove, 2-7-1855.
Vansant, James, Rev., Cumberland co.—Rachel Ireland, Atlantic co., 10-8-1855.
  Richard W., Allowaystown—Alice P. Seeley, Philadelphia, 1-5-1865.
Vanscoit, Nicholas—Anna M. Strock, 12-28-1864.
VanStavens, Francis—Abigail Hunzinger, 4-16-1854.
Vare, Henry—Elizabeth Jones, 4-24-1858.
Vogel, Charles T.—Caroline Kronk, both Philadelphia, 5-23-1860.
Wagner, George—Hannah E. Hudson, 1-13-1859.
Waine, Joseph—Susan Bosure, 5-18-1845.
Walkenshaw, A. M.—Margaret C. Gilfillian, both Philadelphia, 10-15-1864.
Wallace, Ivins Davis—Eleanor Foulk Rediker, 12-24-1863.
Wallens, Jacob—Elizabeth Robbins, 6-4-1850.
Walmsley, William Henry—Annie M. Bunting, Crosswicks, 11-23-1854.
Walters, John N.—Harriet Fayette, 5-1-1852.
  Samuel—Rebecca Wilson, 9-26-1844.
Wamsley, John—Cordelia Frances Dunn, 1-26-1862.
Wannan, George—Phebe Ann Long, 4-4-1848.
Warberton, Peter—Sarah Ann Gibbons, 3-5-1856.
Ware, Andrew J.—Sarah Brown, 7-4-1854.
  Josiah—Elizabeth Horner, 2-16-1860.
Warrick, Edmund H. (s. Joseph and Theodosia)—Priscilla R. Batten (d. Moses and Roxanaa), 2-1-1849.
Warrington, James (s. John and Deborah), Burlington co.—Abigail Lippincott (d. Barclay and Deborah), 3-23-1848.
Watkins, John W.—Sarah H. Johnson, 11-14-1844.
Watson, Edward—Ann McConley, 10-12-1845.
  George—Sarah Albertson, 11-1-1854.
  George—Priscilla Eisle, 2-10-1858.
  Geo. W.—Mary Bideman, 11-29-1858.
  James—Nora Elmira Rapel, 1-6-1852.
  James—Mary Ann Grain, 5-21-1854.

Weatherby, Samuel L.—Susan F. Boyd, 5-15-1852.
  William P.—Emma L Jefferies, 5-21-1862.
Weaver, Henry Clay—Mary Elizabeth Seward, 1-20-1844.
Webb, John H.—Anna Patterson, 12-31-1853.
Weeks, Andrew—Angeline Staar, both Pennsylvania, 4-22-1851.
  Benjamin E —Ann Eliza Hewitt, 5-28-1854.
  Daniel C.—Sarah Jane Weeks, 6-25-1854
  Nicholas Lower Bank—Rebecca A. Wright, 10-6-1864.
Weest, John, Mount Holly—Mary K. Fisher, 12-22-1853.
Welch, William—Rachel Beckett, 8-21-1854.
Wells, Abner—Ann Buzby, 1-1-1854.
  Charles—Elizabeth Ann Middleton, both Burlington, 5-24-1856
  George—Sarah Albertson, 4-11-1844.
  Horatio T.—Ann Maria Berenger, 4-3-1852.
  John—Rachel Braddock, 10-10-1850.
  Philip, Jr.—Catharine Watson, 1-14-1845.
  Samuel —Abigail Warner, 12-30-1850.
  William, Burlington co.—Elizabeth Becking, Montgomery co., Pa., 1-18-1851.
Werner, Anthony—Esther Ann Stow, 5-24-1862.
Werts, Joseph—Susan Ann Moore, 9-20-1853.
Wescot, Reuben—Susan Norcross, 1-24-1863.
Wescott, David A.—Emily C. Smith, 9-28-1862.
  John—Hannah R. Taylor, 3-17-1866.
  Waran—Susan Jaggard, 2-25-1847.
West, Edward—Anna Amanda Clinger, 3-4-1855.
  Elijah E.—Mary Stafford Thackery, 2-1-1854.
  John T.—Patience R. Spiegle, 6-1-1852.
Westcoat, Christopher—Martha Ann Githens, 5-14-1854.
Westcott, Ezra—Martha H. Watson, 10-17-1863.
  Jesse—Eliza Bates, 7-14-1855.
Weverman, Isaac W.—Catharine Swartly, both Montgomery co., Pa., 12-26-1863.
  Wheaton, Joseph P.—Mary Elizabeth Graves, 8-16-1852.
  Miles K.—Elizabeth Walker, 11-11-1865.

CAMDEN COUNTY MARRIAGES—BOOK A 53

Whitacar, David—Elizabeth L. Kesler, both Clarksboro, 12-30-1846.
White, Edmund C.—Mary E. Bateman, 4-6-1845.
  Edmund—Emma Clark, 1-5-1865.
  John F.—Keziah Sickler, 5-4-1850.
  John T.—Lydia C. Sparks, both Salem co., 9-6-1854.
  John W., Ocean co.—Janett Y. Horner, Burlington co., 6-21-1865.
  Josiah, Burlington co.—Mary H. Allen, 10-2-1862.
  Simon Wilmer—Catharine I. Noggle, 10-13-1859.
  Wm. A.—Henrietta S. Wible, 1-2-1858.
Whitehead, Joel—Caroline Hewitt, 4-25-1852.
Whiting, Edward S., Andersonia, Conn.—Emma J. Hurlburt, 6-21-1865.
Whitteir, Cyrus M., Washington, D. C.—Martha Beckley, 6-15-1865.
Wick, Jesse E.—Adaline P. Down, both Turnerville, 12-9-1865
Wickers, Amos—Phebe A. Powell, 4-7-1862.
Wignall, John—Ann Broughton, both Manayunk, Pa., 9-30-1855.
Wikel, Israel E.—Annie Strang, Moorestown—8-15-1862.
Wilcox, William, Brighton, N. Y.—Mary A. Livermore, 11-17-1858.
Wiley, Samuel—Mrs. Hetty Lamar, 10-30-1859.
Wildon, John P.—Matilda M. Robb, 8-10-1846.
Wilkins, Alfred F.—Anna W. Core, both Frankford, Pa., 3-15-1865.
  Amos—Phebe A. Powell, both Gloucester co., 4-11-1842.
  Andrew J.—Elizabeth Jane Hazleton, 12-1-1851.
  James—Sarah D. Rogers, 12-3-1846.
  John—Elizabeth Kline, 11-8-1851.
Wilkinson, Alfred—Charlotte V. Dunn, 9-25-1845.
Willett, Virgil—Lenora Campbell, 8-18-1862.
Williams, George L.—Susan Ann Phillips, 12-9-1847.
  Hiram—Hope Ann Cheeseman, 9-16-1847.
  John—Rachel Pine, 12-16-1848.

CAMDEN COUNTY MARRIAGES—BOOK A

Williams, John C.—Maria Grose, 2-22-1862.
  Jonathan P.—Sarah Jane Shone, 2-6-1851.
  Montraville—Fanny A. J. Riley, 1-26-1855.
  Gerrard—Ann Robinson, 12-25-1862.
  Richard—Mary Emily Rennail, 4-20-1854.
  William—Sarah Brown, 11-15-1845.
Willits, Stephen, Tuckerton—Mary Alma Knorr, Philadelphia 9-20-1865.
Willmot, John S.—Margaret Kincade, 3-27-1855.
Wills, Adon G. (s. Adon and Eliza)—Susannah T. Matlack, (d. Joshua and Amy), 4-15-1858.
  Varney—Hannah Gifford, 12-13-1845.
Wilson, Ephraim, Rev.—Susanna Ganges, 4-10-1858.
  Henry B.—Mary Ann Wilson, 10-3-1854.
  James E. (s. James and Ann)—Esther Bateman (d. Stephen and Maria), 11-7-1850.
  James F.—Phebe S. Sines, both Tuckerton, 9-12-1858.
  John J.—Ann Dunham, 5-22-1858.
  John S.—Amanda Brock, Moorestown, 3-10-1859.
  Joseph C. (s. Eli), Gloucester co.—Rachel H. Boggs (d. Mrs. Ann Perkins), 2-27-1856.
  Thomas—Ann Jameison, Philadelphia, 7-14-1846.
  Thomas Y.—Elizabeth Senor, 9-29-1849.
  William—Jane Conlin, 2-26-1853.
Wiltse, William H. (s. Joseph)—Anna E. Keyser (d. Andrew), 5-2-1863.
Wiltsey, William—Mary Ann Beetle, 6-18-1853.
Winder, Samuel—Sarah Johnson, both Philadelphia, 6-20-1852.
Winner, Abram—Sarah Brown, 9-2-1865.
Winterbottom, James—Mary Ann Hill, 7-14-1864.
Wise, Benjamin F., Philadelphia—Emma R. Repsher, 10-8-1854.
  Edward, Philadelphia—Margaret Ann Bailey, 6-12-1853.
  John—Rebecca Thomas, Gloucester co., 10-6-1856.
  John—Ella Comley, 7-4-1864.
Wisham, Samuel P.—Phebe P. Peters, 1-17-1852.

CAMDEN COUNTY MARRIAGES—BOOK A

Wolfe, Robert—Mary Ann Carr, 12-30-1852.
Wolohon, Joseph, Jr.—Rachel Alexander (wid. of Benj. M.) 9-18-1860.
Wood, Charles K.—Hannah Hoffman, 9-3-1854.
  Edmund T.—Sarah Ann Cooper, 10-7-1847.
  John B. (s. John and Elizabeth C.), Philadelphia—Susan Shivers (d. Richard and Mary H.), 12-9-1862.
  John C.—Sarah Bee, 1-9-1845.
Woodard, Ebenezer—Sarah Briant, 9-6-1852.
Woodington, David C.—Mary Wood, Burlington, 7-11-1853.
Woodling, Henry—Mary Davis (colored), 1-24-1845.
Woodruff, Elmer C. R.—Cordelia Whittington (d. Nehemiah and Louisa), Mt. Vernon O., 5-3-1864.
Woods, Ezekiel—Elizabeth Longworth, both Ireland, 1-5-1856.
  Josiah C.—Marrietta Heritage, Gloucester co., 11-12-1864.
Woolcott, Charles Southwark (s. Benj. and Hannah)—Henrietta Davidson (d. Adam and Mary Ann), 11-1-1860.
Wooley, Abraham—Juliann Boyern (colored), 1-1-1849.
Woolford, George W.—Mary J. Fielding, 4-26-1864.
Woolohon, Elwood—Amy Barrett, 5-30-1857.
Woolsey, Cooper—Sarah Kendle, 4-10-1851.
Wright, Benjamin—Lydia Taylor, 5-24-1854.
  Blith—Sarah Thompson, 6-3-1848.
  George—Elizabeth Ann Bulah, 7-20-1853.
  John—Elizabeth Smallwood Middleton, 2-4-1848.
  Joseph—Mary Joslin, 5-24-1856.
  Willard, M. D.—Annie M. Frambes, both Absecon, 11-21-1844.
Wyle, John—Mary L. Sutton, 12-27-1855.
Wynoker Andrew—Edith Emmon, 2-22-1864.
Yard, William—Mary M. Champion, 4-3-1852.
Yell, John, Milford, Mass.—Matilda Crawford (d. John and Sarah), 7-28-1858.
Yarkes, Charles, Philadelphia—Margaret P. Patterson, 12-19-1844.
Yound, Thomas—Eliza Ann Adams, 11-22-1849.

Young, John—Leah Mawrie, both Chester, Pa., 7-26-1865.
  Robert—Ann Smith, 8-27-1852.
Zane, Harry H., Philadelphia—Elizabeth Fredericks, Baltimore, Md., 5-31-1865.
Zergable, John—Elizabeth C. Stanger, both Glassboro, 2-19-1863.
Zeambleman, Jacob—Mary Zepselum, 7-21-1850.
Zenks, Charles—Elizabeth Rogers, both Philadelphia, 4-6-1858.
Zulker, Andrew—Rebecca Snuffin, 8-27-1850.

CAMDEN COUNTY MARRIAGES

BOOK B

A number of marriages were recorded in both Book A and Book B. These have been omitted in this list.

Abbott, Benj. F.—Beulah C. Horner, 3-26-1866.
   James—Catharine Bird, 7-23-1866.
Abdill, Wm. C.—Rebecca S. Jones, 11-7-1869.
Abel, Joseph H.—Beulah I. Richards, both Turnerville, 12-30-1874.
Aborn, Abner, Swedesboro—Susanna Groff, Woodstown, 9-4-1873.
Abrahams, Jacob, Burlington co.—Sarah J. Sterling, 6-21-1871.
Ackley, George E.—Kate L. Ames, 5-8-1875.
   Harry P.—Minnie Bilderback, both Elmer, 6-18-1878.
Acton, Charles, Salem—Lizzie S. Lippincott, Marlton, 11-14-1864.
Adams, Geo. W.—Mary J. Stites, 9-30-1869.
   George W.—Mary G. Stiles, 11-12-1877.
   Joshua—Matilda Chapman, 12-2-1869.
   William L., Wilmington. Del.—Mary L. Booth, 6-24-1872.
Addlestone, Herman—Annie Sacks, both Philadelphia, 9-2-1906.
Ainsworth, John—Rachel A. Williams, 8-28-1873.
Albertson, Geo. Henry—Catharine Cook, 4-10-1878.
   John—Elizabeth Johnson, 1-20-1868.

Albertson, John S.—Mary J. Lock, 2-26-1874.
Allridge, James E.—Anna Kelley, 9-17-1875.
Albright, William—Lizzie Henry, Philadelphia, 2-2-1878.
Albus, John, Jr.—Maria Morrell, 11-4-1875.
Ale, Emmor—Melvina Unpleby, both Trenton, 3-24-1877.
Allen, James—Catharine E. Dare. 12-27-1875.
  John M.—Mary Ambruster. 11-10-1873.
  Joseph—Margaret A. Chapman, 4-14-1874.
  Joseph C., Bordentown—Emily Beaston, 4-20-1873.
  Percy W.—Emma M. Fougeray, 11-7-1874.
  Robert—Mary E. Frazer, 3-4-1875.
  Turner R.—Ann M. Wilmot, 12-24-1873.
  Wilbert S.—Matilda Price, Bargaintown, 2-18-1874.
  William Fredric—Caroline P. Locke, 4-20-1871.
Allenbark, George—Mary Shane, 9-13-1877.
Allison, Witten—Martha Kennedy, 3-30-1871.
Almy, J. Holder—Dora Clinton, both Philadelphia, 3-7-1902.
Amminghs, Andrew—Anna Warren, 7-6-1866.
Amon, George H.—Abigail Louis Fisher, 1-1-1867.
Amos, Henry—Martha Jacobs, 6-18-1874.
  Joseph—Sarah L. May, 7-28-1875.
Anderson, Alfred—Jane Middleton, 4-1-1875.
  Andrew—Mary S. Starkey, both Red Bank, 11-9-1876.
  Benj.—Mary A. Brewer. 10-10-1868.
  David M.—Eliza McDowell, 6-3-1877.
  John C.—Estella S. Clark, both Hammonton, 2-25-1877.
Andrews, Wm. Redman—Annie Lee, 1-20-1876.
Angeroth, George—Mattie M. Nail, Burlington, 11-22-1873.
  Thomas J.—Ella J. Harrison, 5-26-1874.
Anser, John S.—Clara M. Norton, 2-5-1878.
Anthony, John W.—Rebecca Pascoe both Philadelphia, 10-13-1869.
Apgar, Benjamin M.—Matilda L. Locke, 7-20-1875.
Applegate, Edward, Georgetown—Clara Lippincott, New Lisbon, 1-18-1871.
  Emmor—Maggie L. Johnson, 3-27-1872.
Appley, Carroll L.—Catharine Hews, 4-14-1877.
Armstrong, Henry James—Charlotta Fisher, 3-17-1909.

Armstrong, Lewis C.—Mary Culp, 5-19-1874.
Thomas, Philadelphia—Eliza Willitts, 9-17-1877.
Arnold, John—Mary Hafner, 10-10-1875.
Arthur, Stephen—Lydia Meckin, 7-6-1872.
Ashton, Thomas—Catharine Sheridan, 10-28-1876.
Atkinson, John, Philadelphia—Lillian W. Southwood, 6-4-1903.
Mathew R.—Maria L. Reed, 3-25-1872.
Atterson, James A.—Catharine E. Henry, 7-11-1872.
Auble William H. —Ellie Taylor, 12-2-1869.
Aumick, Richard—Sarah A. Mason, 5-4-1869.
Austin, Henry—Emma Fireing, 11-29-1866.
Avis, Joseph H.—Paulena L. Smith, 11 25-1875.
Ayars, Caleb, Lower Alloways Creek—Catharine Harris Elsinboro, 12-31-1864.
Charles R.—Abbie Morrison, 10-25-1873.
Eugene C.—Minnie Yeager, 12-22-1870.
Bahls, Charles—Josephine Gunther, both Philadelphia, 1-23-1881.
Bailey, Edward—Eliza Harris, 1-13-1875.
Geo. W., Philadelphia—Rebecca Hurff, Hurffville, 12-8-1869.
Henry—Mary A. Harmon, 2-16-1876.
Bailiff, Moses—Sarah Collins, 6-29-1868.
Bair, Andrew, Jr.—Mamie A. Kyle, both Philadelphia, 9-3-1903.
Bakeley, George W.—Miriam Cline, 11-9-1871.
Baker, Chas. A.—Agnes Porter, 12-2-1874.
Levi S., New York—Hepzibah E. Seager, 5-13-1867.
Philip S., Paulsboro—Maria E. Thompson, Berkley, 11-22-1871.
Robert C.—Laura C. Keighton, 5-1-1872.
Baldwin, Charles, Jamesburgh—Kate Wall, 2-6-1866.
Ballinger, Franz, Indianapolis, Ind. — **Martha** Fletcher, Philadelphia, 7-19-1898.
George—Josephine Repman, both Mantua, 2-14-1877.
Jacob—Elizabeth C. Jennings, both Salem co., 1-31-1870.

Bancroft, Harry E.—Mary Buchanan, 11-15-1875.
  William C.—Annie E. Shivers, 8-2-1870.
Banford, John P—Amy Ames, 2-7-1871.
Bannell, Frank C., Tunkhannock, Pa.—Ruth A. Stark, Philadelphia, 5-18-1903.
Bantom, George W.—Rebecca A. Cook, 5-27-1873.
Barcklow, Edward, Moorestown—Sallie Adams, 11-16-1871.
Bareford William, England—Mrs. Deborah Smith, 2-20-1866.
Barker, Samuel E.—Carrie Leconey, both Swedesboro, 11-21-1871
Barkham, Joseph W.—Sarah Brown, 7-15-1876.
Barnes, Allen—Louisa Lewis, 9-21-1871.
  Charles A. Philadelphia—Helen Devault; recorded 9-22-1897.
Barney, Martin M.—Ella Davidson, 12-3-1867.
Baron, Joseph M.—Mary S. Culley, 10-15-1872.
Barrett, John S.—Margaret Stewart, 6-28-1867.
Barton, George C.—Mary J. Henderson, both Philadelphia, 7-8-1868.
Bassett, Wm. H.—Sarah A. Booen, 11-28-1847.
Batchelor, John W., Woodbury—Martha Reed, Cressville, 11-7-1869.
Bateman, Edward S.—Sarah W. Wood, 11-21-1871.
  Henry C., Williamstown—Sarah A. Wilkins, Turnerville, 4-2-1868.
  Isaac—Teressa Cooley, both Newfield, 6-16-1868.
Bates, George E.—Maria Goodenough, Mt. Laurel, 1-25-1877.
  George W.—Sallie J. Lock, 5-10-1877.
  Thomas—Mary A. Marshall, 5-2-1875.
  Wm.—Sarah A. Davis, 10-16-1867.
Batten, Joseph Z.—Margaret Dunn, both Gloucester co., 3-31, 1870.
Baxter, Charles W.—Ellen Escott, 2-23-1873.
  Walter J.—Mary J. Austin, 9-20-1877.
Bayard, Daniel—Ellen Brown, 8-6-1872.
Beans, G. W. Abington, Pa.—Lizzie A. Kane, Willow Grove, Pa., 11-21-1872.

CAMDEN COUNTY MARRIAGES—BOOK B 61

Beary, Eli S., Jr., Philadelphia—Ray A. Donnelly, 12-24-1872.
Beck, Andreas—Maria Buzard, 11-29-1877.
Beckenbach, Anton M.—Carrie H. Wallace, Palmyra, 4.10-1877.
Becker, Theo. Whittock—Emma Brister, both New York, 7-23-1865.
Beckett, George W.—Nellie R. Stillwell, 10-17-1872.
Beckley, Marmaduke, Marlton—Rebecca E. Shreve, 1-24-1872.
  William C., Cross Keys—Harriet Ware, East Bethel, 8-11-1872.
Bee—Charles H.—Sarah Sickler, 11-26-1868.
  Thomas, Mantua—Emma Hires, Turnerville, 12-25-1872.
Beecher, William J., Philadelphia—Ellen J. Shields, 1-21-1878.
Beideman, William—Ella Esleach, 10-20-1872.
Bell, William—Elizabeth Folwell, 9-5-1877.
Bendler, John—Mary Ann Howell, 9-1-1867; also recerded as 3-9-1874.
Benedict, Lewis Hanford, Brooklyn, N. Y.—Emma L. Kellogg, 11-22-1870.
Benham, Joseph H.—Elizabeth Miller, 5-26-1873.
Benjamin, Edward R.—Hannah Harker, 10-2-1873.
Bennett, Aaron—Hetty Bennett, 12-27-1872.
  Charles L., Philadelphia—Tessie Pennington, 7-27-1872.
  Chauncey—Ellen Hart, 12-11-1871.
  Edgar W.—Jeannie Wilmerton, 10-1-1873.
  Edward—Elizabeth Bennett, 12-20-1864.
  James M.—Teenie Stone, 5-30-1908.
Benson, James H.—Laura M. Wright, 9-4-1871.
Bentley, Joseph, Chester, Pa.—Annie M. Hewlings, 5-18-1876.
Berdein, Rudolf, Philadelphia—Bertha Schlicter, 11-1-1897.
Berger, John—Mary Arnold, Montgomery co., Pa., 1-2-1870.
Bernhart, John A., Jr.—Mary L. Bensing, both Philadelphia, 5-7-1903.

Berryman, John M. P.—Mary A. Christy, 12-20-1864.
  Thomas—Isabella Berryman, 5-21-1874
Besser, Jacob W.—Mary Hollworth, 12-18-1873.
  William—Susan Witten, 12-23-1869.
Bibighans, William J.—Mary Ella Thompson, 11-26-1876.
Bickley, Edward—Anna First, both Philadelphia, 7-10-1901.
  Henry E.—Catharine Kugan, both Philadelphia, 12-2-1875.
Biddle, Charles S.—Sarah Wright, both Salem co., 3-15-1870.
  George K.—Anna E. Kelley, 12-25-1873.
  John H., Baltimore—Esther L. Brower, Absecon, 10-4-1866.
  John W., Bridgeton—Elizabeth Thackara, 8-20-1873.
Biles, Augustine S., Philadelphia—Mary Hurff, 5-21-1868.
Bringhurst, William H., Philadelphia—Laura Sharp, 3-7-1878.
Birch, John F., Philadelphia—Mary A. Outwater, 11-12-1874.
Birchmeyer, Theodore M.—Laura Wood, 7-5-1875.
Bischoff, John G.—Ernestine Wagner, 9-6-1868.
Bishop, John T.—Caroline Black, both Chester, Pa., 2-2-1875.
  Theodore T.—Amanda L. Severns, 11-22-1874.
Bitters, Joseph, Jr.—Lottie R. Nagel, 8-3-1871.
  Zachar—Annie Eliza Thomas, 4-12-1877.
Bitting, William—Mary H. Lane, 2-20-1872.
Bittle, Charles C.—Lydia Coxen, 9-20-1868.
  Richard—Mary Cade, 9-23-1877.
Blair, Harry D.—Emma Severns, 2-8-1874.
Blake, John H.—Ann Tillman, both Philadelphia, 2-7-1871.
  Samuel—Margaret H. Batten, 3-3-1866.
  Samuel—Edith Sharp, 11-20-1873.
Blinzinger, John—Clara Platt, 2-23-1874.
Blizzard, George—Mary Bozorth, 10-31-1868.
  John A.—Clara V. Parvin, 3-2-1872.
  Oliver Burton—Augustine Alberta Shaw, 10-10-1877.
Block, David—Rebecca Waller, both Philadelphia, 2-15-1903.
Blodgett, Lyman H.—Ella S. Potter, 10-28-1906.
Blood, Leon C.—Elizabeth Dunn, both Wilmington, Del., 2-2-1910.

Blum, Elbert—Margaret Schnetzler, 4-14-1873.
Boardman, Francis H.— Elizabeth J. Herbert, Philadelphia, 8-19-1867.
Boggs, Edwin R.—Ida M. Powell, 12-24-1874.
 Randolph—Lizzie Croadale, 11-26-1871.
Boice Wm., Philadelphia—Mary E. Macauley, 11-24-1897.
Bolton, Henry L.—Anna Vliet, 10-15-1876.
 Wm. H.—Lottie Couch, 5-15-1869.
Bond, Thomas P., Mullica Hill—Ruth Weatherby, 4-14-1878.
Bonneville, Alton S.—Jemima A. Mason, both Philadelphia, 7-20-1902.
Boutetemps, Joseph—Emma C. Williams, 12-18-1873.
Boogar, Jefferson G.—Anna Sickler, 11-14-1868.
Booker, William—Louisa C. Walton, both Burlington, 9-6-1866.
Bool, Wm. T.—Mary A. Johnson, both Sussex co., Del., 9-8-1869.
Booth, Frank W.—Lydia Wriggins. Philadelphia, 12-27-1876.
Borden, Joseph—Martha C. Paul, 7-17-1877.
Bordman, T Frank—Adelaid S. Page, 2-22-1876.
Borton, Abraham—Mary Ellen Hunt. Burlington co., 4-3-1867.
 David—Anna J. Thomas, 1-17-1871.
Bosch, Charles—Caroline De La Croix, 6-28-1877.
Bosworth, Jeremiah—Elizabeth Ollis, Norfolk, Va., 3-4-1864.
Boultinghouse, Winfield S.—Mary A. Reeves, Woodstown, 11-4-1873.
Bourdeau, Alfred R.—Harriet Pierson, 7-7-1868.
Bourman, Charles P.—Lydia Warnock, 6-21-1877.
Bovell, Henry S,—Maria M. Knaub, 6-8-1878.
Bowers, John W., Philadelphia—Sarah Beck, Westville, 12-14-1873.
Bowker, Chas. W.—Sallie Lippincott, both Philadelphia, 7-4-1866.
Boyer, C. Walter—Mary H. Willets, Jersey City, 2-28-1878.
 Edward—Eliza Miller, 5-2-1866.
Bozorth, John A.—Ella Barnes, 6-24-1873.

Bozorth, Joseph—Ann Stow, 11-29-1856.
  Samuel—Deborah Ann Butler, 1-16-1867.
Brace, Robert W.—Harriet R. Whitecar, both Philadelphia, 7-17-1907.
Braddock, Isaac A.—Anna L. Collings, 6-17-1874.
  William—Priscilla Dilks, 12-26-1870.
  William S.—Rachel Borton, both Burlington co., 1-24-1870.
Bradford, James, New York City—Elizabeth Imogene Robinson, 12-31-1870.
Bradley, David, Philadelphia—Phebe Oney, 12-22-1875.
  William J.—Anna R. Sheldon, Millville, 11-8-1877.
Brady, John S.—Mary L. Carter, 4-21-1878.
  John T., Philadelphia—Amanda E. Sapp, Burlington, 3-29-1868.
Brandriff, Alfred, Millville—Lottie Price, 4-27-1871.
Branson, George—Lizzie E. Borton, 6-24-1876.
Branzant, George R.—Mattie Tomlinson, both Newton, Pa., 4-12-1877.
Bray, William—Eliza Richards, Florence, 3-12-1872.
Breese, J. Warren—Rebecca Wolverton, 6-11-1877.
Brelsford, Chapman—Margaret Hudson, 4-30-1871.
Breyer, Henry A.—Mary A Shute, 11-24-1869.
Briand, Samuel, Jr.—Mary Smith, Medford, 2-17-1866.
Brick, Edward L.—Emma Seeley, both Hurffville, 3-10-1870.
  William—Mary E. Page, Phoenixville, Pa., 12-25-1877.
Bridges, Mark, Maine—Eliza Jane Case, Philadelphia, 5-16-1867.
Briddy (or Priddy) Edward, England — Catharine Hale Brown, 5-18-1871.
Bright, Joseph—Mary Kenneman, 9-14-1872.
Brill, Henry, Glassboro—Martha Ann Bittle, 4-11-1867.
Brindle, Benjamin—Catharine Tucker, 11-9-1873.
Brister, John W., New York City—Elizabeth T. Keeler, 12-2-1867.
Broadwaters, George—Margaret McCann, 4-17-1872.

CAMDEN COUNTY MARRIAGES—BOOK B 65

Brobst, Frederick—Katie Appel, both Philadelphia, 7-4-1901.
Brock, Edgar C.—Blanch Glendora; recorded 9-22-1897.
Brooklian, Nathaniel—Julia Ann Laws, 10-31-1872.
Brooks, Hamilton S.—Helen N. Clarke, 8-27-1873.
  Henry H.—Carrie Maria Alton, 10-21-1880.
  Joseph, Scottdale, Pa.—Lillie D. Patton, 11-17-1897.
  William—Sallie E. Joslin, 9-21-1871.
Broomly, Wilson—Hannah A. Fowler, Ocean co., 10-11-1872.
Brothers, James—Rebecca Ramsey, Philadelphia, 10-31-1877.
  William—Anna Blair, 6-5-1869.
Brotherton, Isaac—Sybella Springer, 4-11-1866.
Brower, Levi—Julia A. Wilson, 5-28-1873.
Brown, Charles, Candia, N. C.—Laura H. Carmen, 12-4-1876.
  Charles H.—Lucinda Gordon, 4-12-1874.
  Charles R—Downingtown, Pa.—Carrie Wigo, 4-18-1898.
  David B.—Mary S. Cliver, 11-26-1868.
  David B.—Mary E. Haines, 5-15-1873.
  David P.—Sarah E. James, 8-23-1877.
  David S., Boston—Anna Lytle, 2-20-1873.
  Edward F.—Elizabeth Hensel, 2-7-1878.
  Jacob—Anna Ford, Pleasantville, 1-26-1872.
  John J.—Emma Harvey, 11-17-1873.
  Jonathan—Annie M. Ward, both Burlington co., 12-27-1871.
  Randel—Eliza Tice, 1-7-1868.
  Richard H., Jr.—Margaretta Shanklin, 7-7-1877.
  Thomas T.—Zipporah Basset, both Glassboro, 10-20-1874.
  W. Q. H.—Lizzie Pancoast, 8-3-1873.
  William—Catharine Costell, 4-15-1868.
  William H.—Rebecca Batten, both Swedesboro, 1-18-1872.
  Winfield—Hannah Ostler, 12-24-1873.

CAMDEN COUNTY MARRIAGES—BOOK B

Browning, Abraham M.—Josephine Cooper, 3-4-1868.
  George G —Dora V. White, 11-15-1876.
  William J.—Belinda Taylor. 1-30-1873.
Bruce, Edwin P.—Lillian E. Stevens, both Philadelphia, 10-23-1904.
  Matteson W., Philadelphia—Martha J Guice, 2-13-1873.
Bruner, Emil, West Philadelphia—Kate Baker, 7-16-1874.
Bryan, Josiah H.—Ella R. Dill, 11-13-1876.
  Thomas—Emma Algor, Monmouth co., 3-11-1873.
Bryant, Charles Hewit—Maggie Hurd, 12-18-1877.
Burch, Theodore, North Carolina—Maria Nidecker, Philadelphia, 9-23-1903.
Buck, Charles—Ellen Hagerman, 10-10-1871.
Buckington, Wevalin I.—Bertha Smith, both Philadelphia, 12-12-1905.
Buckley, Thomas, Philadelphia—Katherine E. Butts, 6-10-1902.
Budd, Alfred—Anna E. Ball, Philadelphia, 3-2-1878.
  Jehu—Hannah H. Browning, 9-5-1877.
  John H.—Harriet Woolford, 5-19-1872.
  Samuel P.—Elizabeth A Williams, 6-18-1866.
  Samuel P.—Maggie Triplett, 12-20-1871.
Budden, John—Rachel Wiltse, 6-6-1866.
  John W.—Laura Long, 9-10-1876.
Budding, Charles H.—Lizzie Burnell, Philadelphia, 10-18-1868.
  William H.—Barbara Dinsdale, 1-14-1876.
Buesing, William—Mary Schdellbacker, 6-28-1874.
Bunts, Calvin—Georgianna Williams, 3-6-1877.
Burden, Joseph J.—Kate I. Ellis, 6-6-1869.
Burgess, Emery, Abington, Mass.—Mary Ann Lewis, 11-11-1872.
Burket, Michael I.—Mary Hammell, 8-7-1867.
Burkett, James—Sarah Skill, 11-24-1873.
  Samuel, Woodbury—Mary E. Westcott, Almonesson, 10-19-1871.

CAMDEN COUNTY MARRIAGES—BOOK B 67

Burnett, Elijah, Baltimore—Ella Hetzell, Philadelphia, 8-8-1866.
  Frank—Louisa Holl, 6-16-1872.
Burr, Gordon L.—Mary M. Murray, 8-19-1873.
  Jonathan—Martha Edwards, 12-6-1869.
Burras, Litton—Caroline Davis, 12-19-1880.
Burrough, Edward – Emily Collins, Moorestown, 11-23-1870.
Burroughs, George W—Louisa Boulton Davis, 1-8-1868.
  Mickle—Emily A. Bruner, 10-1-1884.
  Samuel—Margaret M. Seeley, 3-19-1874.
Burton, Jacob H.—Mary F. Cain, 10-27-1872.
  Jeremiah—Lydia Purnell, 5-22-1873.
  Thomas, Delaware—Amanda Cuff, Salem, 12-18-1873.
  Tillman—Hannah Laws, 8-7-1867.
Bush, Franklin—Annie Morrison, 6-22-1876.
  Israel—Louisa Stansberry, 10-27-1867.
Bussell, William—Maria Penton, 10-12-1863.
Butcher, Edmund J.—Sarah Illingsworth, 4-11-1877.
Butt, William, Philadelphia—Rebecca Sharp, 6-1-1871.
Butts, Wm. H., Portsmouth, Va.—Elizabeth E. Smith, 12-24-1873.
Busby, Isaac—Ruth Kellum, 4-17-1878.
Buzby, Granville N.—Emily R. Williams, 5-28-1877.
  John R.—Sarah Birdsall, 7-14-1867.
  Joseph K., Rancocas—Sabilla Martin, Beverly, 12-25-1867.
Buzine, William L.—Charlotte A. Calvert, 1-21-1872.
Cain, James J.—Mary McClain, 12-27-1866.
  John F.—Christianna Hensel, 3-31-1877.
Callahan, Richard, Philadelphia—Rebecca Leeds, 12-15-1897.
Calverly, Benj.—Maggie Brian, both Philadelphia, 11-25-1868.
Campbell, Alexander—Rebecca Betson, both Moorestown, 7-19-1877.
  Alfred M., Fairfield—Ruth M. Stetson, 3-29-1873.

Campbell, Anthony— Emma C. Gleason, 12-19-1875.
  Davis M.—Eliza E. McGannion, 9-30-1875.
  Henry—Sarah Phillips, 1-18-1873.
  John J.—Lizzie M. Read, 10-6-1871.
  Wilson—Josephine Burdeau, 12-13-1887.
Cann, Thomas, J.—Sarah Eliz. Howell, 11-28-1877.
Cannon, James—Sarah Bradshaw, 11-4-1871.
Cantlin Harry Franklin Philadelphia—Lydia Ann Kline, Chester Pa., 6-17-1901.
Cantrell, Edwin—Jennie Hammond, 6-26-1875.
Caperoon, William—Carrie J. Hults, 4-30-1873.
Capewell, Mark—Whillie Batt, 11-4-1873.
Carey, James W.—Jennie L. Wannan, 3-1-1878.
Carli, Francesco—Felicetta Morrone, both Philadelphia, 6-7-1905.
Carll, Chas. M.—Anna Louisa Githens, both Alloways Creek, 12-21-1864.
Carney, James W.—Maggie Bradshaw, 3-20-1875.
Carpenter, Thomas G.—Anna E. Schilling, both Philadelphia, 6-20-1872.
  William H.—Hattie Lawless, 4-12-1877.
Carr, James A., York, Pa.—Mary E. Johnson, 7-4-1875.
Carson, William—Mary E. Campbell, 3-4-1875.
Carter, Daniel A.—Laura Horner, 10-29-1876.
  Elias—Clara Galbraith, 3-9-1877.
  John J., M.D.—Eliza Knopp, both Philadelphia, 5-25-1872.
  Theodore—Eleanor Carter, 8-24-1873.
Carty, Benjamin—Caroline Morgan, 6-4-1876.
Cashore, James H.—Rebecca King, 1-13-1871.
Casper, Charles, Jersey City—Adeline Ambruster, 4-5-1874.
Casperson, Wm.—Minnie Vansciver, 1-4-1877.
Cassady, Sam'l F.—Lizzie Newkirk, both Pittsgrove, 12-15-1866.
Caster, Henry, Frankford, Pa.—Anna C. Fowler, 6-2-1873.
Cecil, Thomas—Anna E. Weatherby, 9-9-1900.
Chadwick, Wm. A.—Rachel T. Lee, 5-7-1868.

Chamberlin, Charles—Elizabeth Fithian, 4-18-1876.
Chambers, Wm.—Lucy Trafford, both Hammonton, 1-1-1870.
  William H.—Frances R. Torman, both Philadelphia, 4-23-1901.
Champion. Frank E.—Anna M. Risley, both Cape May, 9-8-1877.
  Lemuel—Mary Champion, 10-31-1875.
Chance, William—Mary J. Postly, 11-26-1874.
Chapman, Edward F.—Adelia Doherty, both Philadelphia, 10-4-1877.
Charles, Robert—Sallie Beetle, 12-25-1872.
Charles. Zara—Anna May Bishop, 8-3-1872.
Charrier, Frederick—Emma V. Devinney, 1-13-1870.
Chase, Warren L.—Louisa F. Taylor, 5-20-1873.
  William—Margaret James, 1-23-1876.
Chattan, Wm. W.—Mrs. Harriet L. Lippincott, 8-3-1869; also recorded as 6-27-1867.
Cheesman, Chas. F.—Sallie Sheppard, 5-25-1873.
  Geo. W.—Johanna Horn, 6-22-1829.
  Stephen—Hannah Dolson, 1-7-1871.
  Thos. J.—Martha P. Robinson. 7-28-1868.
  Wm. J., Turnerville—Keziah Jaggers, Wenonah, 10-14-1875.
Chew, Charles E.—Susan Adams, 6-7-1874.
  Chas. W.—Mary E. Bates, 9-12-1866.
  Jehu, Barnsboro—Kate W. Smith, Philadelphia, 3-7-1878.
  John F.—Cornelia Chew, 5-10-1872.
  Joseph P.—Mary A. Cline, 3-13-1852.
  Wm. H.—Rebecca Wood, both Washington twp., 11-30-1865.
Church, Samuel T.—Jennie Kain, 4-2-1872.
  William H.—Laura V. King, 4-3-1876.
Champening, Frank H.—Agnes M. Chew, both Philadelphia, 1-23-1874.
Churchill, William—Clara C. Smith, both Philadelphia, 11-5-1874.

Clark, Charles, Woodbury—Bella Walker, 3-18-1874.
  David, Gloucester co.—Mary McCollum, Port Republic, 7-3-1867.
  George S.—Sarah F. Crispin, 6-4-1874.
  John G.—Lizzie Sage, 10-12-1873.
  Thomas—Sarah Baker, both Harrisburg, Pa., 11-27-1873.
  William C.—Mary E. Warrick, 12-25-1876.
  William H., Jr.—Mary C. Heppard, 10-7-1873.
  William H. H.—Lena S. Blish, 4-17-1875.
Clarke, George H.—Mary A. Cronk, 10-22-1868.
  George T.—Caroline Leitenberger, 1-30-1873.
Clay, Wm.—Elizabeth Worthy, both Philadelphia, 8-20-1870.
Clayton, Charles A.—Mary H. Boyd, 6-7-1876.
  Daniel—Henrietta McCollum, both Atlantic co., 6-1-1873.
  David—Ella Marshall, 4-3-1873.
  John H.—Edith Viola Streeper, 4-19-1876.
  John K.—Sarah A. Reed, 2-19-1872.
Clemens, Frank A., Prussia—Anna Voll, Germany, 1-9-1868.
Clement, Lewis H.—Rebecca C. Smith, 11-7-1876.
  Richard G., Moorestown—Lydia F. Smith, Mt. Holly, 6-24-1869.
  William H.—Mrs. Lizzie H. Hunt, 5-30-1872.
  William H.—Ella S. Parker, 10-27-1875.
  William W., Delaware co., Pa.—Honnah L. Sloan, 12-30-1869.
Clevenger, Leander—Susan Huston, both Burlington, 12-16-1870.
Cliff, Jeremiah—Maggie Hoffner, 10-31-1875.
Cline, Joshua, Atlantic City—Anna Mary Meyers, 11-20-1873.
Cliver, Dillwyn—Sallie Lindell, 7-17-1872..
  Orlando M—Christiana Deets, 2-26-1872.
Clopper, John C.—Lidie Graham, 10-23-1872.
Coate, Wm.—Catharine Fusgan, Germantown, 2-1-1866.
Coates, Azel—Mehitable Tatem, 9-4-1871.
Cochran, Archibald—Rebecca V. Middleton, 2-4-1873.
Colbert, Henry F.—Anna J. Souders, 7-3-1867.
Coles, Chas.—Mary M. Colson, Gloucester co., 6-8-1865.

CAMDEN COUNTY MARRIAGES—BOOK B   71

Coles, Edgar G.—Emma V. Paschall, 10-28-1873.
  Edgar J.—Josephine Williams, 5-3-1876.
Collier, Wm.—Annie Hyde, both Philadelphia, 3-18-1865.
Collings, Geo.—Sarah Carlile, 1-29-1870.
Collins, Charles H.—Ida Cameron, 8-1-1875.
  Samuel—Lina Shaw, 9-8-1873.
  Washington I.—Emma V. Long, both Philadelphia; recorded 10-19-1897.
  Wm. H.—Rebecca S. Thackara, 7-30-1868.
  William I.--Anna E. Albertson, 5-23-1875.
Columbus, Favian S., Washington, D. C.—Sarah Ann Coates, 8-13-1873.
Conet, Howard—Hannah Coleman, 8-20-1875.
Conlan, Francis J.—Martha W. Pearson, 8-4-1873.
Conner, Edward—Carrie Sherman, 6-28-1876.
  George H.—Annie Scheperkotter, 8-13-1877.
  James Givins, Philadelphia—Josephine Estelow, 9-7-1865.
  Wn. Donaldson—Mary Alice Hoxie, 4-30-1868.
Connor, George S.—Josephine Roberts, 5-8-1873.
Conover, Belford, Sarah Weeks, 9-9-1877
Conrey, Isaac—Melisa Beeby, 2-15-1875.
Conway, John—Bella Berryman, 7-24-1876.
  John Thos.—Arabella C. M. Spencer, 2-10-1870.
  Patrick—Sarah Elizabeth Cathgard, 12-19-1885.
Cook, George Alfred—Mary Genelda Wall, both Philadelphia. 10-29-1872.
  Joseph—Ida Bebrick, 3-18-1878.
  William H.—Sarah Githens, 11-19-1873.
  Wm. B.—Martie P. Batten, 9-19-1876.
Coombs, Mathew—Margaret Breyer, 8-17-1872.
  Wm. F.—Angelina C. Sullivan, both Gloucester co., 11-22-1877.
Cooper, Allen W.—Linda Ludavicy, both Philadelphia, 3-22-1898.
  Asabel, Philadelphia—Linnie Plum, 10-29-1868.
  Charles W.—Mary A. Rully, both Philadelphia, 6-10-1899.
  George—Ella F. Kennedy, 12-10-1873.

CAMDEN COUNTY MARRIAGES—BOOK B

Cooper, James, Greenwich—Annie R. Bradshaw, 4-4-1878.
Cooper Nathaniel Nicholson—Margaret J. Clarke, 12-25-1870.
  William L.—Catharine H. Turner, 4-16-1908.
Cope, Tilford H.—Bessie C. Thompson, both Pottstown, Pa., 10-29-1908.
Copel, Charles—Mary Thompson, Philadelphia, 2-2-1878.
Copern, John, Eastport, Me.—Amanda Bertha Fraenks, Hamburg, Ger., 9-16-1875.
Cordery, Samuel L.—Kate Edgar, 6-10-1877.
Cordrey, John S—Martha Kean, 12-16-1874.
Coels, Edmund—Abbie Cook, 7-22-1866.
Corless, James, Germantown—Jennie Potts, Boston, Mass., 4-7-1870.
  Joseph—Eva L. Harrison, 1-1-1878.
Cornelius, Robert—Coralie Stockton, 6-25-1876.
Corre, Charles M.—Anna M. Newton, 5-12-1872.
Corson, Harrison J.—Roselma Hill, 4-1-1874.
  James—Anne Wood, 4-16-1866.
  John G.—Jennie Thatcher, 7-2-1876.
Wm. H.—Elle Johnson, 10-15-1866.
Cossaboon, Chas. P.—Sarah Ann Newbern, 8-13-1865.
Costa, George—Lydia M. Kier, 11-29-1874.
Costell, Hill S.—Catharine Loper, 10-28-1873.
  Jonn S.—Ida Snuffin, 7-25-1875.
Cotner, John W.—Louise Vanstavens, 9-8-1868.
Courter, John D.—Laura R. Braker, 10-17-1876.
Coventree, Charles W.—Lizzie Paul, 4-18-1877.
  George C.—Mary J. Courter, 11-29-1876.
Cowan, Nathan F.—Sally Ann Ackley, 1-22-1877.
Cowell, Joseph, Jr.—Clara Wieland, both Philadelphia, 12-20-1908.
Cox, Benjamin T.—Jennie M. Robertson, 9-3-1873.
  Charles F.—Ida Pike, 12-12-1875.
  Charles I.—Ellen McCann, 4-17-1872.
  Charles Edward (colored)—Mary C. Lockman, 4-26-1875.
  Ephraim—Ida A. Valentine, both Westville, 2-28-1871.

CAMDEN COUNTY MARRIAGES—BOOK B 73

Craft, Joseph—Susanna Chew, both Hurffville, 5-17-1865.
Norman, Philadelphia—Laura Virginia Davis, 7-16-1877.
Craig, James—Mary Baikley, 12-13-1868.
Crain, William—Barbara Zimmerman, 2-20-1869.
Cramar, Charles J.—Sarah Bunting, 9-10-1876.
Crammer, Hiram A.—Mary I. Schrader, 1-1-1868.
James A.—Anna R. Dobbins, both Moorestown, 7-21-1873.
Crane. Jacob F., Franklinville—Mary E. Hugg, 12-14-1869.
John Gaskill—Ella Wriggins, 12-24-1876.
Crank, Charles W.—Amy E. Fowler, 4-27-1873.
Cranston, James—Hannah L. Husted, 11-2-1874.
Craycroft, Wesley—Elizabeth McIntire, 7-17-1872.
Cregor, James—Mary L. Lerenck. 6-10-1872.
Creighton, Lewis M.—Fannie Test, 8-8-1872.
Crispin, Theodore—Margaret Davis, 7-11-1866.
Crist, George H., Williamstown—Emma S. Schanck, Weymouth, 5-7-1876.
Crowell, Frank E.—Annie R. Wells, 6-20-1877.
Crowley, Thos., Pleasant Mills—Hester Hankins, Batsto, 5-27-1868.
William H.—Susanna E. Vandegrift, 5-6-1877.
Cuff, Leonard—Ellen Jones, both Salem, 9-4-1874.
Cundiff, George H., Maryland—Mary Neale, Philadelphia. 3-1-1874.
Cundy, Collin R., Chester co, Pa.—Sarah Ann Hall, Delaware co., Pa., 11-20-1864.
Cunkle, Edgar Ewens—Bessse W. Hetrick, both Harrisburg, 8-18-1903.
Cunningham, John R.—Mary E. Pitman, 3-9-1848.
Oliver, Philadelphia—Rebecca Quick, 1-23-1869.
Cuney, Samuel T.—Amanda M. Kemble, 12-25-1876.
Curdy, Samuel—Rebecca Griffin, 1-20-1876.
Curley, John C.—Emily Earling, 10-31-1875.
Currie, Howard—Rebecca S. Armstrong, 6-28-1875.
John—Emily J. Flower, 12-9-1858.
Dailey, Jacob, Bridgeton—Mary Keene, 1-18-1866.
Millard Filmore—Emily Virginia Asendorf, 10-23-1877.

CAMDEN COUNTY MARRIAGES—BOOK B

Dalby, Herman R.—Clara L. Wells, both Philadelphia, 1-6-1898.
Dallas, Richard S.—Carrie Stewart, 3-10-1874.
Daniels, Enoch—Rebecca Bozorth, 8-4-1871.
   Percy H.—Allise E. Collins, 7-4-1872.
   Samuel T.—Mary E. Stackhouse, 4-23-1871.
Dare, Edward—Emily Walker, 8-11-1869
   William—Frances E. Burdick, both Syracuse, N. Y., 8-7-1869.
Darlington, Thomas P.—Patience A. Force, both Gloucester co., 11-14-1870.
Darr, Alfred—Ellen Starn, 4-7-1878.
   William S.—Rebecca Stewart, 10-4-1875.
Davidson, David D.—Mamie T. Reilley, 6-5-1878.
   James J.—Margaret T. Rulon, both Swedesboro, 12-21 1870.
   Joseph E.—Mary E. Rudden, 5-23-1872.
   Samuel T.—Emma Sawyer, 5-5-1875.
   William—Hannah Mawhinney, 12-28-1873.
   William M., Philadelphia—Rachel T. Lee, 8-27-1868.
Davis, Abram—Elmira Sigars, 6-1-1876.
   Amer—Ellen J. Simpson, both Delaware co., Pa., 8-20-1873.
   Benj. C., Jr.—Annie M. Palmer 1-13-1870.
   Edward—Eliza Harris, 1-13-1875.
   Elijah T.—Emma Jane Shinn, 1-6-1867.
   Francis H.—Clara C. Beuhler, 6-2-1872.
   George Washington—Rebecca L. Shinn, 2-7-1878.
   George W. — Isabella Ethridge, Gloucester co., 3-11-1873.
   Geo. W., Milford—Gertrude Ware, 4-25-1871.
   George W.—Lizzie Davis, 1-8-1874.
   Jacob—Mary Wilson, both New York City, 1-18-1873,
   James—Anna Laws, 12-25-1880.
   John E., Philadelphia—Clara Lenard, 8-1-1877.
   Joseph M.—Margaret Glenn, 6-29-1870.
   Trial, W.—Annie Duble, 4-17-1875.

CAMDEN COUNTY MARRIAGES—BOOK B

Davis, Wm. C., Philadelphia—Mary A. Vansciver, 8-19-1868.
Wm. H., Bristol, Pa.—Annie E. Munyan, 5-8-1873.
Day, Henry F.—Sarah M. Woods, 11-1-1876.
Deakyne, Wm. J.—Margaret Huston; recorded 9-17-1897.
Deal, Daniel—Mary E. Johnston, 7-24-1899.
DeBarth, Joseph R.—Caroline M. E. Kiehl, 6-30-1909.
Decker, Henry H-—Harriet Butcher, both Philadelphia, 3-15-1883.
Deckman, Wm. A., Dublin, Md.—Susanna Adams, Burchville, Md.; recorded 10-5-1897.
DeCook, James, Jr., Philadelphia—Sarah L. Churges; recorded 9-23-1897.
DeFreast, Charles R., New York City—Mary E. Beckett, 8-27-1867.
DeHart, Peter—Sarah Huntington, 1-3-1869.
Delamater, John S., Philadelpoia—Emma C. Wood, 4-7-1868.
Delaney, James A.—Adelia G. Burley, 12-27-1871.
Demarest, Stephen E.—Mary L. Price, 8-23-1872.
Dempsey, James—Florence Ida Schaeffer, 2-22-1909.
Dennis, Wm.—Georgianna Carter, 1-25-1873.
Deno, Walter—Ida Detwiler, 5-5-1876.
Deny, Daniel—Elizabeth Cook, 1-11-1868.
Dermitt, Charles H.—Anna M. Harker, Pennsylvania, 11-1-1875.
Derrick, Wm. F.—Anna M. Warrington, 1-15-1873.
DeShields, John, Eastern Shore, Md.—Emeline Sullivan, Philadelphia, 7-25-1871.
Devereaux, James—Elizabeth Walker, both Newcastle co., Del., 5-3-1869.
Devine, Samuel M.—Emma Weeart, 4-27-1878.
Devinney, Geo. H.—Martha Bacon, 4-25-1872.
Dewey, James H.—Stella Melissa Williams, 4-5-1877.
Dewson, John—Emma Sutten, 1-8-1866.
Dibble, Oscar Charles, Philadelphia—Eliza Josephine Partridge, 12-24-1876.
Dick, William—Catharine Murphy, 3-13-1872.
Dickerson, Charles—Maria Crandoll, 7-30-1873.

Dickinson, Elleanan—Frances Woodward, 12-26-1867.
Dicks, George L , Wenonah—Sarah Stevenson, 3-14-1872.
Dickson, George W.—Martha Davis, 11-28-1872.
  Thomas E.—Ann M. Dickson, 7-2-1873.
Dietrich, Frk. August—Juliana Born. 4-27-1775.
Dilks, Ephraim, Deptford—Elizabeth A. Weldie, 1-13-1866.
  John—Olive E. Hallowell, 6-23-1875.
  Thomas, Gloucester co.—Abbie Miller, 3-20-1873.
Dill, Henry A.— Mary E. Taylor, 5-5-1869.
  John H., Philadelphia—Amelia Murray, 1-15-1872.
  John W.—Annie Powell, 6-6-1872.
  Samuel P.—Mary Peckman, 6-18-1872.
Dillon, William H.—Anna M. Rudderow, 4-15-1874.
Dilmer, Charles—Catharine Meggs, 2-19-1876.
Dilmore, Benj. H.—Hannah P. North, 11-9-1871.
  George J.— Mary E. Laughlin, 7-10-1872.
Dixon, George—Elizabeth Poole, Bridgeton, 7-13-1872.
  John—Abigail Hewitt, 9-10-1870.
  Ralph—Lizzie M. Renny, both Philadelphia, 6-10-1900.
  Samuel—Elizabeth Camal, 10-7-1869.
Doan, Elwood—Hester Wilson, 9-8-1867.
Dobleman, John L.—Anna E. Field, 5-14-1843.
Dolicat, Richard—Ann Eliza Williams, 6-15-1874.
  Doll, Paul John, Philadelphia—Mary Gibson, 11-3-1903.
Dorner, Wm.—Mary Mineo, Philadelphia, 11-11-1898.
Dorrell, Smith—Sallie Vansciver, Moorestown, 12-18-1876.
Doty, Clarence, New York City—Hannah Amanda Lamb, 1-30-1867.
Dougherty, Abner—Kate Murray, 10-2-1873.
  Isaac—Josephine Browning, 4-1-1875.
Doughton, Wm. Henry—Mary L. Horner, 2-29-1872.
Douglass, George, Bridgeport, Conn.—Ellie Heaton, 4-9-1873.
Douney, Timothy, Philadelphia—Matilda Mulhall, 1-17-1898.
Douty, Thomas, Beverly—Josephine Nichols, 1-1-1873.
Dover, Alfred—Achsah H. Johnson, 11-26-1867.
Downs, James R.—Anna M. Weigner, 12-27-1871.

CAMDEN COUNTY MARRIAGES—BOOK B 77

Doyles James H.—Emma Kinsil, 11-29-1875.
Drake, Franklin H.—Kate U. Lee, 7-5-1872.
Dreuffus, Jacob, Philadelphia—Anna A. Yost, 5-10-1873.
Drew. David, Philadelphia—Lizzie M. Gifford, 2-25-1866.
Driver. George W.—Mary S. Moulton, both New York, 10-18-1866.
Duble, John R.—Lizzie Nicholson, Williamstown, 3-10-1875.
  Joshua H.—Sarah A. Thompson, 11-25-1876.
DuBois, Wilford O —Sabilla P. Newkirk, both Upper Pittsgrove, 10-23-1866.
  Wm.—Clara E. Leadbester, 2-15-1899.
Dudley, Daniel, Jr., Moorestown—Rebecca Merriel, 12-24-1863.
  Darling—Anna H. Parker, both Moorestown, 2-8-1872.
  Joseph A.—Clara M. Haines, both Burlington co., 8-15-1873.
Duffee, Henry—Elizabeth Goss, 5-31-1874.
Duffel, Reuben—Sarah Cheesman, both Frankford, Pa., 12-24-1872.
Duffield, Benj.—Mary Lamb, 1-7-1869.
  George—Anna Brewin, 10-9-1873.
Duffy, George W.—Leonora Jones, both Philadelphia, 7-9-1876.
Duran, Ganeswood M.—Anna S. Thompson, both Bordentown, 5-7-1873.
Dunn, John—Martha Pfiffer, 12-8-1877.
  William H.—Sallie Baker, 8-21-1873.
Dyer, Lewis W.—Mary Jackson, Philadelphia, 4-15-1876.
Eiler, Robert F., Philadelphia—Angie Hutchinson, 11-16-1871.
Earley, William—Anna Edwards, both Philadelphia, 1-21-1869.
Eastburn, Benjamin F.—Lizzie Wynkoop, both Bucks co., Pa., 3-26-1878.
Eastlack, James H.—Miriam Pursglove, 3-22-1877.
Eckhardt, William C., Moorestown—Hannah Roberts, 1-18-1872.

Eddy, William H.—Adda S. Blatherwick, 12-5-1876.
Ederlin. Wm. R.—Anne C. Shivers, both Philadelphia, 11-16-1865.
Edwards, Benjamin H.—Lizzie Downs, 5-8-1868.
  Henry G.—Mattie Myers, 12-31-1872.
  Isaac Henry—Anne Trotter. 6-26-1872.
  James L.—Ella A. Maxwell, 3-27-1869.
  John—Mattie Stillwell, 9-7-1873.
  John A.—Mary E. Hagerty, 9-13-1873.
  Joseph G.—Effie Jaggers, 8-29-1876.
  Peter—Mary Ann Harris, 12-20-1877.
Eich, Sebastian—Catharine Seitz, 1-4-1878.
Elberson, Isaac—Hannah G. Pluck, 10-12-1868.
Eldridge, William—Laura Douglas, 10-30-1876.
Elfreth, Charles—Mary A. Bruden, 6-3-1872.
Elliot, S. Augustus—Miriam A. Minnick, 11-9-1875.
Ellis, Asson—Caroline K. North, 12-30-1877.
  Isaac K.—Mary Murphy, 10-8-1874.
  Jessie—Mary E. Voorhees, 10-10-1877.
  Josiah H.—Helen Wolohon, 5-1-1874.
  William C.—Mary Taylor, 11-19-1871.
Elmer, William—Elizabeth J. Goulblen, 11-11-1869.
Elwell, Charles—Mary A. Chew, 6-30-1872.
  Charles H.—Ellen R. Dow, 8-4-1869.
  Isaac V.—Josephine A. White, 3-25-1870.
Embley, Charles O.—Mary Phifer, 9-5-1872.
Emery, Charles L.—Laura E. O'Donnell, 12-2-1873.
Emmet. David—Ruth Naylor, 9-29-1868.
Engle, Jehu—Anna R. Quicksall, 2-8-1872.
  John R.—Ella R. Burr, both Philadelphia, 6-25-1901.
English, Chas. B.—Jennie Charles, 7-1-1876.
  Charles, Sr.—Lizzie McE. Rowand, 10-13-1874.
  John, English Creek—Mary E. Bowen, Unionville, 2-19-1866.
  Wilson—Ray Corson, 6-1-1876.
Enrich, Gaston W.—Josephine L. Wilkins, both Upper Providence, Pa., 8-16-1875.

CAMDEN COUNTY MARRIAGES—BOOK B 79

Ernst, George Wilson, Philadelphia—Emma E. Wilkinson, 6-13-1872.
Erven, William—Mary Jane Jellitt, 10-13-1875.
Essig, William F.—Catharine Havengro, both Philadelphia, 12-22-1901.
Etherington, Lewis, Bridgeton—Eliza Venable, 12-26-1877.
Etris, John Land—Martha Louise Stigale, 6-15-1904.
Evans, Alfred C.—Angelina Jackson, both Moorestown, 11-27-1871.
  Charles—Amelia Kendell, 4-15-1871.
  John W., Tuckahoe—Jane A. Brayman, 6-28-1868.
  Joseph P.—Ella Moore, both Hammonton, 12-31-1872.
  Joseph S., Marlton—Sallie C. Riggins, 2-5-1874.
Evaul, Jacob—Lucinda M. Evaul, both Bethel, 12-21-1877.
  Joel H.—Amanda Horner, 4-11-1867.
  John—Ella M. Hoppera, both Palmyra, 1-25-1877.
Evering, Budd—Sophie Sing, 8-16-1874.
Everly, John—Friderick Isese (?), 5-16-1868.
Everman, John W.—Georgiana Savage, 1-31-1870.
Ewens, Charles—Emma Johnson, both Philadelphia, 7-17-1868
Fair, William Allen, Stapleton, N. Y.—Hope L. Haines, New Dorp, N. Y., 7-20-1907.
Farnham Abbott—Rachel Hews, 5-28-1877.
  Charles—Kate Magourly, 2-12-1875.
  Thomas—Kate M. Daisey, 4-30-1878.
Farquar, Leroy—Mary Ann Harned, 9-23-1876.
Farquhar, Daniel—Sarah McWhinney, 1-20-1875.
  John R.—Virginia Moore, 8-20-1873.
  Joseph—Laura Murphy, 12-2-1877.
Farr, Charles—Rebecca Esler, 10-1-1871.
  James L.—Anna Devault, 6-14-1876.
Farrell, John A.—Mary I. Hillman, 12-9-1873.
Fennimore, William H.—Elizabeth Horneff, 7-19-1875.
Fenton, Frank A.—Annie Lewis, 1-7-1868.
Ferat, Charles M.—Mary A. Wrifford, 11-29-1877.
Ferbig, Franklin M.—Mary Bishop, both Burlington co., 8-31-1870.

Ferguson, James—Catharine O'Conner, 2-4-1868.
Ferrell, Charles W., Pine Grove—Mary Young, Glassboro, 6-22-1877.
Ferry, John—Jennie Trimble, 12-25-1873.
Fetters Henry—Mary Ann Car, Philadelphia, 1-17-1869.
Fidler, Theodore—Mary Wilkins, 10-10-1868.
Field, Thomas D.—Louisa Hoffman, 7-11-1872.
Fieriglio Bragio—Maria Rosa Fieriglio, both Philadelphia, 10-11-1905.
Fifield, Harry—Emma R. Pine, 8-9-1877.
Filer, Enoch—Abigail A. McCullough, both Hurffville, 9-5-1870.
Fink, George W.—Mary V. Mathers, both Port Royal, Pa., 7-6-1908.
Finley, Albert W.—Sarah Ryan, 7-13-1872.
Fish, Charles L.—Martha Logue, 12-25-1873.
  George W.—Mary P. Garwood, 11-19-1873.
  William—Mary E. Johnson, 12-24-1873.
Fisher, George W.—Annie Channel, 4-30-1877.
Fitchett, William—Jane Showel, Jersey City, 10-30-1872.
Fitzsimmons, Charles H.—Anna Carey, 4-6-1875.
Fizone, ——— —Arabella Fish, 10-21-1873.
Flaig, John—Caroline Jorgan, 1-15-1866.
Flanagan, Robert L.—Victoria L. Collyer, 1-6-1878.
Fleming, Samuel Wilson, Harrisburg, Pa.—Mary Melvina Sauther, 10-7-1875.
Flemming, John D.—Lydia Green, 12-30-1868.
Flenner, Benjamin H.—Adeline F. Cole, 4-29-1872.
Fletcher, Franklin—Amanda Taylor, 7-21-1867.
Flint, Aaron—Elizabeth Griffey, 10-17-1869.
Fooy, Richard—Alice A. Gross, both Philadelphia, 4-2-1875.
Ford, Benjamin—Mary Ann Patterson, 8-14-1869.
  George—Elizabeth Mlller, 12-22-1868.
  Isaac, Mannington—Hannah E. Wright, Yorktown, 12-3- 1874.
  William—Emma Farrow, 3-1-1873.
Foresman, William S.—Amanda Bird, 4-19-1876.

Forest, Daniel—Lizzie Bennett, 11-30-1875.
   Joseph—Adeline Loughlin, 9-21-1873.
Formas, Julian J.—Edith Smith, both Philadelphia, 6-24-1903.
Forsyth, David K.—Annie W. Wolfsen, both Philadelphia, 10-25-1902.
   Joshua—Louisa Hatch, 2-21-1878.
   William, Saltsburg, Pa.—Elizabeth Graham, 12-24-1866.
Fort, Rob. N.—Emma F. Creeley, both Burlington, 2-24-1876.
   William S.—Rebecca A. Brown, both Burlington co., 3-3-1869.
Fortiner, Alfred—Ann Rumford, 7-24-1869.
Foster, Franklin Linwood, Auburn—Helen Rebecca Watson, 7-16-1877.
   William—Sarah Gibbs, Heightstown, 2-7-1878.
Fountain, Marcy—Mary E. Ingram, 8-22-1872.
Fowler, Richard, Matawan—Anna P. Beatty, Trenton, 5-3-1878.
Fox, Daniel G.—Maggie M. Hewitt, 10-1-1871.
   George Washington—Laura Shinn, 7-6-1876.
   John—Martha Riedel, both Philadelphia—2-2-1898.
   Wm. H.—Emma Conrad, 1-27-1877.
   Wm. M., Kent co., Md.—Caroline Bowen, Roadstown, June, 1868.
Frame, Osben—Emma E. Waters, 9-15-1873.
Francisco, Wm.—Mary Dare, 6-10-1877.
Frand, Martin—Mary J. Lees, 8-17-1871.
Franey, James, Philadelphia—Jane Campbell, 8-11-1867.
Frank, August, Florida—Ellen Sarah O'Neal, Ireland, 4-2-1878.
   Charles—Mary C. Lee, 3-16-1869.
   Michael—Emilie L. Stanton, 9-4-1875.
Frazer, William—Abbie Abbott, 7-13-1874.
Freas, George J.—Lizzie Wall, 5-20-1874.
Fredericks, Joseph—Bella Stretcher, 6-30-1873.
Freeman, Chas.—Elizabeth Curing, 8-1-1868.

French, Thomas, Gloucester co.—Rebecca M. Nicholls, Oscalosa, Ia., 2-5-1870.
Frey, William R.—Sadie Arthur, both Philadelphia, 12-26-1908.
Friepse, William, Philadelphia—Sue Kerfis, 10-11-1877.
Fritchie, Marcus—Mary Winner, 8-12-1873.
Fryling, Jos. G.—Sarah E. Harley, 5-10-1877.
Fuets, George D.—Maria Hurlocke, 7-13-1874.
Fullerton, John Mallin—Amy L. Brown, 10-15-1877.
Furgray, Arthur R—Ella Z. Funk, 4-11-1872.
Furrow, Elijah H.—Cordelia Fitzchew, 10-12-1876.
Gaines, Noah—Elizabeth Fisher, 8-5-1852.
Galbreth, Richard—Emma J. Cowperthwaite, 4-27-1873.
Ganan, James—Jane Harvey, 1-10-1874.
Gandy, Peter W.—Ellen V. King, 3-24-1874.
Gardess, Joseph—Mary Ann Willis, 12-14-1871.
Gardiner, Joseph E., Turnerville, Mary Walker, 12-5-1869.
Gardner, Joseph E., Marlton—Mary E. Mathis, Rancocas, 9-15-1872.
Garrison, Charles—Sarah Louisa Mackey, 5-30-1867.
Garwood, C. C.—Henrietta Strickland, Atlantic co., 7-2-1867.
  Daniel B.—Ella Louis, 9-8-1873.
  John L.—Ida E. Olive, 8-29-1872.
  John W.—Elizabeth W. Borten, both Burlington co., 12-1-1869.
  Joseph F., Turnerville—Patience Watson, Gloucester co., 5-4-1869.
  Robert F.—Sallie H. Martin, both Burlington co., 2-5-1868.
  Wm. H.—Susan Ann Holland, 3-19-1873.
Gaskell, Edward, Buddtown—Lydia Gaskill, Mt. Holly, 7-8-1866.
Gates, Aaron—Susan A. Willis, 3-1-1869.
  Franklin E., Cumberland co.—Mary E. Cobb, Coxsackie N. Y., 6-16-1867.
Gaubert, Theo. F.—Eliza Easton Caddy, 5-9-1871.
Gauff, Samuel—Elizabeth Kniser, 7-27-1866.

Gaul, Harry R.—Sallie A. Newton, 11-20-1873.
Gaunt, John—Anna E. Lehman, 12-26-1867.
Richard—Mary Eliza Cook, both Massachusetts. 4-13-1867.
Geiger, Andrew D.—Emma McPherson, 11-7-1878.
William, Reading, Pa.—Elvira A. Thompson, 7-16-1868.
Gemmill, Henry Clay—Helen Bringhurst, both Philadelphia, 1-12-1904.
Gerhard, Peter J., Philadelphia—Sabina Goodwin, 11-2-1868.
Gersenderfer, Otto—Emma Hilderman, both Philadelphia, 5-26-1898.
Gibbs, E. Howard—Florence Bowker, 11-11-1872.
Giberson, John C.—Eleanor A. Leslie, 4-3-1872.
Josiah E.—Emily C. Woodrow, 9-2-1866.
Gibson, John W.—Sarah Gurn, 1-25-1866.
Samuel—Mary Lewallen. 2-18-1872.
Giddings, Walter O—Jennie P. Hoag, 4-14-1886.
Gideon, Wm. D. Glassboro—Clara V. Sweeten, 9-24-1871.
Gifford, Daniel—Temperance Foster, both Millville, 3-10-1866.
Daniel L.—Harriet Smith, both Glassboro, 8-7-1872.
Francis A.—Adeline L. Trout, 11-7-1868.
Henry J., Rochester, N. Y.—Mary F. Warren. 2-11-1864.
Jacob R , Williamstown—Hannah A. Allen, 9-21-1873.
Gill, Henry—Sarah Ennell, 12-31-1859.
William—Lydia Fitch, 10-10-1868.
Gillette, Edward S.—Margaret Fisher, both Philadelphia, 4-30-1898.
Gilman, Ambrose, Philadelphia—Rachel S. Wilson, 1-12-1873.
Gilmore, Robert—Charlena Tice 3-2-1873.
Gilpin, William—Florence Dych, both Philadelphia, 3-25-1898
Githens, Jesse—Rachel Patrick, 7-4-1867.
Glee, William—Mary Hoffman, 5-25-1868.
Glover, Joshua—Maria B. Wheaton, 9-4-1877.
Godfrew, Wm. M.—Annie E. Stevenson, 12-5-1872.

Godfrey, Samuel S., Philadelphia—Annie J. Leake, Millville, 10-4-1871.
Golden. Samuel H.—Harriet A. Albertson, 10-25-1871.
Goldhaler, Jacob—Helen Breen, 9-23-1898.
Golding, Edward—Rebecca Rorke, 2-11-1867.
Goldsmith, Martin—Emma Fellows, 8-27-1869.
Goldy, Leander W.—Julia Mudoon, 8-22-1872.
Goodbody, Fred C., Ireland—Maggie L. Bateman, Williamsport, Pa , 4-13-1898.
Goodwin, Thomas A.—Susie B. Montgomery, 11-28-1878.
Gordon, Joseph M.—Annie Wiltse, 8-6-1871.
Gorman, Robert J.—Hattie North, both Philadelphia, 3-3-1869.
Gorvey, Frank—Maggie A. Riley, 4-24-1878.
Graeff, Augustus Nicholas, Philadelphia—Emma Ada Saurman, 2-12-1908.
Graffen, Harris, Philadelphia—Mary A. Carman, 1-18-1866.
Graham, Chas. E.—Anna E. Valentine, 4-3-1878.
  William—Louisa Kennedy, 3-30-1871.
Gray, Peter S.—Mary E. Smith, Philadelphia, 5-28-1871.
Green, John W.—Lizzie Larmouth, 1-11-1870.
  Wm.—Barbara Zimmerman, 2-20-1869.
  Winfield—Mary Purnell, 6-21-1873.
Greenige, Washington—Mary J. Driggits. 6-3-1867.
Greenwood, James—Mary Ann Devlin, 3-9-1866.
Gregory, William—Anna Brindle, 2-20-1873.
Greis, Hugo—Caroline Doerr, both Atlantic co., 8-12-1866.
  Otto, Philadelphia—Susan Serrien, Gloucester co., 5-16-1871.
Grey, Martin, Salem—Mary Jane Dunham, 2-21-1867.
  Philip—Anna Foggard, 5-27-1871.
Griffee, Stephen—Anna Jacobs, 11-29-1868.
  William—Mary L. Chew, 1-9-1867.
Griffin, Ephraim—Eliza Jane Finch, 12-29-1870.
  John M., Philadelphia—Lydia Byers, 8-12-1873.
Griffith, Isaac—Lizzie Wilson, both Philadelphia. 6-1-1871.
  Joseph B.—Harriet Murphy, both Chester co, Pa., 8-16-1870

CAMDEN COUNTY MARRIAGES—BOOK B 85

Gross, Owen B.—Frances A. Coates, 9-9-1877.
Grosscup, Henry C.—Elizabeth Barrett, 4-28-1872.
Grover, Harry B.—Eliza Mallman, 1-7-1869.
  W. B.—Hannah L. Leaving, 5-13-1877.
Grube Herbert E.—Flossie O. Hagenback, 5-17-1908.
Grupp, William—Emeline Yehner, Trenton, 8-24-1873.
Gumben, Jeremiah—Louisa Caroline Eldridge, 2-1-1872.
Guthridge, James—Annie Stokes, 3-6-1909.
Guthrie, Oliver E.—Mary Bennett, Millville, 10-5-1868.
Haas, Jacob—Chataring Donbach, 9-19-1869.
  William—Bertha Shack, both Philadelphia, 10-5-1885.
Hackney, Joseph—Adle Munroe, 9-13-1877.
Haden, William—Harrietta Weintz, 6-1-1868.
Hage, William—Cecelia Willie, Philadelphia, 9-8-1867.
Hager, Jacob—Anna D. Wilson, 8-97-1866.
Hagerty, William, Shicklerville, Pa.—Lydia McCormick, Mill Creek, Del., 8-4-1876.
Hageue, William—Lucy Finney, Woodbury, 12-18-1874.
Haines, Charles—Bertha Hartle, 4-23-1873.
  Elwood, Burlington co.—Sallie Harris, Palmyra, 8-30-1877.
  Joseph—Elizabeth C. Jewell, 8-13-1874.
  Joseph G.—Fannie E. Cramer, both Philadelphia, 1867.
  Millard F. Burlington co.—Lizzie S. Flenard, Mt. Holly, 12-1-1876.
  Mordecai F., Rancocas—Hannah A. Cox, 4-3-1872.
  Wm.—Margaret Baker, 1-16-1869.
Hall, Hosea—Sarah Shorts, 9-19-1869.
  Issac—Mary Townsend, 10-4-1872.
  Jesse, Jr.—Sallie Cavanaugh, 11-15-1868.
  Theodore F.—Anna Devine, both Philadelphia, 7-22-1867.
  William H.—Mary M. Sheppard, 10-11-1874.
Hamilton, Robert J., Frankford, Pa.—Sarah Mills, 9-3-1872.
Hamlyn, George F.—Rosa F. Tebbett, Hammonton, 12-16-1873.
Hammell, George—Elizabeth Pike 4-5-1872.
  Harry M., Philadelphia—Elena B. Applegate; **recorded** 8-9-1897.

Hammell, Horace—Isora Morris, 11-2-1871.
  Israel, Ohio—Jane Newton, 12-30-1868.
  John—Anna Reese, both Philadelphia, 1-7-1871.
Hammond, Mitchell, New York—Laura Thorn, 11-5-1870.
Hampton, Henry—Sarah C. Richman, both Ewingsville, 10-8-1870
  John D.—Hannah I. Wallen, 12-25-1873
Hand, Aaron—George Anna Smith, 5-27-1873.
  Frank S.—Anna M. Pedrick, 5-20-1876.
  Joseph, Jr.—Emma S. Fairfield, 9-3-1873.
  Ludlam—Deborah Beek, 10-4-1869
  William—Eliza Jane Souders, both Malaga, 10-18-1865.
Handy, Franklin—Martha A. Cooper, 7-4-1872.
  Ishmael—Harriet Ann Mandz, both Philadelphia, 8-4-1872.
  Samuel—Martina Harris, 4-9-1876.
Hankinson, Robert D. S., Monmouth co.—Elizabeth Gaines, 3-18-1869.
Hanmer, Samuel—Clara A McKeever, 7-29-1877.
Hannah, Frank S.—Evelena Stratton, Pennsgrove, 10-17-1874.
Hannold, Howard M.—Louisa King, both Hurffville, 11-3-1872.
Hanson, Joseph E.—Sarah E. Brinnisholtz, 5-28-1872.
  Sameul D.—Sallie E. Truxton, 4-5-1875.
Harbison, Hugh—Bertha Pinkert, 7-23-1875.
Harden, Jacob M.—Amanda Hartley, 2-21-1867.
  Stephen—Levinia Hardy, 9-13-1869.
Hare, John Q.—Mary E. Stow, 10-31-1873.
  William—Mary C. Smith, 9-14-1873.
Harker, Charles—Anna Bowers, 8-3-1874.
  John—Anna Mary Schell, 12-6-1871.
Harkins, Ambrose—Annie Ellis, 11-3-1864.
  Henry R.—Wilhelmina M. Shaw, both Millville, 7-4-1866.
  William—Emma Baker, both Philadelphia; recorded 9-20-1897.
Harkness, Nathan—Jemima Vansant, both Bristol, Pa., 4-23-1868.

Harley, Edward—Ida V. Severns, 6-13-1877.
John, Philadelphia—Susan Godfrey, 6-29-1876.
Harp, Samuel—Rachel Hough, 1-7-1774.
Harris, Benjamin, Mary Harkins, 1-17-1876.
  George W.—Kate Hull, 10-13-1873.
  James—Rebecca Matlack, 7-4-1867.
  John—Mary Benson, 9-13-1885.
  Wm. H., Burlington co.—Mary C. Cox, 5-5-1870.
  W. P—Mary Whilldin, 7-8-1869.
Harrison, Albert—Georgean Annica, 10-22-1877.
  Charles—Rebecca Thompson, 2-21-1878.
  Edward G., St. Michael, Md.—Eleanor L. Waithman, 1-14-1875.
  George—Mary Brown, 9-27-1845.
  Granville Willard, Philadelphia—Jane Maria Dennis, 5-4-1878.
  Samuel J.—Mary R. Burroughs, 4-15-1875.
  Walcott, Philadelphia—Sarah E. Hart, Brooklyn, 3-18-1878.
Hartman John C.—Lizzie Dawns, 6-16-1872.
  Philip, Cincinnati—Rachel Johnstone (or Johnson), 10-6-1872.
Harvey, Varney—Ann E. Walker, 6-19-1873.
Hassert, Charles—Mina Halshart, 1-8-1874.
Hatch, Joseph—Caroline I. Treagg, 11-14-1872.
Haun, Wm F. M.—Martha Countryman, 4-12-1876.
Hausman, Wm.—Bertha Krattenmacher, both Germany, 7-5-1869.
Havens, Albert J.—Lou M. Garrison, 6-28-1877.
Haviland, Francis—Elizabeth Tripler, 10-8-1874.
Hawkins, Stephen—Mary Baker, 2-10-1868.
Heater, Theodore W.—Emma Caverly, 1-1-1877.
Heath, John R. Thompson—Jennie Westle, Coatesville, Pa., 8-1-1874.
  William—Margaret Kellum, both Eastern Shore, Md., 6-5-1871.
Heimbach, Richard, White Haven, Pa.—Ella M. Lester, Luzerne co., Pa., 4-25-1876.

Helbert, Henry—Mary L. Schubert, 8-3-1869.
Helmbold Charles H.—Emma Ferris, 4-4-1875.
Helms, Thompson—Sally C. Urbar, 3-25-1877.
  Wm H.—Sallie White, 8-19-1867.
Helomeboy, Theodore—Mary C Henry, both Philadelphia; recorded 10-21-1897.
Hembold, David—Georgiana Worley, 6-13-1875
Hemphill, Elijah Dallett, Allentown, Pa —Rebecca Mickle, Philadelphia, 11-22-1871.
Henderson, Benj. F.—Anthor Sheppard, 8-4-1872.
  Robert B —Martha Naylor, both Philadelphia, 12-29-1875.
Hendricks, William R., Bridgeton—Mary R. Applegate, 1-1-1872.
Hendrickson, Andrew I.—Elizabeth Warrington, 2-12-1868.
Henison, Thomas F.—Anna Nelon, both Ireland, 12-2-1866.
Henny, Alphonso—Marteine Blacscold, 8-25-1868.
Henry, Charles S.—Addie M. Lucas, 1-5-1876.
  David M.—Annie Dugan, 11-5-1877.
  John S., Philadelphia—Mary Jane Tweed, 3-10-1868.
  William—Elizabeth Burns, 3-13-1876.
Hensel, John—Alice Young, 10-12-1873.
Heppar, Joseph—Hannah Locke, both Philadelphia, 8-18-1909.
Heppard, Joseph—Elizabeth Stites, 8-6-1868.
  Samuel M.—Mary R. McWilliams, 4-15-1874.
  William D., Philadelphia— Priscilla Powell, Leesburg, 1-1-1871.
Herber, John—Ella Smith, both Atlantic co., 5-15-1877.
Herforth, Charles—Ottilia Reidel, both Philadelphia, 12-3-1875
Heritage, Arthur—Mary Augusta Upham, both Hurffville, 1-5-1865.
  Charles I., Gloucester co.—Susannah Turner, 8-3-1862.
  Elijah, Gloucester co.—Sarah J. Fisler, 1-16-1873.
  Harrison—Elizabeth K. Turner, both Gloucester co., 4-23-1868.
Hersey, Samuel—Elizabeth Clark, both Salem, 6-14-1873.

Heston, Alfred M.—Abbie L. Mitchell, 12-30-1875.
Heusman, William F.—Mary J. Clift, 10-12-1873.
Hewlings, Geo. W.—Pauline Plummer, 10-31-1875.
  John N.—Sarah J. Hope, 9-1-1872.
Hiddermass, Albert— Maggie Foster, both Philadelphia, 11-14-1897.
Higginbottom, Joseph—Sarah Robinson, 1-19-1873.
Higgins, Charles—Mary E. Burroughs, 1-6-1877.
Hildebrand, Charles—Elizabeth Ritter, both Germany, 8-13-1868.
Hill, Chas. B.—Catharine Ewings, 4-30-1866.
  Gabriel P.—Anna H. Johnson, 9-20-1872.
  James R.—Eleanor Hines, 9-12-1872.
  John Z.—Mary E. Helms, 12-20-1868.
  (or Thill), Theodore—Annie Dundas, 6-2-1886.
  William H.—Hester J. Conover, Atlantic City, 12-26-1868
  William H.—Matilda M. Price, 11-5-1873.
Hillman, Chas. H.—Jane Peyton, 2-2-1878.
  John Ford—Kate Sorver, 10-27-1868.
  William—Annie Collins, 1-23-1876.
Hillyer, Howard, Pennsylvania—Fannie Elizabeth Olmsted, New York, 6-28-1868.
Hinchman, Jacob—Mary E. Birdsall, 12-2-1869.
Hinds, Thomas—Mary Oney, 10-10-1872.
Hinkle, Aaron—Cornelia Comley, 10-27-1877.
  Adam—Mary Ann Kelly, 1-4-1875.
  Geo. N.—Mary Dougherty, 2-7-1866.
Hinman, William, Clarksboro—Mary A. Yonker, 11-22-1877.
Hires, Phineas S., Bridgeton—L. Louise Swing, Cumberland co., 5-9-1872.
  Samuel—Emma H. Goldshall, both Gloucester co., 9-5-1872.
  William M.—Eliza M. Whitelock, 5-16-1877.
Hitchner, Rollins F., Atlantic City—Martha H. Mead, Salem co., 9-20-1876.
Hoagland, Charles M.—Clara R. Mahoney, 12-24-1872.

CAMDEN COUNTY MARRIAGES—BOOK B

Hoffman, George C.—Mary J. Braddock, 9-7-1872.
  John, Bridgeton—Rebecca J. Pedrick, 6-7-1873.
  John—Henrietta M. Stout, both Royalton, Conn., 11-6-1899.
  John A.—Sarah A. Dixson, 2-1-1874.
  William L.—Elizabeth Bryan, both Philadelphia; recorded 9-11-1897.
Hogan, Chas. M.—Helen Clark, 12-30-1875.
Holderness, Thomas—Lillian DeWolf, both Philadelphia, 1-24-1904.
Holdgate, Stephen, Trenton—Elizabeth Burns Warden, 4-14-1870.
Holl, George—Laura Stockton, 6-25-1873.
Holland, Franklin—Hannah E. Snyder, 4-15-1867.
  William A.—Henrietta D. Scheperkotter, 12-31-1869.
Hollis, Chas. J.—Martha A. Harris, 8-9-1874.
Hollohan, Martin—Sarah A. Wardle, Cape Island City, 9-13-1869,
Holmes, Benjamin— Mary Elizabeth Smith, Turnerville, 11-1-1876.
  John C., Cranberry—Louisa M. Powell, 3-7-1871.
  Johathan B.—Catharine H. Downs, Elton Wis., 6-12-1876.
Holster, Clarence E.—Jennie Lewis, 3-31-1873.
Holston, Atwood, Clayton—Marion Ross, 11-13-1876.
Holt, Francis B.—Sarah Catharine Robertson, 6-15-1862.
  William—Betty Buckley, 7-18-1873.
Holton, Clarence E.—Jennie N. Lewis, Easton, Pa., 3-31-1873.
Homeyard, Henry—Theressa S. VanMeter, both Philadelphia, 8-24-1871.
Hoover, William V.—Joanna Fish, Bridgeton, 3-20-1876.
Hopkins, Charles I.—Mary Stoughten, 9-11-1867.
  George Hicks—Amelia M. Glover, 11-12-1867.
Hopper, Harry, St. Louis, Mo.—Elizabeth A. Brown, 7-31-1871.
Horn, Emanuel, Philadelphia—Flora Levi, New York, 4-2-1906.

CAMDEN COUNTY MARRIAGES—BOOK B 91

Horn, John—Rachel Clark, 5-23-1878.
Hornberger, Henry L., Philadelphia—Mary Ann Hurff, 2-13-[1868.
Horner, Asa P.—Mary G. Githens, 3-14-1871.
  Benajah A.—Anna A. Ross, 5-22-1867.
  Benjamin—J. L. Eacritt, 10-7-1873.
  Chas. Henry—Lizzie McMahon, 10-31-1877.
  Edward—Tillie McCain, 3-14-1869.
  Ezra—Anna M. Scroggy, 10-19-1870.
  George E.—Ollie Tenbner, both Philadelphia, 5-22-1901.
  Joseph—Laura Gowie, 1-31-1877.
Houghtaling, James—Anna Headley, 7-5-1868.
Houston, Charles—Leanna Waters, 6-8-1873.
Howard, Frederick—Maggie Lezenby, 3-25-1873.
  John W.—Hannah Beckett, 1-11-1871.
  Lee—Annie Lafferty, 6-30-1875.
  Wm.—Mary J. Childs, both Manayunk, Pa., 12-31-1876.
Howell, Ellis W.—Lydia Osler, 11-18-1875.
  Frank W.—Jennie Marshall, 10-1-1876.
Howes, Henry W.—Villie C. Bain, 6-5-1867.
Hudson, A. S., Woodbury—Emma E. Davidson, Philadelphia, 12-24-1876.
  Edward Augustus—Mary Martha Surdam, both New Brunswick, 7-4-1877.
  John L.—Sallie Castle, 8-25-1875.
  William—Emma Beadle, 7-16-1876.
Huey William—Keziah Shee, 9-23-1868.
Huff, James—Sarah Gormley, 3-16-1874.
Hughes, Samuel S.—Leonora Curtis, 5-27-1867.
Huling, William H.—Anna C. Corletta, 4-1-1877.
Hulme, Joseph S.—Abigail Wille, both Burlington, 6-4-1867.
Hummell, Joseph, Charlton, N. J.—Emma Adams, 12-31-1868.
Humphrey, Francis—Mary Jane Down, 3-21-1873.
Humphries, George—Mamie Coy, Palmyra, 4-16-1877.
Hunt, George S.—Clarissa Cook, 1-1-1877.
  Henry, M. D.—Theresa Hugg, 1-31-1866.
  James—Mary A. Hewitt, 8-20-1869.

Huntsinger, George—Sarah J. Darnell. 12-24-1872.
Hurff, Brooks—Margaret Gant, both Chestnut Ridge, 8-28-1870.
  Jesse L.—Sarah E. Prosser, both Turnerville, 3-10-1870.
Hurlbut, Eugene R.—Maria A. Gray, Ingrafter, O., 12-2-1869.
Hurst, James—Lucy Sadler, Palmyra, 6-22-1876.
Husted, George—Amelia C. Mayers, 10-12-1873.
  William—Julia C. Wallace, 7-1-1877.
Huston, Wm. H.—Josephine Crispin, 12-24-1875.
Hutchins, James, Burlington co.—Mary L. Baylor, Burlington, 3-25-1878.
  Wm. H., Cleveland, O.—Sallie Watkins, Minersville, Pa., 1-8-1877.
Hutchinson, John G.—Joanna Phillips, Mt. Holly, 10-30-1876.
Hutton, Richard—Jane Esher, both Philadelphia, 8-5-1874.
Hyatt, Leander—Kate Shute; recorded 12-28-1876.
Idell, Charles I.—Lizzie E. Dubell, 7-30-1873.
Iliff, Benjamin, Philadelphia—Rachel Evans, Pottsville, Pa., 12-6-1871.
Ingham, William H.—Mary E. Maxwell, 1-28-1869.
Ireland, Edwin—Susan A. Weiser, both Millville, 5-16-1871.
  Thomas—Jane Hinerdinger, both Chester, Pa., 7-29-1870.
  Wm. Henry, Frankford, Pa.—Sarah Ann Bilson, 9-15-1875.
Ireton, Eugene W.—Josephine Wilkins, 11-23-1876.
  Franklin—Anna M. Richardson, 3-6-1867.
Irish, William E.—Anna Hufty, 11-23-1871.
Irons, Walter—Lettie Calhoun, both Philadelphia, 4-2-1901.
Isley, Frederick—Mary A. Dutton, 12-16-1873.
Irvine, William S.—Mary D. Stultz, 12-1-1877.
Jackson, Andrew—Amanda H. Reynolds, 6-5-1876.
  Franklin P.—Minerva Thompson, 5-24-1877.
  Gideon L.—Mary E. Burey, 12-18-1872.
  Immanuel, Washington, D. C.—Sallie Godfrey, 11-29-1874.

CAMDEN COUNTY MARRIAGES—BOOK B   93

Jackson, James P.—Mary Douglass, both Woodbury, 1-10-1869.
  Marcellus L.—Addie Burgess, both Hammonton, 4-5-1873.
  Miles—Mary A Gray, 7-7-1871.
  Thomas D.—Mary Gaskill, both Delaware co., Pa., 3-18-1875.
  William—Sarah A. Bowser, Philadelphia, 10-8-1885.
Jackway, Andrew—Lucy Stewart, 4-25-1878.
Jaggard, Ambrose E., Almonesson—Clara Batten, 12-23-1876.
  Edward S.—Theodosia Warrick, 3-25-1875.
Jaggers, David R.—Eliza McMann, 9-28-1869.
  David R.—Agnes Berrymont, 6-12-1876.
James, John L.—Lucinda L. Brooks, 6-22-1872.
  William—Ellen Wier, 7-12-1873.
Jamison, Samuel P.—Phebe M. Hyland, both Philadelphia, 7-9-1874.
  William—Annie Greenage, 11-18-1866.
Jarges, Abraham—Adna Greis, 12-30-1866.
Jarman, Wm. S.—Pauline S. Appleton, 11-24-1876.
Jefferies, Wm. H.—Maria Outwater, 9-8-1870.
Jefferis, Clinton D.—Anna P. Troth, 5-28-1868.
  Joseph C.—Lizzie Smith, 3-4-1872.
Jennings, Edward D.—Bathsheba Cheesman, Turnerville, 8-11-1872.
  George E. A., Philadelphia—Mary F. Wright, Beverly, 12-14-1871.
  Robert, Jr., Pittsburgh, Pa.—Rachel Elwell, 2-3-1898.
Jennison, Mathew H.—Margaret Carson, 6-8-1868.
Jess, Lorenzo—Mary R. Haines, 11-5-1860.
Jessup, John W.—Harriet Gardiner, both Gloucester co., 3-17-1870.
Jester, Daniel—Margaret E. Hughes, 5-1-1877.
Jobs, Samuel—Debbie E. Chamberlain, 4-11-1877.
Johns, Frank J., Scranton, Pa.—Emma E. Applin, 3-9-1898.
Johnson, David H.—Clara V. Hillman, 9-10-1874.
  Harry J.—Mamie A. Brenner, both Philadelphia, 3-30-1901.

Johnson, Henry L., Jr.—Frances E. Poole, 10-19-1876.
  Jacob—Rachel Weeks, 7-4-1872.
  James—Sarah A. Woolford, 7-9-1871.
  James—Elizabeth Cross. Andalusia, Pa., 9-9-1877.
  James Henry—Elizabeth Johnson, both Philadelphia, 1-20-1872.
  James P.—Amelia K. Wood, 12-19-1875
  John—Elizabeth Shackler 7-31-1870
  John—Clara R. Hinkle, 2-25-1875.
  John Henry, Smyrna. Del.—Margaret Sarah Weeks, 12-31-1871.
  John, Sr.—Mary F. Richards, 10-22-1868.
  Joseph K.—Mary Corson, 4-17-1872.
  Nelson W.—Anna M. McCown, 3-5-1874.
  William E.—Maggie Dingler, 2-25-1874.
  William H.—Amelia Hubbs, both Westfield, 12-1-1868.
  William H.—Sarah Bryant. 3-11-1872.
Johnston, John, Jr.—Kate Shephard, 7-12-1877.
Jolley, John, Doylestown. Pa.—Sarah Parvin, 1-20-1876.
Jones, Asher—Sarah W. Norcross, 7-3-1875.
  Benj. Y.—Mary E. Peterson, 11-16-1873.
  Charles H.—Jennie Greenley, 7-14-1872.
  Charles H., Vincentown—Caroline H. Ensel, 12-20-1876.
  Edwin F.—Mary Elizabeth Butcher, 6-10-1877.
  Henry Isaac, Philadelphia, Mary A. Mathias, 1-30-1878.
  James—Ella Martha Pope, 5-31-1883.
  Jarvis C., Tuckerton—Abbie A. Birdsall, 10-19-1874.
  John—Mary Ann Nelson, Pehnsylvania, 6-11-1868.
  John C.—Amanda M. Deacon, both Burlington co., 1-28-1869.
  J. Paul—Elizabeth Wilsey, 1-4-1872.
  Thomas—Beulah Thorn, 3-9-1869.
  William—Elizabeth Thompson, 9-11-1870.
  William—Elizabeth Chambers, 8-5-1872.
  William H.—Mary H. Paul, both Philadelphia, 7-23-1871.
  William H.—Sarah A. A. Walker, 12-25-1871.
Jordan, J. Albert, Iowa—Emeline Hackett, 2-21-1872.

CAMDEN COUNTY MARRIAGES—BOOK B 95

Jordan, James C.—J. F. Williams, 11-11-1872.
Joslyn, C. R.—Carrie Lyman, 12-25-1873.
Joyce, Joseph—Beulah L. Pike, both Moorestown, 10-1-1874.
Jillerd, Edward E —Annie E. Till, both Philadelphia, 6-14-1877.
Juff, Charles H.—Elizabeth Higginbotham, 9-25-1872.
Jump, J. Henry, Maryland—Anna E. Venable, Marlton, 2-11-1868.
Justice, Charles F —Fannie L. Beckett, 11-21-1872.
Kahn, Joseph, Norfolk, Va.—Sarah Stewart, 9-23-1874.
Kaiting, Thomas—Mary Kaiting, 11-9-1871.
Kean, Peter, Rancocas—Augustine Adams, Port Republic, 10-23-1872.
Keene, Chas. W.—Fannie E. Middleton, 5-8-1877.
  Samuel C., Boston, Mass.—Mary A. Campbell; recorded 11-9-1897.
Keffer, William—Hannah Simpkins, 2-20-1857.
Keighton, Robert G.—Lizzie A. Howell, 2-14-1877.
Kelley, Benj. F.—Mary A. Clifton, 12-14-1870.
  Edward—Anna Bradley, 9-11-1871.
  Edwin—Rachel M. West, 9-29-1877.
  James—Maggie Trimble, 7-25-1875.
  Peter, Catharine Smith, 7-3-1871.
Kelly, Isaac—Harriet D. Powell, 5-17-1868.
  James J.—Fannie J. Andrews, 7-30-1872.
  John—Edith E. Burt, 8-28-1872.
  William—Mary Caroline Naylor, Torresdale, Pa., 10-8-1867.
  Winfield S.—Mary J. Reynolds, 2-9-1873.
Kemp, Howard—Eveline R. Taylor, 6-5-1873.
Kennady, David—Mary A. Jeffries, Frankford, Pa., 3-31-1875.
Kennedy, Geo. W., Baltimore, Md.—Omelia Bectel, 5-28-1866.
  Robert C. M.—Emily Alice Clayton, both Philadelphia, 6-8-1904.
Ketterer, William—Nellie Weymer, 1-22-1872.

Kevil, Henry—Elizabeth Johnson. both Philadelphia, 12-10-1871.
Key, William—Elizabeth Taylor, 4-27-1864.
Keys. Robert, Pittsburgh. Pa.—Margaret McIsaac; recorded 7-3-1878.
Kiker. Matthias—Frances Fortiner, 11-18-1869
Kille, Henry, Philadelphia—Sarah Stokes, Burlington co., 1-8-1874.
King, Henry P.—Rachel E. Wannan, 3-23-1869.
  Herbert Paul, New York—Reba Mulford Ely, Philadelphia, 6-13-1905.
  John E.—Hannah Knowles. both Philadelphia, 1-2-1869.
  Thomas E.— Roseanna E. Treadway, both Salem, 12-25-1873.
Kinsey, John W.—Lizzie L. Davis, 12-24-1876.
Kinsley, Lewis—Sarah Hess, both Philadelphia, 9-3-1873.
Kirby, William G.—Harriet Dilks, both Westville, 12-30-1873.
Kirk, Isaac B.—Elizabeth Grupp, both Bridgeton, 3-30-1866.
  Jesse G.—Mary E. Griffith, 11-20-1867.
  John R.— Emma Goodway, 10-22-1871.
Kirkbride, Job—Jane R. Kirkbride, both Burlington co., 7-9-1867.
  Josiah R., Mt Holly—Mary Ella Fogg, Briegeton, 12-31-1865.
Klapp, Joseph—Caroline Ingraham, both Philadelphia, 9-3-1873.
Kleinstner, Wm.—Agnes Mitchler, 9-6-1869.
Klemm, William G.—Laura V. Hoffman; recorded 5-23-1870.
Kline, Charles—Hannah Bray, Burlington co., 9-13-1873.
  Harry—Bridget M. Sutton, both Norristown, Pa., 10-25-1902.
Knauff, W. W.—Mary Elizabeth Sell, 5-7-1877.
Knaugh. John Philbert—Maria Miller, both Germany, 6-8-1867.
Knight, Abram C.—Margaret Ritzell, 2-7-1878.
  Elias M.—Annie C. Clair, both Westvllle, 5-1-1877.

Knight, Frank, Philadelphia—Ruth Ann Hall, 11-15-1864.
George—Mattie S. Johnson, 12-20-1876.
James—Mary A Wilson, 8-25-1869-
Knipe, Theo D.—Emma Adler, 10-20-1872.
Knox, John W.—Mary E. Bohm, 12-23-1875.
Kolle, Jacob, Pottstown, Pa.—Ella Jones, 9-30-1870.
Krager, Albert—Alice Burt Crowley, both Philadelphia, 3-26-
Kriser, William—Rosie Schick, both Philadelphia, 3-1-1898.
Krause, Walter R., Sanatoga, Pa.—Elsie K. Haus, Pottstown, Pa., 9-22-1909.
Krusen, Howard H., Richboro, Pa.—Ann Roberts, Newton, Pa., 12-26-1876.
Kuemmerer, William, Philadelphia—Catharine Friede, Lebanon, Pa., 5-16-1875.
Kupp, Henry E., Birdsboro, Pa.—Lydia F. Stretch, Philadelphia, 6-2-1875.
Kurfis, George—Alice Smith, 11-22-1871.
LaDow, Sylvanius—Annie E. Bailee, both Dividing Creek, 1-2-1873.
Lafferty, Charles D.—Adelaide Pimlot, 9-12-1867.
Edward W.—Mary D. Neald, 12-4-1869.
Edward Walbridge—Virginia Rapp, Philadelphia, 5-23-1874.
Laird, Ferdinand—Eva Beeber, 2-11-1872.
Lamar, Charles F.—Bertha Neal, 5-5-1906.
La Maria, Robert—Ann Widdows, both Philadelphia, 1-24-19 3.
Lambert, Benj. F.—Caroline S. Wilkins, 6-20-1867.
Lamplugh, Jacob, Wilmington, Del.—Sarah Boots, 5-2-1867.
Lane, Wm. H.—Arametta Baker, 2-28-1850.
Langerdorf, Geo. D.—Ella Heisler Jeffris, 1-1-186 6.
Langhed, David H.—Mary H. Young, 7-22-1870.
Lanning, Charles—Cornelia Albertson, both Trenton, 12-18-1873.
Larzelere, Samuel M.—Sarah Ida Rudderow, 12-24-1874.
Latcham, Charles C.—Elizabeth A. Lovell, 5-28-1868.
Laughlin, George W.—Anna Livezy, Germantown, Pa., 4-24-1872.

Law, Howard—Mary Ann Clark, 6-2-1873.
Lawson Henry Clay, Philadelphia—Ella Hatch Fagan, 11-27-1897.
  Samuel H.—Lizzie Hill, both Philadelphia, 12-26-1871.
Lawton, Benjamin—Mary Ketterer, 9-11-1873.
Lay, Arthur, Woodbury—Emily L. Archer, 3-31-1878.
  Charles B.—Mary E. Sweeten, 9-13-1874.
  Isaiah—Mary Foster, 6-26-1876.
Lazirus, William C.—Ella V. Hurley, 7-21-1877.
Leach, Stephen J.—Sarah A. Buzby, 11-3-1869.
Leaming, Jacob M., Salem—Sallie R. Hubbs, Beverly, 8-28-1875.
Leap, Benj. H. Gloucester co.—Lizzie C. Turner, Turnerville, 4-18-1867.
  George h.—Ella F. Moore, 11-20-1877.
Lear, Theodore, Brooklyn, N. Y.—Mary L. Sparks, Salem, 8-31-1871.
Lebair, John W.—Mary E. Striker, both Jersey City, 3-14-1871.
LeChard, Joseph—Almeda Willett, 8-26-1872.
Ledward, Thomas C.—Jennie Coulter, 7-3-1868.
Lee, Edwin F.—Maggie Kirkwood, Millville, 1-31-1873.
  Frank—Sarah Becket, 9-7-1876.
  Isaac Rhodes, Philadelphia—Pinkie Thurston Smith, Richmond, Va., 12-7-1901.
  James—Anna M. Sparks, both Penns Grove, 12-25-1874.
  Joseph C.—Evelyn Walthall, 5-17-1875.
  Samuel B.—Anna Sheets, 10-31-1874.
Leech, Arthur, Philadelphia—Florence M. Moore, 11-22-[1909.
Leeds, Charles H.—Sallie P. Wooster, 7-11-1872.
  Jacob, Mary E. Charles, 4-19-1873.
Lefevre, Charles H.—Ardrienette L. Livermore, 4-24-1873.
Lehman, William—Mary Painter, 5-14-1877.
Leib, Andrew G., Bethlehem, Pa.—Csrrie Smith; recorded 11-4-1897.
Leming, Henry O.—Kate Delamater, both Pennsylvania, 10-12-1875.

CAMDEN COUNTY MARRIAGES—BOOK B 99

Leslie, Phenigal A.—Hannah Eastlack, both Deptford, 4-3-1864.
  William G.—Mary E. Marshall, both Philadelphia; recorded 5-2-1901.
Letellier. Alphonse—Elsie Delaferte, 2-12-1878.
Letherbury, William H. L.—Emma Forbes, 12-24-1876.
Leverick, Charles—Mary A. Wilson, 6-22-1875.
Levering, John W.—Mary E. Green, 11-26-1872.
Levingston, Joseph R.—Mary M. Fults, 7-12-1875.
  Thomas H.—Anne Hays, 7-29-1872.
Levins, Charles W.—Julia A. Johnson, 7-27-1872.
Levy, Frank—Sarah E. Hammond, 4-25-1869.
Lewallen, Abraham—Theodosia Appley, 4-14-1871.
  John G.—Sallie E. Holton, 5-4-1871.
  Wm. H.—Kate Bilhart, 5-24-1871.
Lewis, Charles H., Pittsburgh, Pa.—Mary C. Cairote, 6-13-1875.
  Chas. M.—Jane C. Black, both Philadelphia, 12-19-1868.
  Selan Howard—Margaret J. Loane, both Philadelphia, 6-27-1900.
  Walter S., Jefferson—Isabella A. Stewart, Mullica Hill, 3-14-1878.
Lezenby, Samuel W.—Anna Letitia Dodd, 12-4-1865.
Lichten, Samuel—Jennie D. Madenfort, both Philadelphia, 7-3-1900.
Lightcap, Franklin—Sarah M. Solomon, 10-17-1872.
Likeness, Edwin S.—Josephine O. Dodd, 5-30-1832
Lilly, Richard P.—Sadie A. Leach, both Philadelphia, 1-9-1902.
Linch, Calvin E.—Theodosia R. LaDow, 2-18-1873.
Lincoln, Silas S., Philadelphia—Mattie Loring, Portland, Me., 9-29-1876.
Lindermuth, Byron—Martha Nuller, both Marietta, Pa., 4-9-1903.
Lippincott, William R.—Abbie E. Hollingshead, both Burlington co., 11-6-1873.
Lloyd, Malcolm—Anna Howell, 6-10-1869.

Lloyd, Peter M.—Emaline Sanderlin, 9-2-1877.
 Smith, Burlington co.—Anna Little, Burlington, 11-30-1876.
Lock, Joseph—Lucy Hooper, Mt. Holly, 3-21-1874.
Lockhart, Otto K.—Margaret E. Morton, 12-31-1871.
Lockwood, William, Paulsboro—Mariah Wright, 9-9-1866.
Logan, William— Mary R. Smith, 9-19-1875.
Lonagan, William H.—Martha Guy, 10-15-1873.
Long, Hugh A.—Louisa P. Crandal, both Mantua, 1-15-1873.
 John S.—Mary Ella Darnell, 10-30-1876.
Longtoft, William—Emma Courtenly, both Philadelphia, 4-6-1877.
Lord, David C.—Mrs. Anna E. Brown, 1-3-1873.
Lore, William C.—Lizzie D. Parvin, 9-7-1867.
Loveland, Benj. F., New York—Sallie R. Carter, 4-9-1864.
Lowe, Edward, Barnsboro—Susan Hendrickson, 6-30-1868.
Lummis, Jonathan—Marian F. Potts, 6-11-1868.
Lynch, Alexander—Fanny Coley, 9-1-1867.
 William C.—Jessie M. Robertson, both Philadelphia, 7-25-1901.
Lynn, Joseph—Lydia Camden, 2-18-1875.
MacGowan, Mariin Luther, Scotland—Susie D. Scott, Boston, Mass. 5-4-1879.
Mackin, James M., Charlston, S. C.—Emma Murray, 11-7-1876.
MacNichol, James—Rachel A. Hand, 8-12-1868.
MacMinn, Benj. H.—Mary Stevenson, Wallingford, Pa., recorded, 10-19-1897.
Madara, John—Nettie Carr, both Woodbury, 7-17-1869.
Madgin, Wm. H.—Anna E. Scott, 4-2-1872.
Magee, Lambert J.—Anna Gerard. 11-11-1876.
Magoun, Theodore W.—Mary E. White, 11-28-1870.
Maguire, Jerome—Amelia LaBlothier, 6-25-1866.
Mallack, William H.—Mary Stovel, both Trenton, 1-11-1877.
Malone, Wm. Jos.—Emma R. Galloway, both Philadelphia, 5-20-1877.
Malson, Frederick—Ida May DeHaven, 11-22-1877.
Malthameyer, John, Jr.—Elizabeth C. Eichel, 7-2-1867.

Manlove, James—Emma Tull, both Philadelphia, 10-31-1898.
Manly, Edward, Burlington co.—Sophia Stewart, Hestonville, Pa , 2-9-1871.
Mantz, Frederick—Anna Daumler, both Philadelphia, 11-2-1876.
Mapes, Mark H.— Anna King, Burlington, 5-6-1866.
  Richard J.—Mary E. Fountain, Philadelphia, 9-5-1877.
Maremback, Leabine—S. V. A. Smith, 9-3-1865.
Margerum, B. Albert—Elizabeth Thatcher, both Bustleton, Pa., 10-20-1908.
Marks, Lewis—Lydia Ann Smith, 10-13-1866.
Marple, Frank E., Leeds, Me.—Amelia M. Courier, 1-6-1898.
  John R.—Elizabeth Walker, 8-20-1873.
  John W.—Lydia Sutts, 9-18-1873.
Marshall, Charles—Hannah Moore, 2-11-1866.
  Frank W.—Sallie H. Leeden, both Clayton, 10-12-1876.
  Jesse—Emma Louisa Rommelman, 3-18-1876.
  Joseph—Margaret Hooper, Philadelphia, 11-12-1875.
  Nathan D.—Anna C. Sloan, 11-3-1875.
  Richard H.—Florence L. Cope, both Philadelphia, 2-22-1909.
  Robert, Medford—Charity Stratton, 12-23-1874.
  William L.—Virginia W. Davis, 7-13-1871.
  William—Fanny Huston, 10-1-1866.
Martin, James W.—Susanna Hodges, 6-1-1876.
  Joseph, Manahawkin—Abbie S. Marshall, 4-12-1877.
  Samuel—Mary Ann Fletcher, 6-13-1876.
  Theodore P.—Mary J. Lindhurst, 10-1-1871.
Mason, George B.—Hannah Morgan, both Philadelphia, 1-23-1898.
  Joseph—Sallie E. Walker, 3-13-1878.
  Richard C.—Etta Knight, 6-30-1875.
  William F.—Emma L. Thompson, 8-29-1873.
Mathers, Leander H.—Emmarentha Rambo, 9-5-1867.
Mathes, William H.—Sarah Boardman, 6-15-1872.

Mathews, George W.—Mary A. Keller, both Chester, Pa., 3-24-1878.
Mathis, Andrew J.—Kate A. Githens, 7-26-1871.
  Charles, Jr. — Celinda Force (wid.) both Moorestown, 12-4-1868.
  Geo. W.—Louisa Hand, 3-5-1868.
  Geo. W.—Louisa Hawk, 3-5-1869.
  Joseph A.—Mary Wood, 7-1-1866.
Matlack, Aaron G. — Cornelia Padelford; recorded 6-17-1872.
  Charles—Mary E. Matthews, 11-12-1870.
  Edward S.—Annie Stone, 10-4-1876.
  Ellis H.—Emma Stiles, 3-6-1873.
  Franklin—Mary Gilmore, 7-30-1873.
  Isaac—Kate Andrews, Clayton, 1-12-1876.
  Isaac D.—Kate D. Wiltshire, both Medford, 7-7-1872.
Matthes, Charles E.— Annie T. McKeever, 12-22-1873.
Mattix, David—Adah Campbell, 5-17-1871.
Mattocks, Albert F.—Louisa Lockman, 3-5-1873.
Mattox, Wesley S., Manumuskin—Amanda Phifer, 11-25-1872.
Mattson, Charles Lock—Mary C. Farr, 11-22-1877.
Mawson, Simeon J.—Abbie Duffield, 12-4-1877.
Maxwell, Edward W.—Harriet L. Breyer, 9-7-1871.
  Hugh H.— Ellen Hefferman, 10-18-1871.
Mayhew, Charles—Mary C. Williams, 5-2-1867.
McAdoo, Robert—Hessy Berryman, 4-2-1865.
McAndless, James—Eliza Ferduson, 6-1-1869.
McBride, Jesse E., Trenton—Mary C. McGowan, 6-26-1873.
McCabe, Wm. S.—Charlotte E. Bender, 1-1-1878.
McCandless, Thomas G—Mary Spence, 1-15-1902.
McCarter, George—Anna Brown, 8-7-1872.
McCarvey, Robert, Trenton—Emma V. Green, 9-29-1867.
McCauley, Melson M.—Elizabeth A. Bendler, both Baltimore, Md., 8-6-1876.

McCleutchen, Wm. Taylor—Sarah Whiteker, both Philadelphia, 1-17-1877.
McCloskey, Thomas—Hannah Doran, 7-18-1870.
McClure, James—Elizabeth Richards, both Bunker Hill, 4-9-1869.
McCollister, Robert—Bella S. Donald, 5-25-1873.
McCracken, Archibald—Ella D. Evans, 4-30-1874.
McCrystal, John H.—Agnes Kelly, both Philadelphia; license granted, 9-20-1897.
McCullough, J. W.—Sarah E. Stevenson, 3-9-1876.
McCurtney, Andrew—Elizabeth Hunter, 8-22-1837.
McDarrow, Luke—Martha G. Wills, 11-14-1867.
McDowell, James, Rachel E. King, 5-4-1875.
McElwee, David—Emma E. Alloway, Vincentown, 12-26-1873.
McGlaughlin, Thomas—Sarah Saunders, 6-11-1871.
McGonigle, Isaac—Jennie McLain, 9-16-1868.
McIlvaine, George—Sarah Locke, 1-6-1874.
  Henry—Hattie H. Kessler, 11-17-1873.
  James S —Lizzie V. Taylor, both Philadelphia, 1-5-1876.
McKeen, Jacob W., Clayton—Clara Newman, 8-7-1875.
McKeighn, Wm.—Sarah Hawkins, both Williamstown, 4-14-1868.
McKibben, Sam'l—Sallie Eyles, 12-27-1866.
McKinley, William H.—Carrie L. Osler, 7-31-1873.
McLaughlin, John—Mary A. Kinkade, both Philadelphia, 2-12-1873.
McMane, Chas. Ed.—Elizabeth Blair, 1-18-1877.
McMichael, John—Anna E. Rue, Amboy, 2-10-1878.
McMullen, James—Minnie F. Cooper, both Villa Nova, 2-24-1907.
McNeil, John, Jr.—Lora A. Fortiner, 11-15-1876.
McPhelin, Patrick, Philadelphia—Mary Gillen; license granted 9-30-1897.
McPherson, Richard—Margaret Hadley, 12-21-1874.
Mears, John H.—Emma H. Abrams, 1-9-1870.
Measy, John—Rebecca Dotterer, 12-9-1875.

Mecray, James— Rachel C. Stevens, both Cape Island, 1-19-1868.
Mellon, William—Emma Platt, 6-28-1870.
Menehin, Robert—Ann Grace, 9-8-1867.
Meredith, Reuben W., Millville—Anna Wells, 5-6-1872.
Merrick, Augustus, Rahway—Emma Reeve, 5-5-1867.
  Lewis—Mary A. Foulke, 4-25-1872.
Mersels, Wm. H.—Phebe Merritt, both Jersey City, 8-4-1867.
Mesirov, Isaac—Zippa Robbins, both Philadelphia, 6-22-1907.
Metzer, Joseph J.—Amanda S. Carpenter, 10-1-1869.
Meyer, Adolph H., Philadelphia—Isabella H. Keyser, Montgomery co., Pa., 7-13-1876.
Middleton, Benjamin P.—Leonora H. Burket, 9-10-1875.
  Dan'l—Abrgail H. Albertson, 12-4-1873.
  Frank B., Philadelphia—Sallie A. Albertson, 4-30-1868.
  Jessie—Anna Donnem; recorded 3-23-1878.
  William—Emma E. George, 9-4-1870.
Middledetch, Robt. H., Ridley Park, Pa.—Eliz. Armstrong, 9-19-1898.
Miles, Henry G.— Emma Paul, 8-1-1877.
Miller, Allen J., Pennsylvania—Elizabeth Pritchett, 8-4-1875.
  Caleb L.—Emma Norcross, 12-31-1873.
  Charles B., San Antonio, Tex.—Josephine Helmstadt, Philadelphia, 8-7-1870.
  Edward F.—Susan Morgan, 2-16-1877.
  Edward J.—Hannah Jennings, 12-2-1877.
  Ephraim H.—Maggie J. Price, 4-14-1877.
  George—Lucy Doran, 12-4-1870.
  George, Cecil co., Md.—Lizzie Taylor, 11-4-1876.
  Isaac—Anna Smith, 6-14-1871.
  John—Henrietta Tourtelot, 3-17-1873.
  John W.—Mary Ann Norwood, 8-24-1873.
  Robert S.—Anna Fullen, 4-24-1871.
  Thomas—Agnes Shocker, 8-22-1867.
  Wm. D.—Mary Ann Mapes, 11-24-1871.

CAMDEN COUNTY MARRIAGES—BOOK B   105

Mills, Henry, Smithville—Mary A. Gates, 12-24-1874.
  James L., Pitt co., N. C.—Annie E. Hill, Philadelphia, 12-6-1871.
  Wm. H., Baltimore — Martha Parker, Tuckerton, 8-12-1865.
Mines, Christopher, J., Jr.—Mary A. Cavanaugh, 8-25-1868.
  Jesse—Emma J. Sapp, 6-10-1866.
Mingin, Joseph,. Williamstown—Annie Keen, Philadelphia, 10-9-1868.
Minnick, Chas. H.—Mehitable Vandergrift, 7-18-1868.
  Wm. B.—Mary E. King, 4-6-1873.
Minus, George H.—Georgianna Rumsey, 11-13-1873.
Miskelly, Charles—Emma Earley, 9-20-1872.
  Nicholas—Catharine Woolmer, 1-15-1871.
Mitchell, Charles, Philadelphia—Virginia White; recorded 9-3-1897.
  George F.—Anna Homan, both Bridgeport, 8-2-1866.
  Henry R., Philadelphia—Lizzie H. Roberts, 10-22-1872.
Mitten, Wilmer, Moorestown—Emma B. Ogg, Fredericksville, 4-29-1876.
Moffit, Edward S.—Anna R. McCartney, Easton, Pa., 10-8-1872.
  George D.—Sarah A. M. Columbus, 5-2-1874.
Mooney, Wm. J.—Eleanor Armstrong, both Philadelphia, 4-17-1902.
Moore, Darius—Harriet Wilson, 12-24-1874.
  Edward S., Hopewell—Mary Lizzie Davis, Deerfield, 11-27-1867.
  Franklin—Rosanna Park, both Woodbury, 12-22-1870.
  George W.—Kesiah Batten, 5-4-1875.
  Henry Watson—Susan Vandergrift, 5-11-1877.
  James—Amanda C. Corels, 12-20-1873.
  John—Priscilla N. Wills, both Burlington co., 2-11-1869.
  Joseph Ballard—Elizabeth Alice Oston, Philadelphia, 7-18-1877.
  Joseph J.—Fannie Lodge, 10-14-1869.

Moore. Timothy C.—Martha W. Jackson, 9-2-1873.
  William Henry—Mary Ann Spencer, 11-27-1877.
  Wm. J.—Anna M. Richmond, 8-16-1876.
Moncrief, Nathan L.—Isabella Chew, Barnsboro, 8-22-1866.
Monil, William A.—Mary M. Bland, 1-2-1876.
Monroe, Henry F., Atlantic City—Bernice A. Price, 12-14-1874.
Moran, Michael—Elizabeth Johnson. 12-4-1868.
Morgan, David—Annie C. Pidgeon, 9-8-1873.
  Eli B.—Altha B. Huston, Stroudsburg, Pa., 7-21-1883.
  George H.—Lizzie Davis, 12-24-1877.
  John—Ellen P. Richards, both Hurffville, 8-20-1870.
  Joseph—Mary Freeman, Philadelphia, 6-2-1870.
  Randall W.—Ella Clark, 1-5-1875.
  Wm. H.—Hannah A. Cotton, both Westville, 4-2-1872.
  William T.—Emily Horner, 12-25-1873
  Wm. Penn—Mary Emma Warrington, 11-28-1875.
Morrell, Charles, Trenton—Elizabeth Elwell, 4-17-1867.
  George F.—Rebecca Lewallen, 6-25-1871.
Morris, Benj. Lafferty—Ella H. Peake, 1-8-1876.
  Chas. W.—Hannah E. Piper, 1-5-1873.
  Griffith, Oneida co., N. Y.—Mary A. Jacobs, 11-21-1876.
  John H.—Eleanor H. Steen, 11-21-1872.
  Joseph F.—Oceanna Howell, Delaware City, Del., 5-25-1873.
  Joseph J.—Mary E. Wright, 6-13-1872.
  William F.—Rachel E. Patterson, Delaware City, Del., 6-15-1873.
Morrow, John J., Wilmington, Del.—Anna Maurice, Bridgeport, 10-21-1871.
Morse, Melvin R., Weymouth—Kate A. Hudson, Mays Landing, 10-9-1871.
Morton, Wm. B.—Mary Bennent, 2-5-1865.
Moses, Elwood S., Montgomery co., Pa.—Margaret Gayner, 10-13-1875.
Moslander, William, West Creek—Sarah Jane De La Cour, 10-30-1856.

Mott, Alfred B.—Anna Adams, both Pennsylvania, 6-9-1876.
Moulton, John—Anna Watson, 10-9-1867.
Mount, Charles H., Easton, Pa.—Sallie T. Reynolds, 4-27-1871.
   David Alston—Maude E. Hudson, 6-20-1877.
Mowers, Daniel—Clara Anthrem, 10-29-1873.
   Lewis—Willamina Vogt, 11-27-1873.
Mulford, Robert A.—Jemima Foster, 9-2-1874.
Mulholland, John R., Philadelphia—Mary E. Johnson, 12-1-1868.
Mulligan, Wm., Philadelphia—Mary Anderson 12-21-1876.
Mullin, Chas.—Ida Davis, both New York City, 12-24-1874.
Mulliner, Chas. Watson—Anna M. Ross, Landisville, 4-13-1878.
Mund, Henry, Philadelphia—Elizabeth Link, Wilmington, 7-4-1875.
Munster, Wm.—Priscilla St. Clair, 6-16-1875.
Munyan, Alfred B.—Angie Scott, 8-8-1875.
Murphy, John W.—Annie D. Frankle, 11-1-1876.
   Leonard—Maggie C. Evans, both Jobstown, 3-11-1872.
   Matthias—Mary C. Smith, 8-10-1872.
   Wm. W.—Mary A. Thackara, Medford, 12-25-1872.
Murray, Edward—Elizabeth Lockman, 10-31-1872.
   Joseph H.—Georgie Lindsey, 10-25-1877.
   Peter—Ellen Penton, both Philadelphia, 1-22-1877.
   Samuel—Florence Flanigin, 6-7-1876.
   Wm. V.—Sarah Jane Boyd, 10-26-1875.
Muschamp, Stanley C.—Eliza Anderson, 6-3-1874.
Myers, Abraham, Bridgeton—Annie E. Chew, Mantua, 1-1-1870.
   Charles — Amanda E. Smith, both Philadelphia, 11-9-1866.
   George W.—Sallie D. Wells, 2-21-1877.
   Robert—Anna Stevenson, 10-25-1873.
Mytinger, Lewis A.—Gertrude S. Locke, 2-26-1875.
Nack, Jacob—Adeline Lipsett, both Hainesport, 11-6-1875.

CAMDEN COUNTY MARRIAGES—BOOK B

Naile, Fred'k J., Philadelphia—Emma J. Patterson, 9-13-1866.
Nassau, Edward Alex, Philadelphia—Emma A. Weaver, 8-28-1874.
Neal, John B., Glen Riddle, Pa.—Amelia C. Gillette, 6-5-1870.
Nealy, John—Anne Morris, both Philadelphia, 8-6-1866.
Negar, Louis—Augusta Voight, both Philadelphia, 6-25-1871.
Neipling, Chas. L., Malaga—Mary Butler, 11-11-1871.
Nelson, Charles—Harriet Price, Absecon, 6-9-1866.
Nelson, Lewis—Nancy W rth (colored), 7-2-1873.
  Richard — Mary A. Edwards, both Philadelphia, 3-16-1865.
Newcomb, Charles A.—Elizabeth T. Chambers, 7-23-1876.
  John—Keziah Newcomb, both Salem, 1-11-1865.
Newman, John, Bergen—Fanny Hampton, Philadelpha, 6-13-1867.
Newton, Charles—Mary A. English, Mt. Holly, 4-8-1873.
Nichols, Charles A.—Blanche Long, both Philadelphia, 11-25-1897.
  Peter—Elizabeth Crosdale, 12-7-1873.
Nicholson, James N.—Fannie Miller, 11-6-1874.
  Jesse S., Bethel—Anna A. Paul, Pemberton, 10-5-1869.
  John, Five Points — Jane Lippincott, Hurffville, 7-1-1875.
Nichuals, Theo. W.—Clara W. Phifer, 6-21-1875.
Nield, Thos. H., Frankford, Pa.—Manetta Phifer, 4-21-1867.
Nixon, George, Philadelphia—Ida T. Lewis, 5-21-1874.
  Josiah A.—Georgianna Bakeley, 7-29-1869.
Noble, Lewis Z.—Cornelia A. Fredericks, 11-14-1876.
Norcross, Forman—Anna Willy, 11-6-1868.
  Thomas—Ellen L. King, 11-26-1871.
Norris, Charles, Philadelphia—Mary E. Irelan, Salem co., 3-11-1876.
North, Levi C.—Emily J. Booth, Philadelphia, 12-5-1871.

CAMDEN COUNTY MARRIAGES—BOOK B

North, Richard—Mary Ann Weaver, 1-13-1872.
William—Mary Williams, both Spring Mills, 1-19-1878.
Norton, John Wier—Frances E. Willats; recorded 4-24-1878.
Nosif, Ira—Marie Gosson, both Philadelphia, 1-31-1906.
Nowry, John—Helena Sturr (or Stunn), 10-2-1877.
Nuttall, Joseph J.—Julia Shelhorn, Wilmington, Del., 12-24-1871.
Odenheimer, John Wm.—Olivia I. Miller, 4-3-1878.
Offenbach, Carl Richard—Marie Willet Finigan, both Philadelphia, 12-9-1902.
Ogden, Wilford F.—Lizzie Crawford, 11-8-1875.
Wm. M.—Lydia A. James, both Philadelphia, 10-14-1874.
Okie, Richardson—Clara Mickle, 9-5-1872.
Oler, Benj. D., West Philadelphia—Josie G. Ellis, Greenville, 1-10-1875.
Oliphant, Jeseph L.—Lucy Budd, Pemberton, 6-11-1873.
Oliver, George W., Philadelphia—Isabella B. Hopkins, 6-29-1873.
Hilliard—Mary E. Heavylow, 12-7-1873.
Oram, Theodore G.—Jennie G. Officer, 10-2-1869.
Orf, August Henry, Philadelphia—Lizzie Kaufman, 11-24-1897.
Ornes, Joseph—Emma R. Crispin, 12-17-1871.
Orr, Alfred L.—Nellie E. Serriel, both Philadelphia, 3-7-1907.
Osborn, Alanson B.—Nellie Garrigan, 1-9-1872.
James, Allowaystown—Julia A. Robertson, 5-20-1872.
Osborne, Charles H.—Emma Tash, 1-8-1874.
Osgood, Wm. L.—Lotta R. Brown, 2-3-1866.
Osler, Amos W.—Priscilla A. Bennett, 2-6-1868.
Charles—Lizzie Hayden, 1-24-1873.
John—Maggie O'Hare, Philadelphia, 2-14-1874.
William H.—Rebecca Adams, 6-10-1872.
Ott, Anthony—Magdalena Golback, 9-1-1873.
Ottinger, George W.—Emma C. Fish, 3-20-1877.
Owens, Cornelius—Mary Pierson, Philadelphia, 5-24-1909.

Packer, Benjamin R., Philadelphia—Mary Ann Myrose, 9-13-1877.
Page, Frank P., Mt. Holly—Lizzie Allen, Vincentown, 10-7-1876.
  George W.—Mary J. Clark, 3-5-1876.
  Henry, Philadelphia, Fanny Rogers, 7-19-1868.
  Joseph A.—Martha A. Gercke, 5-31-1875.
  Thomas S., Columbus—Lizzie Leconey, Swedesboro, 7-9-1868.
  William—Louisa M. Merry, Philadelphia, 2-25-1868.
Painter, William—Sarah Jane Nofels, 3-4-1871.
Palasco, John—Annie Ellis, 9-9-1866.
Palmer, Harry C., Jr.—Irene Brinmer, both Philadelphia, 2-3-1898.
Pancoast, David J.—Sarah Emma Abbott, Unionville, 12-21-1876.
Parent, George—Elizabeth Luressa Atkins, both Allentown, Pa., 9-9-1871.
Parker, James E.—Sarah E. McBride, 4-29-1871.
  Samuel S.—Elizabeth Ann Johnson, 7-10-1871.
  William—Hattie McIlvaine, 10-31-1869.
  Wm. C.—Mary Morse, both Philadelphia, 10-11-1877.
Parkhill, Charles—Clara Payne, both Harrisburg, Pa., 6-10-1871.
  Oley J. H.—Linda Portler, both Philadelphia, 6-28-1904.
Parks, Charles Edward—Lucinda R. Wall, 1-16-1870.
  Jacob — Sarah Elizabeth Chew, both Hurffville, 4-13-1865.
  Jacob M., Gloucester co.—Mary E. Steelman, Hurffville, 3-11-1869.
  Levering—Mary Brickwell, 12-21-1872.
  Samuel R.—Mary J. Wiatt, 9-3-1871.
  William S.—Annie Lyle Rushton, both Chicago, Ill., 11-26-1902.
Parmenter, Henry—Mary R. Hays, Philadelphia, 11-12-1871.
Parsons, Albert, Hattie Goernley, 9-7-1872.
  Charles J. H.—Lydia F. Sailor, Pennsylvania, 2-15-1871.

CAMDEN COUNTY MARRIAGES—BOOK B 111

Parsons, Richard W.— Mary A. McIlvee, both Medford, 10-26-1871.
William—Angeilne Smalley, both Salem, 7-4-1868.
Paterson, Daniel—Rebecca S. Treadway, 9-6-1873.
Patroni, Giovanni, Philadelphia—Anna C. Perkins, 9-14-1869.
Patterson Charles W.—Emma Albertson, 6-9-1875.
Henry—Isabel Eagen, Philadelphia, 6-7-1877.
Patton, Charles H.—Gertrude B. Larzelere, 5-10-1877.
Paul. William H.—Clara Adams, 8-29-1876.
Paynter, Charles A.—Sadie Singer, Philadelphia, 4-22-1877.
Peachy, Samuel—Emma E. Reynolds, both Odessa, Del., 2-5-1872.
Peacock, Thomas C.—Mary M. Dandinger, 11-19-1871.
Peak, John W.—Lucretia Stockton, both Mt. Holly, 10-20-1869.
Peale, James N., Chico, Cal.—Ida F. Hewlings, Woodbury 7-27-1876.
Pearce, Woodruff—Maggie Griffin, 4-19-1877.
Pearson, Daniel, Philadelphia—Christianna Gohune, Reading Pa., 12-3-1870.
Pease, Cornelius—Annie Reed, 10-11-1872.
Peasley, Wm. A.—Josephine Dow, 7-31-1869.
Peck, Daniel—Margaret Lalocker, 5-13-1870.
Peckman, Fred'k A. J.—Emma J. Dill, 4-15-1872.
Pelton, Charles E.—Kate Lott, 8-6-1871.
Penn, Wesley, Williamstown—Mary Beebe, 10-8-1871.
Pennbelser, Benjamin—Sophie E. McAllister, 8-8-1877.
Penney, John, Burlington co.—Julia Palmer, 7-20-1866.
Punningtnn, Alford R.—Lucy A. Briant, 11-26-1885.
Pennock, George B., Bordentown—Emma Cowperthwaite, 12-16-1876.
Pennypacker, Thomas M.—Annie L. Lore, Salem, 6-16-1871.
Penrose, Evan R.—Kate M. Bisnbaum, both Philadeiphia, 6-19-1869.
Peoples, Samuel A.—Clara S. Phillips, 1-13-1876.

112 CAMDEN COUNTY MARRIAGES—BOOK B

Perkins, Edward W.—Anna H. Dudly, both Moorestown, 7-10-1872.
Perrine, George—Kate Swing, 7-13-1873.
Peters, William L.—Rachel Watson, Turnerville, 6-2-1874.
Peterson, Charles H.—Elizabeth Conway, 7-8-1868.
  John H., Piermont, N. Y.—Rebecca McClain, 12-25-1869.
  T. E.—Susan Pierce, 10-30-1872.
  William K.—Margaret Applegate, 3-16-1873.
Peto, Francis—Isabella Folwell, 8-8-1875.
Petouse, Frank—Laura V. Vernon, 8-11-1872.
Pew, Isaac H.—Maggie McManus, 8-22-1870.
Pfeiffer, Fred'k P., M.D., Philadelphia—Emma Rowand, 10-9-1866.
Pidgeon, Charles H., Jr.—Anna E. Ellis, 4-19-1874.
  Isaac H.—Mary E. Hendrickson, 12-24-1867.
Pierce, Abraham—Josephine Biddle, 12-4-1877.
  Samuel, Altoona, Pa.—Maggie E. Metuck, 5-17-1877.
  Ward—Nancy Watson, Furffville, 8-30-1865.
Pierrie, Frank H., Philadelphia—Bessie T. Maris, 11-12-1869.
Pierson, Daniel—Sarah Hunter, both Philadelphia, 5-5-1867.
  Lewis C.—Lizzie C. Down, 8-14-1876.
Pike, David, Burlington co.—Mary H. Higbee, Wrightsville, 6-3-1876.
  John—Margaret Vickers, 5-18-1874.
Pine, Alfred—Mary Ann Wells, 3-21-1871.
  Henry H.—Abigail A. Cline, 10-12-1875.
  Henry S.—Caroline Cattle, 9-23-1869.
  William H.—Lidie Haines, 12-10-1871.
Pinyard, Theodore—Addie Goodwin, 7-16-1877.
Pitman, Dana—Mattie Jackson, 8-30-1873.
Plum, John M.—Elizabeth K. Todd, 11-16-1865.
  Reuben H.—Hannah Saunderson, 6-25-1876.
  Samuel—Ruth Stetser, 5-4-1877.
Plummer, Wm. H.—Mary E. Roork, both Salem, 10-18-1876.
Polk, Benj. B.—Julia A. Colding, 10-1-1874.

CAMDEN COUNTY MARRIAGES—BOOK B   113

Polk, Eiijah C.—Annie M. Moore, 5-27-1885.
  John G.—Hannah Lewis, 10-28-1869.
Pool, Thomas—Mary Haney (colored), 5-6-1873.
Poole, George P. J.—Mary F. Evans, 2-11-1874.
Porch, Samuel, Williamstown—Damaris Clohosey, Philadelphia, 4-30-1868.
Porter, James, Jersey City—Lizzie Lindon, Philadelphia, 11-11-1870.
  John—Rachel Fries, 12-3-1873.
Porteus, Francis L.—Mary Fithian Hood, 9-30-1875.
Powell, Edmund B., Spring Mill—Hannah Zimmerman, 4-15-1871.
  George—Maggie Barrett, 8-16-1885.
  George W.—Edith Sharp, 12-1-1873.
  Richard J.—Susan Ella Hill, Woodbury, 11-30-1876.
  Robert M.—Georgie F. Hires, 10-14-1847.
  Samuel A.—Mary A. Satour, 3-1-1867.
  Samuel P., Almonesson—Mary Emma Stewart, Hurffville, 3-31-1878.
  Thomas—Emma Matlack, 1-9-1878.
Preston, Robert, Trenton—Anna M. Hayes, 5-5-1867.
Price, Isaac M.—Kate Locke, 8-7-1872.
  (or Rice) Richard—Mary C. Brown, 11-30-1874.
  William—Ann E. Bacon, 6-19-1875.
Prickett, William H.—Jennie Thomas, 11-18-1875.
Priddy, Edward England—Catharine Hull Brown, 5-18-1871.
Priest, Edmund H.—Mary Ann Snyder, 1-25-1872.
  George W.—Catharine Wallin, 2-26-1872.
Priestly, David Albert—Auguste Julianne Rhodes, 11-12-1876.
  Charles—Mary A. Thompson, 7-5-1875.
Pruitt, Josiah—Edith Tillman, 5-31-1873.
  Peter—Sarah Lockum (colored), 8-10-1872.
Purdy, Geo. Starr, Danbury, Conn—Sarah E. Chiles, 10-2-1873.
Purnele, James Robbins—Ada Maria Sperry, 12-12-1877.
Quicksell, Jos. S.—Linda W. Martin, 3-29-1878.
Quinn, George W.—May Yeager, 1-28-1872.
  James M.—Josephine Smith, 8-2-1871.

Rafferty, Peter—Bridget Haforan, 5-6-1868.
Rainsford, Walter—Emma Schoentag, both Philadelphia, 4-1901.
Rambo, Samuel F.—Amanda Holmes, 10-19-1872.
Randall, Aaron B.—Mary Ellen Fenton, 8-12-1871.
 Chas. H., Eatontown—Lydia A. Throckmorton, Long Branch, 5-23-1876.
Randles, Robt. Lynn—Josephine Kelly, 4-10-1867.
Randolph, Asa A. F.—Adeline M. Elwell, both Shiloh, 12-13-1871.
Rapp, Charles H.—Mary Fisher, 12-8-1868.
 Franklin—Melissa Kinkade, 3-22-1869.
 Thomas—Sophia Allgayer, 5-12-1872.
Rapport, Joseph—Esther Beariut, both Philadelphia, 8-15-1903.
Ray, Daniel C.—Annie L. Rogers, 10-15-1874.
Read, Edward—Rebecca Dixon, 2-17-1857.
 Rufus, Cohoes, N. Y.—Emma J. Pew, 4-9-1872.
 William T.—Lulu McCormick, 1-15-1874.
Reader, John—Silla Grindle, 12-16-1875.
Reall, Joseph H.—Fannie H. Carter, 5-5-1872.
Redfield, Robert H.—Jane McCurdy, 2-20-1872.
Redheffer, Amon A.—Elizabeth J.. Getz, both Philadelphia, 7-6-1870.
Reed, George W. B., Baltimore, Md.—Mary Austin, Lancaster, Pa., 3-7-1867.
 Jacob—Matilda Brisler, 12-16-1875.
 Joel—Mary A. Jones, 7-12-1873.
 Joseph H.—Lydia N. Peacock, both Burlington co., 10-9-1869.
 Norman B., Milesburg, Mich.—Maria Phillips, Detroit, Mich., 6-23-1875.
 William, Philadelphia—Carrie Tucker, 11-4-1876.
Reeve, Harry H.—Sallie Michener, both Philadelphia, 7-24-1870.
 Joshua M.—Almira McDonald, 4-26-1873.
Reeves, Wm. C.—Ella Z. Creeley, 3-7-1877.

Register, Horace G., Philadelphia—Mattie Conard, 10-7-1885.
  Isaac M.—Ruth Wood, 1-25-1873.
Rehig, Owen—Mary Rehig, Carbon co., Pa., 10-1-1869.
Reilly, Franklin—Catharine Sahford, 5-22-1866.
Renier, George C., Gloucester co.,--Lizzie A. Wood, 11-20-1872.
Reinhard. David—Rebecca S. Wolf, 12-28-1868.
  Edward—Louise Jennis, 3-12-1868.
Repsher, Frank L.—Josephine T. Dodd, 8-8-1870.
  Wm. Penn—Amanda Gainer, Philadelphia, 10-16-1867.
Restein, Julius—Pauline Vogel, both Philadelphia, 9-3-1805.
Reuhling, Gustav—Mary Wreistner, both Philadelphia, 5-30-1905.
Reynolds, James—Virginia Osborn, 11-3-1874.
  Nelson R.—Alice S. Ranier, Trenton, 4-26-1876.
  William—Emma Matilda Senior, both Philadelphia, 2-27-1859.
Rhoads, John H.—Ella Swing, 8-27-1873.
Rice, Joseph—Emma McGuire, 7-10-1871.
  Peter—Emma Jane Rhoads, 12-24-1876.
  (or Price) Richard—Mary C. Brown, 11-30-1874,
  Thomas B.—Susanna G. Lake, 1-1-1869.
Richards, Benj. F.—Josephine Cook, both Turnerville, 2-10-1866.
  Philamon. Duncannon, Pa.—Adeline McCulley, 9-10-1866.
  Thomas J.—Ann Kelley, both Philadelpha, 6-19-1873.
  William F.—Helen Monroe, both Atlantic City, 6-28-1873.
Richardson, Edward Augustus—Emma Miller, 7-21-1877.
  John C.—Amelia Thomas, 9-31-1875.
  John M.—Anna M. Hogan, West Chester, Pa., 3-31-1909.
  Robert I.—Anna Taylor, Tuckahoe, 8-5-1867.
Richie, John—Louisa Cowgill, Mickleton, 12-13-1875.
  William H.—Joanna D. Foster. 3-28-1875,
Richmond, George—Alwilda Robinson, 11-2-1874.
  George C.—Cornelia J. Ellis, both Delenco, 3-9-1877.
Ridge, Moses Marshall—Rebecca A. Chew, 6-23-1875.
Ridgeway, Franklin—Sallie A. Green, 12-25-1873.

116 CAMDEN COUNTY MARRIAGES—BOOK B

Ridings, Thomas—Eliza Edwards, both New Castle, Del., 10-3-1873.
Rinear, Charles, Mt. Holly—Mary E. Perry, 7-9-1871.
Riggs, George C., Elwood—Mary J. Adler, 1-1-1873.
Righter, J. E.—Emma V. Dolbow, both Wilmington, Del., 6-3-1872.
Rightmire, W. G.—Lydia VanSciver, 6-9-1869.
Righton, Samuel—Louisa Opdyke both Roxborough, Pa., 2-20-1868.
Ritter, Frank S.—Emma J. Davis, 2-15-1902.
Roath, Joseph H.—Anna M. Zimborman, 6-28-1871.
Robb, Amos S.—Tabitha Godfrey, 8-29-1872.
Robber, Henry—Elizabeth Ramseager, 3-14-1874.
Robbins, George Henry—Cornelia Barger, both Philadelphia, 11-5-1903.
Roberts, Anos C.—Susannah V. J. Richards, 2-23-1870.
  Millard F.—Netty Mundy, 9-26-1877.
  Pancoast—Jennie Evans, 12-22-1868.
  Pancoast—Addie L. Wolf, 6-25-1873.
  Stacy L.—Harriet K. Roberts, both Philadelphia, 12-1-1869.
Robertson, John—Jennie R. Huston, 10-13-1875.
Robinson, Edward C.—Millie W. Wilson, 2-17-1877.
  Felix B. Absecon—Hope Anna Walker, 6-9-1874.
  Harry C.—Melvina Field, 5-15-1878.
  Isaac K.—Louisa Jones, 6-13-1875.
  Isaac W.—Mary E. Corson, 12-11-1866.
  John—Kade Davenport, both Philadelphia, 7-31-1872.
Roby, Edgar—Ann Brittain, 11-7-1868.
Rodgers, James—Susie V. Chambers, 11-25-1873.
Rogers, Daniel R.—Rachel Sinclair, 1-14-1873.
  Elmer Q. C.—Ruth Anna Matlack, 5-25-1871.
  Thomas—Maggie Brothers, 10-27-1872.
Rogerson, Thomas—Amanda Morgan, Gloucester co., 6-25-1872.
Roland, John Lewis—Amelia B. Clement, 8-18-1871.
Roles, John—Louis Thomas, 5-4-1872.

Rollo, Wm. L.—Mary Isabel Tyman, 12-17-1872.
Romine, Thomes, Wilmington, Del. — Hattie S. Channell, Millville, 6-3-1868.
Roop, Franklin—Rosie Doughty, Philadelphia, 1-1-1868.
Root. Archie Conrad, Philadelphia—Blanche E. Lingerman, Summerton, Pa., 6-9-1908.
  David S.—Alzina F. Hoffle, both Philadelphia, 4-26-1877.
Rosade, Herman—Sophia Nowton Chase, 5-28-1876.
Rose, John—Sophia Frazier, both Philadelphia, 3-3-1878.
  Wm. F.—Mary C. Whitlock, 4-8-1869.
Rosell, Charles L.—Mary Lowe, 3-28-1877.
  Elias J.—Mary F. Fisher, both Hurffville, 12-19-1875.
Roseman, George W.—Martha A. Long, 9-2-1845.
Ross, Joseph—Lizzie B. Hartle, 4-8-1873.
  Richard R.—Anna V. Newton, 5-2-1872.
Roth, Edward Francis—Ellie Elizabeth Harris, 10-6-1867.
Rounds, George—Julia Beecher, 10-1-1873.
Rowan, Edwin H.—Annie W. Shuster, 6-15-1872.
Rowand, Elwood F.—Mamie J. Epley, 9-13-1876.
  Henry H.—Mary E. Day, 2-15-1876.
Rowles, William M.—Mary Ellis, 7-6-1877.
Rubart, James—Mary E. Sayre, 8-24-1873.
  John—Sarah Weeks, 10-6-1876.
Rudrow, Asa, Woodbury—Emma Jane Cook, 5-1-1872.
Rudderow, Harris—Rebecca Davis, Philadelphia, 7-16-1874.
Rudderow, Wm. A.—Annie T. Schubert, 11-24-1898.
Rue, John, Mt. Holly—Mary Cuthburt, 1-20-1875.
Ruley, Edward— Minerva W. Gehris, both Philadelphia, 11-24-1909.
Rumford, Samuel B., Chester, Pa.—Emma Clayton, 4-20-1878.
Runger, William F., Glassboro, Tillie Heventhall, 8-27-1876.
Rush, Geerge, Philadelphia—Martha Purcell, Morton, Pa., 1-15-1901.
Russ, Eben J., M.D., St. Marys, Pa. —Clare H. Hindle, 7-28-1875.
Russell, Henry—Anna M. Dare, 3-31-1876.

CAMDEN COUNTY MARRIAGES—BOOK B

Russell, Hugh –Emeline Alston, 11-26-1873.
  Willis G.—Anna J. Todd, 1-19-1873.
Rutherford, John—Carrie Ingersoll, both Cape May co., 12-24-1874.
Ryan, Dennis—Margaret Rox, 1-3-1858.
Saake, Charles—Katie Messner, both Philadelphia, 4-21-
Sage, Isaac—Catharine H. Smith, 4-7-1874.   [1903.
Sagiers, David M.—Anna R. Budd, both Gloucester co., 2-
Sailor, William H.—Rachel E. Keen, 2-5-1872.   [15-1872.
Salmon, Wm. H. C., Worcester, Eng.—Annie Craft, 12-15-1898.
Salvage, Benj., Lewes, Del.—Anna Y. Davis, Milford, Del., 12-17-1901.
Samples, John L.—Mary H. Thompson, 4-21-1909.
Sanders, John—Sarah Simpson, 1-11-1872.
Sands. Daniel—Arria Derrickson, 11-16-1874.
  Samuel P.—Emily V. Lescher, 6-28-1877.
Sapp, Benj. Louis—Kate Boyle, 6-19-1875.
Satchell, Charles H.—Rebecca Webb, 7-18-1872.
Saulsbury, James—Elizabeth Parmer, 6-22-1873.
Saunders, George F.—Malinda Munday, 7-1-1874.
Sauseline, Charles—Rachel Humphries, 4-11-1872.
Savege, Lewis—Rachel Carter, 3-6-1873.
Sawyer, Chas.—Elizabeth Megonigle, Philadelphia, 8-7-1866.
  Charles A.—Martha Hatton, 6-16-1873.
  William O.—Kate Jester, Philadelphia, 11-15-1877.
Soylor, Wm. D.—Florence Mitchell, both Philadelphia, 12-14-
Sayres, Albert—Eliza D. Hunt, 6-20-1877.   [1904.
Sayrs, Charles—Sarah Smith, 8-7-1872.
Schafer, Herman—Josephine Jones, 8-15-1876.
Schaffer, Peter—Ann C. Beller, 3-6-1874.
Schamely, James—Julia Travis, both Gloucester co., 12-9-1865.
Schauffler, Edward W., Constantinople, Turkey—Mary A. Haines, Burlington co., 8-3-1869.
Schell, Sam'l F.—Elizabeth Giberson, 12-20-1877.
Schellinger, Clarence Mulford, Philadelphia—May Spooner, 7-16-1871.

CAMDEN COUNTY MARRIAGES—BOOK B 119

Schellinger, Thomas, Cape May—Mary E. Clark, Philadelphia, 5-10-1877.
Schick, Max, Philadelphia—Barbara Kiel, 4-15-1875.
Shingles, William—Anna Nickel, both Philadelphia, 7-5-1885.
Schoefer, John, Pottsville, Pa.—Clara Tracey, 1-5-1869.
Schofield, James C.—Emma Karge, 6-13-1875.
   John—Annie Wilkinson, 11-16-1872.
   Joseph S.—Lizzie Murray, both Roxboro, Pa., 6-9-1873.
Scott, Anthony, Milltown—Maggie Wagner, New Brunswick, 4-15-1876.
   Jonathan—Georgie Kahler, 11-30-1873.
Schutz, Theodore B.—Phebe Schreen, 11-15-1874.
Schuyler, Henry—Marietta C. Schofield, 1-18-1874.
Scudder, Jacob V.—Jennie Sterling, 9-2-1871.
Scull, Reeve D.—Sadie A. McDonnell, both Philadelphia, 12-22-1902.
Seagraves, Thomas, Woodbury—Matilda Orund, Manchester, 4-15-1876.
Sela, Charles A.—Margery E. Johnson, 1-1-1872.
Selah, Charles A.—Sarah E. Henry, 7-14-1875.
Sell, George H.,—Elva A. Hunter, Burlington, 5-17-1377.
Sellers, Geo. B.—Clara M. Plum, 4-6-1876.
Severns, Augustus—Ida R. Mines, 9-9-1875.
   Samuel H.—Lydia J. Smith, 10-11-1873
Severs, Samuel—Clara Gilbert, Masonville, 3-13-1878.
Seybold, Charles—Lizzie Walker, 4-1-1873.
Sexton, Mahlon B.—Amelia Asling, 2-5-1870.
Shanklin, Joseph K.—Hannah Shaw, 3-6-1872.
Sharp, Charles H.—Mary C. Fiering, 12-20-1871.
   Franklin—Arabella E. Frazier, 12-23-1875.
   Jonathan P.—Mary E. Matlock, 10-19-1872.
   Samuel D.—Sarah S. Pearce, 12-6-1866.
   Samuel P.—Caroline Hillman 12-31-1880.
   Samuel S.—Josephine Matlack, 6-24-1873.
Shattuck, George, Connecticut—Caddie M. Rowans, 4-16-1867.

Shaw, John R.—Georganna Peterson, 2-5-1878.
  Louis K., Newport—Clara E. Haun, 9-30-1876.
  William G., Otsego co., N. Y.—Lucy A. Crandell, Philadelphia, 11-3-1869.
Shawcross, Samuel—Mrs. Geo. Murry, both Philadelphia, 9-6-1873.
Sheer, Samuel H.—Anna L. Penn, 5-21-1873.
Sheets, Wm. D.—Sarah Casperson, both Gloucester co., 2-24-1853.
Shelly, John—Martha J. Dale, 10-19-1872.
Shelton, Murray—Sarah C. Parker, both Philadelphia, 12-8-1898.
Sheppard, Joseph C.—Mary Camp, 11-23-1877.
  Wm. Otis, Orange—Parthena Hickman, 11-8-1876.
Sheridan, Wm. H.—Sarah J. Parks, 3-26-1866.
Shewell, William Mt. Holly—Sarah M. Street, 7-29-1875.
Shields, Samuel H.—Susanna Vuntier, 12-27-1875.
Shiers, Augustus—Sallie J. Jacobs, 1-3-1874.
Shill, Raymond A., Jr.—Lizzie Lindale, 4-17-1879.
Shimp, Benj. F.—Sarah A. Hofflinger, 12-15-1874.
  Philip—Susanna Trotter, 8-1-1874.
  Richard—Rebecca Huston, 10-13-1875.
  William—Sarah J. Tuckert, 11-30-1872.
Shinn, Allen B.—Ella V. Hunter, 7-9-1871.
Shivers, Bowman H.—Dora Hall, 5-28-1873.
  Joseph R.—Abby Bell, both Moorestown, 4-25-1867.
  Josiah—Ida Bell Casperson, 12-12-1877.
  R. Levice—Mattie A. Browning, 12-8-1870.
  William M.—Lucy V. Carman, 6-30-1875.
Shoemaker, Hiram J.—Eva A. Burt, both Bridgeton, 1-1-1873.
  Robert W., Gloucester co.—Sue Lewallen, 11-28-1872.
  Walter—Maggie French, 10-25-1877.
Short, Theodore A.—Sarah J. Hunter, both Philadelphia, 11-1-1905.
Shotwell Wm. H.—Martha C. Alloway, both Marlton, 5-27-1867.

CAMDEN COUNTY MARRIAGES—BOOK B 121

Shraden, Wm. H.—Emily Bell, 12-12-1867.
Shuman, John D.—Mary Ann Ryan, 1-31-1877.
Shuster, Clayton, Jr —Mary E. Shimp, 12-31-1872.
Shute, Winfield S.—Harriet H. Price, 10-12-1871.
Sickler, Horatio—Anna McClees, both Bucks co., Pa.—5-29-1868.
  Jacob—Clarinda Ware, 7-31-1875.
Simkins, David—Sarah Thompson, 3-25-1874.
  Harry—Clara P. Bakeley, 1-16-1873.
Simmons, Robert A., Rickmond, Va., Pamelia B. Shinn, 4-15-1876.
Simons, David H.—Hannah E. Green, 4-30-1868.
Simpkins, David H.—Melissa J. Dexter, 10-28-1876.
  Joseph—Adah Perkins, 12-1-1870.
  Joshua C.—Sarah S Thomas, 4-4-1874.
Sinclare, Andree Middleton—Mary E. Gillen, 2-11-1877.
Sitler, John—Eilzabeth Matlack, 12-15-1872.
Siveler, Levi—Annie R. Weber, 9-4-1875.
Skill, John F. Hamilton—Pernell Carty, both Gloucester co., 6-15-1876.
Skinner, George W., Barnsboro—Rachel Chew, Hurffville, 7-26-1876.
Sleeter, Frederick—Mary C. Albertson, 7-31-1875.
Slim, Sam'l—Mary B. Horner, 3-26-1868.
  William—Anna M. French, 11-14-1872.
Sloan, Joseph I.—Ella J. McGuire, Bordentown, 6-29-1873.
  Nathan—Amy C. Pedrick, Pedricktown, 10-26-1873.
Small, Abel H.—Margaret Pond, 8-22-1870.
  John W.—Mary E. Carels, 12-23-1873.
Smiley, Christopher— Sarah Gibson, 12-13-1871.
Smith, A. A., Leomister, Mass.—Lydia M. Winchester, Malden, Mass., 3-26-1874.
  A. B. Cooley—Emma E. Countryman, 12-24-1867.
  Alexander—Mary E. Rodgers, 1-16-1869.
  Chas.—Atlantic H. Deets, 2-22-1866.
  David S.—Annie Miller, Philadelphia, 10-13-1877.
  Edward—Sarah McManus, 1-24-1865.

Smith, Edward—Frances Morrill, 10-2-1875.
  Edward—Maggie Camel, 9-21-1875.
  Frank—Virginia Harris, 6-10-1872.
  Franklin H.—Sarah Evans, 11-20-1875.
  Frederick—Frederica Greiker, 2-24-1868.
  Frederick—Julia Hays, 2-17-1872.
  George—Emma Holland, 2-16-1875.
  George E.—Caroline Hughes, 6-17-1877.
  George L.—Mrs. Maria Kimberly, 11-8-1866.
  Gilbert W.—Emma V. Nicholson, 9-1-1872.
  Hamilton S.—Liszie Hart, 9-8-1871.
  Jacob—Mary M. Hera, 2-15-1868.
  Jacob—Edith Evans, 11-12-1876.
  James L.—Mary H. Neil, 10-1-1871.
  John—Emma B. Pine, 4-19-1868.
  John—Eliza Barham, both Hammonton, 12-27-1876.
  John F.—Mary A. Holt, 6-6-1874.
  John L., Bridgeton—Martha A. Crammer, Manahawkin, 6-23-1866.
  Joseph Howard—Hannah Etherington, 11-17-1873.
  Larkin—Mary Whitaker, 9-1-1869.
  Max—Ida Lemisch, both Philadelphia, 6-21-1908.
  Richard—Amelia Barber, 1-17-1876.
  Richard Y.—Avalinda Green, Philadelphia, 9-24-1876.
  Richardson A.—Mary Emma Boileau, 6-15-1870.
  Sam'l K.—Carrie Beebe, both Salem, 12-18-1872.
  Thomas—Elizabeth S. Budden, 11-30-1876.
  William—Mary E. Miller, 12-7-1872.
  William C., Moorestown—Mary T. Matlack, Fellowship 3-20-1871.
  Wm. H.—Bridget Gant, both Wrightsville, 10-21-1875.
  Wm. L.—Georgianna Ivins, 6-23-1872.
Snethan, Thos. B.—Harriet Ants, both McDonough, Del., 12-31-1868.
Snider, John—Charlotta Ivens, 8-5-1866.
Snively, George W., Philadelphia—Helen B. Tyler, 6-17-1868.

Snuffin, Elwood—Anna Farrell, 1-3-1871.
Snyder, Andrew E.—Anna R. McCulley, 12-25-1866-
 Clarence—Mary Wood, both Pennsylvania, 4-25-1877.
 Henry R.—Achsah S. Hinchman, 5-1-1867.
 Jacob K.—Emma M. Ayres, 10-28-1875.
Sockum, Elisha—Ellen Oney, 12-22-1858.
Souder, Joseph—Rebecca Ann Magee, both Gloucester co. 3-7-1866.
Southwick, Charles—Ruth Tunnelin, 9-12-1872.
Spangler, Edwin J.—Gertrude Horner, 9-16-1875.
 John F., Philadelphia— Annie M. Gilmore, 10-9-1876.
Sparks, Benj. F., Philadelphia—Catharine F. Anthony, 6-3-1873.
Spear, Charles A., New York—Helen Cooper, Philadelphia, 7-23-1873.
 Edward G.—Mary E. Wolfe, both Philadelphia, 3-20-1906.
Spencer, Samuel—Sarah Shall, 1-9-1869.
 William—Mary Ann Randles, 4-2-1865.
 William—Anna Dobbins, 3-24-1874.
Springer, Augustis—Elizabeth Landschurtz, 1-6-1878.
Sprowl, Albert—Christina Westcott, 12-15-1872.
 Thos. J.—Almira Kimble, 4-26-1866.
Stackhouse, Jonathan, Jewlstown — Elizabeth Bryan, Wrighstown, 9-20-1877.
Stafford, Charles C.—Martha S. Hillman, 2-3-1875.
 Richard—Isabella Clark, 7-4-1867.
 Thomas—Ann Wood, 1-12-1871.
Standland, S. T.—Anna E. Gregory, 9-23-1872.
Stanger, Jacob F.— Eliza S. Doyle, 1-11-1872.
Stanton, Jas. P.—Alice H. Dilks, 9-4-1876.
 Miles—Gertrude M. Gailand, both Philadelphia, 11-25-1906.
Starn, George E.—A. Clow Odling, 10-26-1876.
Stearns, George—Anna Cline, both Mt. Holly, 3-10-1869.
Steckney, George A.—Laura V. Bell, both Philadelphia, 12-14-1876.
Steele, William A., Philadelphia—Millicent A. Severns, 12-18-1873.

Steelman, Wesley, Somers Point—Rachel Godfrey, Seaville, 5-9-1866.
Stehr, Augustis, Sarah M. Campbell, 12-26-1876.
Steinmetz, Wm. W.—Annie Mehan, both Philadelphia, 6-20- [1871.
Steinmeyer, Samuel C.—Kate Tenney, 12-23-1872.
Stephens, Jonathan R.—Harriet Wright, 7-30-1874.
  Thomas—Mary W. Collins, 6-26-1873.
  William J.—Mary C. Berryman, 1-3-1875.
Stephenson, Joseph—Sarah E. McKeever, 6-15-1875.
Stern, George E.—A. Clow Odling, 10-26-1875.
Stethens, Frank J.—Sarah Jane Paullin, 12-29-1875.
Stetser, Chattin—Jennie Harris, 8-21-1877.
  Jacob F.—Josepihne Simpkins, 2-11-1874.
Stevens, Daniel—Sophia Francis, 11-5-1871.
  John—Mary Ann Butler, 10-27-1875.
  Samuel C.—Annie F. Barnes, 3-10-1873.
Stevenson, Chas. D—Sallie Compton, 11-2-1875.
  Charles C.—Mary Ellen MacDonald, 12-20-1871.
  Daniel O.—Lizzie Moffit, 5-14-1876.
  Josiah—Martha Dare, 1-7-1870.
  Moses—Sarah Carey, 2-5-1873.
  Parry—Isabel Ashley, 2-27-1873.
  William B.—Susie D. Packer, both Woodbury, 3-9-1871.
  Wm. L.—Elizabeth Vanhorn, 12-30-1872.
Steward, Henry—Sarah Young, 6-12-1873.
  John—Delia McKale, 11-28-1872.
Stewart, Augustus—Emma S. Porch, both Almonesson, 12-18-1871.
  Corbin G.—Charlotte B. Quinn, both Philadelphia, 2-4-1903.
  Hugh C.—Alice Leach, 2-6-1876.
  James—Alice R. Rosten, both Woodbury, 11-2-1871.
  John L.—Mary E. Dunn, both Mullica Hill, 3-14-1878.
  John T.—Louisa A. Mathis, 12-31-1872.
  Leonard—Rebecca C. Barrett, 9-28-1874.
  Lummis M.—Mary H. Rafine, 12-24-1868.
Stiles, Benjamin, Jr.—Anna W. Wilson, both Moorestown, 3-4-1849.

Stiles, Charles H.—Lizzie Price, both Burlington, 1-10-1872.
   Mire—Georgia Anna Alloway, both Marlton, 3-14-1877.
Still Samuel—Mary Wood, 4-16-1871.
Stillwell, Frank—Louisa D. Saphor, 1-2-1878.
Stimson, John—Emma Turner, both Philadelphia, 8-21-1907.
   John Chase—Alice B. Cogill, 5-2-1867.
Stocker, Frederick—Fannie Baker, 6-11-1874.
Stockton, Benj. S.—Lizzie Ball, both Philadelphia, 9-22-1866.
   Robert F.—Matilda Hill, 4-16-1876.
Stokely, Henry E.—Laura Pennington, both Philadelphia, 11-5-1871.
Stokes, Charles—Alice Dayton, 8-27-1866.
   Charles W., Heightstown—Anna G. Rogers, 1-1-1873.
   Joseph E., Medford—Louisa Miller, Bound Brook, 6-8-1868.
   William E.—Hannah J. Arthur (colored), 5-24-1872.
Stompler, Otto—Magdelain Fogg, 11-10-1877.
Stone, Arthur G.—Mary McKinley, 10-23-1908.
   Isaac C.—Lydia W. Wright, 3-23-1876.
   Jacob C.—Mary L. F. Owen, 2-14-1866.
   Joseph M.—Sarah Lillian Tyler, 9-18-1876.
Storey, William H.—Lucinda Bennett, 8-7-1873.
Storms (?), Charles H.—Rebecca A Gill, 2-20-1868.
Story, Joseph—Sarah Davis, 10-28-1874.
Stow, S. Harris—Rebecca A. Hults, 6-8-1872.
Stowe, John—Susan Morgan, 2-16-1877.
Strain, John M.—Ella V. Shill, 2-10-1876.
Strock, Frank A.—Emma J. Ayres, 10-1-1874.
Stratton, Andrew B.—Margaret P. Griffey, 5-22-1869.
Streeper, William S.—Sallie Murphy, 8-3-1876.
Streen, Thomas—Maggie A. Nuller, 4-15-1875.
Streker, George W.—Ettie Abdill, 11-29-1877.
Strickland, Elwood J.—Mary F. Steelman, 2-1-1869.
   Horace P.—Mary C. Brewer, both Gloucester co., 1-31-1871.
Strifel, Charles G.—Ella Mooney, both Philadelphia, 10-13-1902.

String, Charles James—Jane Ramsey McKeen, 10-31-1877.
Stringer, Samuel A.—Ella Collings, 8-8-1877.
Strong, Richard A.—Belle J. Shane, 9-1-1873.
   Thomas M.—Sarah B. E. Rankins, 2-11-1868.
Stroud, Charles H.—Ella Keyser, 8-19-1875.
Stryker, Lawrence V.—Joannah Fine, 10-11-1868.
Stubbs, Alfred—Mary Harvey, 5-2-1866.
   Alfred—Sarah S. Harrison, 8-9-1874.
Styles, Harry C.—Jennie A. Gordon, 12-31-1871.
Subers, Richard C.—Lydia Chapman, 7-14-1876.
   Robert S.—Kate Green, 12-24-1873.
Suiter, William—Serena Sayres, Salem co., 4-27-1871.
Summerill, F. Mason, Jr.—Emma Frances Lansdown, both Philadelphia, 6-20-1904.
Summers, Ezra E.—Lydia Steelman, Atlantic co., 1-14-1874.
Sureton, Andrew H.—Kate A. Jackson, 9-14-1871.
Sutton, Benj. F.—Emily S. Hummell, 6-26-1866.
   Hope—Sallie Woodroe, 4-26-1866.
   Joseph—Gussie Shaw, 12-31-1875.
Swayne, Robert—Mary Ann Cugley, 1-9-1867.
Swingell, William—Mira B. Vanlier, 5-13-1873.
Sweeton, Jesse—Susannah Tribbitt, 1-1-1878.
Swop, Edward—Mary McColey, 1-7-1874.
Tait, Robert W., Westdale, Pa.—Mary E. Burns, Philadelphia, 11-7-1867.
Talbott, Frederick—Elizabeth Breffit, both Germantown, 1.
Tarkington, Wm. S.—Alice Jones, both Philadelphia, 3-17-1867.
Tarlton, John W.—Sophie Mike, 1-15-1874.
Tatem, Wm. A.—Anna E. Emley, 6-20-1867.
Tauser, Thomas W.—Hannah G. Focer, 11-27-1867.
Taylor, Charles—Alice Carney, 11-18-1869.
   Edward O.—Lizzie McClaskey, both Philadelphia, 12-29-1900.
   Geo. W.—Martha Finney, 11-24-1872.
   Harry W.—Maggie M. Woodward 6-24-1873.
   Isham—Carrie A. Carman, both Philadelphia, 10-10-1876.

CAMDEN COUNTY MARRIAGES—BOOK B 127

Taylor, James B., Cincinnati, O —Ella C. Collius, 5-8-1873.
  Joseph A., Mt. Holly—Margaret B. Ireson, 12-3-1875.
  Joseph W.—Anna C. Stockton, 2-10-1877.
  J. P.—Mary C. Metz, Detroit, Mich., 8-21-1876.
  Reuben— Rachel Lockwood, 11-6-1872.
  Samuel—Sarah Jane Loper, Cape May co., 5-15-1867.
  Wesley—Elizabeth T. Prickett, 2-11-1870.
  William C.—Esther B. Kinsley, 4-13-1867.
  William E., Petersburg, Va.—Georgianna Webb, Accomac co., Va., 9-25-1873.
  Wm. H.—Mary C. Adams, 7-5-1868.
Tenniswood, William H.—Alice C. Miller, 4-14-1870.
Test, Henry M.—Kate P. Wright, 5-30-1870.
Thill, Theodore—Annie Dundas, 6-2-1786.
Thoman, William W.—Rebecca Johnson, 12-31·1866.
Shomas, George W., Philadelphia—Virginia S. Monell, 6-12-
  Henry—Mary Jane Pengood, 1-7-1869.   [1878.
  James—Elizabeth Lavery, 5-5-1877.
  Samuel -Martha Mulford, both Hurffville, 3-3-1870.
  Stephen L. Matilda Chadwick, 3-9-1867.
  William H.—Frances A. Adams, 9-11-1833.
Thompson, Allen Major, Philadelphia—Hollis G. Forbes, 12-1-1875.
  Ayers H.—Laura Osler Smith, 8-12-1822.
  Chas. H.—Anna D. Coley, 12-19-1876.
  Edward—Mulinda Mowry, 1-22-1873.
  Isaac T., New York—Kate McCully, Burlington co., 12-24-1870.
  William—Catharine Burton, 3-3-1873.
  William H.—Margaret Thompson, 12-20-1866.
Thomson, Samuel S.—Elmira Houck, Stroudsburg, Pa., 7-22-
Thorn, Ellwood—Drusilla Morgan, 4-9-1868.   [1868
  Richard—Phebe Fitzer, 3-17-1869.
Thorne, Joel E.—Annie E. Nicholls, 8-24-1872.
Thornton, John E.—Sylvia E. Rives, 5-29-1873.
Thorpe, Edwin—Mary C. Paul, 7-4-1871.
Tice, Chas. A.—Jane Gallagher, Philadelphia, 1-2-1878.

Tickell, James D., Port Republic—Miranda McCollom, 4-22-1872.
Till, George—Caroline Harden, 1-29-1874.
  John—Matilda Lockwood, Kent co., Del., 12-24-1873.
  Wesley J.—Annie H. Enders, 4-29-1875.
Timberman, Chas. H.—Sallie H. Smith, both Upper Alloways Creek, 1-21-1869.
Titus—Reuben, Pedricktown—Annie B. Mitchell, Salem co., 8-6-1870.
Todd, Robert—Abigail A. Long, 5-20-1869.
Tomlin, Henry H., Mullica Hill—Caroline E. Tomlin, 3-27-1866.
Tomlinson, Charles W.—Roxanna Warrick, 1-17-1884.
Tonkins, John—Mary C. Mounce, both Gloucester co., 10-21-1871.
  Theodore F.—Amanda M. Mowers, 1-17-1867.
Toomey, Wm. P.—Marietta Steelman, 2-6-1876.
Toronson, Israel—Henrietta Passely, 3-20-1872.
Torrens, James—Josephine Howell, 11-24-1873.
Toultz, Gillman—Sarah E. Long, 9-14-1872.
Townsend—James C.—Laura V. Patterson, 1-10-1874.
  James H.— Elizabeth Hughes, 12-11-1872.
Townshend, William—Clara B. Fulton, 5-29-1877.
Troney, Angelo—Maggie O'Hara, both Philadelphia, 5-3-1878.
Toy, Charles—Eunice Rudderow, 3-25-1875.
  Chas. H., Palmyra—Celestia Swing, 7-12-1877.
Trader, William—Anna Vanderslice, 3-6-1870.
Troth, Jonathan H.—Emergine L. French, both Medford, 11-27-1869.
  Wm.—Rebecca Thomas, both Mt. Holly, 7-1-1866.
Trueax, John—Anna E. Peters, 7-20-1871.
  Wm.—Lizzie Hellermus, 3-3-1866.
Trullender, John—Hannah Sullivan, 3-14-1877.
Truman, John, England—Elizabeth Merrott, 10-20-1866.
Trupp, Aloys—Teresse Schuster, both Philadelphia, 7-4-1908.
Truscott, John—Martha Ball, both Germantown, 6-27-1866.

CAMDEN COUNTY MARRIAGES—BOOK B 129

Trusty, Cornelius—Anna B. Bryant, 10-29-1868.
Tucci, Paolo— Rosa Colahese, both Philadelpha, 10-27-1909.
Tumbleston, Wm. H.—Mamie A. Levy, both Philadelphia, 7-1-1872.
Tunnell, Caleb—Mary E. Heuson, 4-8-1871.
Turkington William C.—Terresa Smith. 9-24-1871.
Turnall, George—Sarah Miller, 6-20-1872.
Turner, Andrew F.—Charlotte R. Lewis, 11-20-1868.
  Burroughs. Turnertown—Emily B. Wilkins, 11-30-1871.
  Chas. A.—Cornelia Munroe, 12-18-1877.
  Charles L.—Laura Becker, both Philadelphia, 7-4-1901.
  Gilbert—Eliza Summers, both Atlantic co., 12-9-1873.
  John H.—Amanda Iredell, 11-27-1873.
Tussey, Gideon C.) Salem, Maria L. Somers, Woodstown, 1-1-1878.
Tuttle, Harry F.—Mary R. Woodfall, 12-25-1873.
Tweed, John A.—Hannah Batcheler, both Williamstown, 3-13-1878.
Upham, Albert S.—Mery Elizabeth Keene, 9-28-1876.
  Benj. F.—Jane Hughes, 10-18-1865.
Upright, Michael—Barbara Beale, 5-26-1868.
Urrangst, Howard, Elverson, Pa.— Florence K. Fisher, Hoseybrook, Pa., 11-29-1909.
Vanaman, David, Williamstown — Mary E. Russell, 4-10-1876.
Vandegrift, Marmaduke Watson — Elizabeth Worthington Terry, both Bucks co., Pa., 1-17-1867.
Vane, Anthony M—Mary E. Hedges, both Philadelphia, 2-17-1878.
VanHest, David—Mary E. Williams, 6-24-1869.
Vanhorn, William D.—Elizabeth A. Firth, 1-1-1876.
Vannaman, B. C.—Jeannette Solly, 1-25-1872.
Vanness, Jacob F.—Catharine Fox, 2-22-1866.
Vanpelt, Michael F.—Eliza A. Adams, 4-30-1873.
VanSciver. Henry C.—Mary E. Haines, both Moorestown, 6-8-1868.
Vanstavern, Edward—Lacetta Joline, 9-23-1872.

Venable, Charles C.—Mary J. McIntire, 3-20-1872.
Loran—Martha H. Pruitt, Philadelphia, 5-19-1875.
Vickers, David L.—Joanna L. Shinn, 2-25-1877.
James H., Philadelphia—Annie S. Good, 4-19-1876.
Voght. Albert L., Philadelphia—Beulah Hickman, 12-29-1897.
Wagner, Rudolph—Eleanor M. Cresswell, both Philadelphia, 1-24-1899.
Walcott, Benjamin Louis, Mt. Holly—Josephine Cairoli, 12-27-1875.
Walker, Benjamin, Delaware—Joan Conway, 11-25-1876.
Benjamin F., Baltimore—Mary F. Harmer, 10-9-1872.
Charles H.—Victoria R. Wood, 11-19-1868.
Edmund C.—Anna C. Snyder, both Philadeiphia, 6-9-1906.
James—Sarah Stanley, 4-22-1869.
John, New York City—Mary R. Cline, 6-6-1867.
John—Ann McVey, 4-17-1876.
Thomas C.—Sarah Conley, both Philadelphia, 10-11-1902.
Walkley, George V.—Elizabeth Morris, 6-7-1871.
Wall, Charles—Josephine Gaul, 11-15-1868.
Wallace, Clement W.—Mary E. Stetser, 12-1-1877.
David P., Philadelphia—Jennie Meyer, 11-14-1897.
Edward F., Paulsboro—Victoria Cox, Westville, 2-24-1872.
Frank, Trenton—Kate Weeks, 2-22-1872.
Wolstenholm, William—Sarah E. B. Finny, 12-21-1873.
Walter, J. Alfred, Philadelphia—Gertrude P. Lippincott, 1-31-1898.
Walton, John W., Williston, Pa.—Henrietta D. Emley, Burlington co., 2-3-1870.
William M., Woodstown—Amelia A. Vincent, 3-1-1874.
Waples. Handy—Ida Virginia Ingram, 11-25-1876.
Ware, Benjamin—Sarah Nichols, 5-5-1875.
Daniel D.—Rachel Ann Cheesman, 2-21-1871.
George B.—Katie Osler, 11-4-1876.
Joseph H., Marlton—Tema Robertson, North Hammonton, 11-27-1876.
Warner, Alfred—Lucind Cork, July, 1872.

CAMDEN COUNTY MARRIAGES—BOOK B 131

Warnock, Robert—Clara Plum, Bethel, 10-4-1877.
Warren, A. W., Olathe, Kan.—Lowanda Lake, Hammonton, 8-8-1877.
  George—Jane Williams, both Washington twp., 9-1-1865.
Wasserott Paul D.—Alice Dungan, both Philadelphia, 5-29-1875.
Washington, Payton Geo., Springfield, Mass.—Ida M. Ashley; recorded 10-28-1897.
Waterson, Alexander, Philadelphia—Hannah Garr, 10-8-1873.
Watson, Charles—Hannah Mary Wilson, 4-5-1876.
  George W.—Rebecba P. Stetzell, 6-16-1873.
  Jacob—Elizabeth A. Batten, 11-8-1869.
  Peter S.—Margaret Bittle, 12-20-1867.
  Philip—Elizabeth Parks, 4-1-1875.
  William H.—Eliza Beans, 4-6-1871.
  William M.—M. E. Templeton, 12-16-1875.
Watt, Robert P.—Melissa Rubart, 3-14-1875.
Way, Edwin F., Belvidere—Annie M. Miller, 12-29-1875.
Wayman, Chas.—Mary A. Miller, 1-9-1873.
Weatherby, John W.—Susan Park, 10-11-1868.
  John H.—Jennie A. Marintyn, Philadelphia. 6-13-1872.
Weaver, Daniel P.—Maggie Banner, both Philadelphia, 7-3-1901.
  William—Sallie Bigelow, 6-20-1872.
Webb, John W.—Mary G. Wise, 9-11-1873.
  Martin—Marietta Sharp. 4-3-1870.
  Matthias—Ellen Stout, 2-4-1857.
  Samuel—Ida Virginia Downing, both Philadelphia, 8-21-1876.
Webbs, G. W.—Susan Croak, 5-28-1877.
Wedmore, Clifford K.—Edna E. Bookhaumer, both Philadelphia, 10-16-1909.
Weeks, Daniel C.—Josephine L. Nash, 4-12-1875.
  Josephus S., Westville—Margaret Boulton, 10-27-1868.
Weintz, Frederick—Virginia Fredericks, 4-8-1867.
Weiss, Henry—Sadie Weiss, both Philadelphia, 3-26-1905.
Waist, John—Annie A. Greenman, 8-30-1869.

CAMDEN COUNTY MARRIAGES—BOOK B

Welsh, Robert Meadville, Pa.—Anna Josephine Smith, 12-24-1867.
Weldon, Alfred, Philadelphia—Alice Carnahan, Kansas City, Mo., 11-2-1876.
  Henry—Matilda Way, 2-5-1873.
Wells, George W.—Mary Ellen Beebe, 12-27-1877.
  John—Elizabeth Harris, 8-11-1877.
  Joseph B.—Mary E. Hinchman, 11-28-1872.
  Melcour—Mary A. Collins, Lumberton, 7-6-1870.
Wescott, Augustus, Pensacola, Fla.—Lucinda Scott, Maryland, 9-1-1872.
West, Cornelius—Susan Gates, 9-7-1871.
  George S.—Mary J. Charles, 4-25-1878.
Westcott, George—Sallie A. Birmingham, 12-21-1873.
  John L.—Deborah J. Fortiner, 8-6-1872.
  Thomas D.—Elizabeth Lee, Elizabeth, 10-1-1872.
Westerfield, Alfred M.—Charlotte M. Nadine, both Newark, 9-27-1875.
Weston, George, Long Island—Henrietta Jones (colored) Salem, 7-8-1870.
Westwood, Frank—Henzy Forrest, 5-1-1872.
Weyer, John H., New York—Phalina Vandyke, Philadelphia, 4-3-1876.
Weygand, Charles F., Philadelphia—Kate Connelly, 6-5-1867.
Weygandt, Geo. H.—Maggie Summers, both Philadelphia. 9-30-1866.
Whaling, John—Anna Hammond, 5-8-1875.
Whall, George Elliott—Mary C. Lytle, 12-20-1877.
Wharton, Joseph—Mary Wetherell, 7-10-1871.
Wheaton, William—Lena Bakley, 6-6-1876.
Wheeler, Charles E.—Kate W. Harris, 12-12-1872.
Whiffin, Jesse—Mary Ann Heusen, 5-15-1875.
Whippey, William R.—Carrie V. Lock, 12-21-1873.
Whiston, William—Margaret Bird, 10-10-1867.
Whitaker, John B.—Mary S. Cordery, both Bridgeton, 3-3-1874.

CAMDEN COUNTY MARRIAGES—BOOK B 133

Whitaker, N. Reed. Washington, Ia.—Mary W. Prickett Vincentown, 11-18-1869.
White, Charles F.—Louisa Philips. 6-19-1872.
  John, Pattonsburg—Mary Richie, 8-30-1873.
  John H., Millville—Mary E. Cossaboon, 7-3-1873.
  J. Orlando—Elizabeth Starr, 10-25-1871.
Whiteker, Wm. Dayton—Anna Kruse, both Bridgeton, 2-10-1876,
Whitehead, David—Josephine Ridgeway, 5-13-1871.
  John—Emma Settle, 3-23-1872.
Whitelock, Thomas B.—Georgie W. Colley, 12-24-1873.
Whitman, Chas. B., Detroit. Mich.—E. Nelz, 9-17-1877.
  Geo. W.—Louisa O. Haslam, Philadelphia, 3-14-1871.
Whittle, Thomas Stewart—Catharine McCain (McCan?), 1-9-1878.
Wilder, William H.—Ella M. Harper, 1-29-1871.
Wildin, David E.—Rose E. Richman, 4-15-1874.
Wiley, Anthony W.—Eliza E. Erwin, both Philadelphia, 6-5-1871.
Wilkes, George—Celesta Kimbal, both Philadelphia, 5-12-1867.
Wilkins, Ezra—Marianna Brannin, 9-24-1868.
  Henry—Ann Margaret Jones, 3-30-1871.
  John—Annie Turner, both Turnerville, 1-30-1868.
  Richard C.—Laura C. Stokes, 6-1-1874.
  Theo. H.—Maggie Mayhew, 10-1-1873.
  Theodore S.—May E. Wilson, 8-18-1872.
  Thomas J., Turnerville—Martha Scott, Westville, 12-24-1874.
  Thomas W.—Hannah G. Edwards, both Medford, 3-22-1870.
Wilkinson, Ayres—Ann Jane Bloomer, 11-5-1870.
  Charles—Sarah J. Vance, 12-28-1870.
Willard, Russell—Mary E. Ernon, 11-1-1877.
Williams, Abner, Philadelphia—Catharine J. Smith, 5-16-1850.
  Alexander—Rebecca Ann Lord, Mauricetown, 5-2-1866.

Williams, Alfred H.—Lizzie A. Pine, 12-25-1876.
 Benjamin—Abbie Turner, Turnerville, 9-12-1872.
 Charles—Rebecca Mason, 5-2-1872.
 Charles A.—Katy Mullen, 12-25-1871.
 Charles P.—Julia E. Nerld, 4-16-1877.
 Frederick S., Cape May co.—Mary E. Seeley, Wilmington, N. C., 10-25-1872.
 George—Caroline C. Hill, 11-24-1872.
 George W.—Sarah Croak, 5-28-1876.
 Henry, Baltimore—Margaret DuBois, Poughkepsie, N.Y., 6-4-1871.
 James P.—Rebecca Heill, 12-24-1870.
 Jesse—Mary Warner, 9-9-1868.
 Levi—Matilda Devall, both Gloucester co., 7-14-1869.
 Russell M.—Mary J. George, 3-29-1875.
 Thomas A. J., Millville—Wilimina M. Beideman, 12-25-1871.
 Thomas H.—Elizabeth M. Cain, 11-11-1871.
 William G.—Harriet E. Cowperthwaite, 7-3-1873.
Williamson, Abraham—Ellen Miller, 1-8-1873.
Willing, Frederick—Hannah Hillman, both Philadelphia, 10-8-1873.
Willis, John W.—Sarah ———, 10-27-1872.
 Samuel—Hannah E. Laws, 8-26-1875.
Willitts, William—Anna H. Mansfield, 4-26-1875.
Willoughby, J. A., Breckenridge, Colo.—Ann Iszard, Mays Landing, 5-23-1877.
Wills, Benajah, Marlton—Maggie Cecelia Bate, 6-6-1878.
 Henry S.—Susannah Elmira Jones, 8-20-1871.
 Kendell L.—Anna M. Wells, March, 1872.
 Sam'l M.—Rebecca R. Borden, 1-15-1867.
 Solomon—Mary Ann Fisher, 3-11-1872.
Wilmot, John W.—Jane E. Hardin, 4-9-1873.
Wilson, Arthur G.—Josephine G. Ridge, 12-24-1868.
 Edward—Lizzie M. Prickitt, 9-10-1876.
 Frank W.—Rachel Hand, 6-23-1873.
 George—Maria Walker, 1-15-1872.

CAMDEN COUNTY MARRIAGES—BOOK B 135

Wilson, George—Ida Emily Sweeton, 9-15-1873.
 George Henry—Sarah Rebecca Risley, 3-5-1877.
 John—Mary Peters, 8-5-1871.
 John—Chrissie Sheets, 2-27-1876.
 John K.—Carolina Rudderow, Bethel, 3-15-1877.
 Richard—Jane Clark, 4-27-1869.
 William—Mary E. Murray, both Philadelphia, 10-5-1869.
 William C.—Kate Babnew, 9-26-1873.
 William H.—Ruth A. Murray, 10-22-1872.
 William M.—Martie Henderson, 10-8-1875.
Wiltsey, Benjamin F.—Almeda Barber, 9-10-1875.
Wiltshier, Alex T.—Susanna Painter, both Marlton, 7-27-1871.
Winkworth, Jabez—Alena Wykand, 9-4-1870.
Winn, Isaac W., Jr.—Maggie D. Rightly, both Bristol, Pa., 3-13-1873.
Winner, Arthur H., Trenton—Mary M. Morgan, 1-18-1876.
 Joseph H.—Sallie E. Parks, 5-11-1868.
 Joseph H.—Sarah Auvach, 8-12-1873.
Winslow, Wm.—Sarah Clark, 5-18-1878.
Winsmore, James S., Philadelphia—Keziah G. Dyer, 11-11-1867.
Wisner, Henry C., Asbury Park—Mary Bartram, 12-20-1876.
Woertz, Henry E., Philadelphia—Anna C. Morgan, Clayton, 11-22-1876.
Wolcot, Henry, Ocean Port—Catharine Bath, Mantua, 11-2-1876.
Wolf, David, New York City—Mary M. Kley, Philadelphia, 2-22-1872.
 George—Maggie Wolf, 9-3-1874.
Wolfe, Robert—Mary Lewallen, 4-5-1871.
 Henry, Norfolk, Va.—Cornelia Capewell, 7-17-1869.
Wood, Abel J.—Mariam H. Beckley, 4-27-1869.
 John—Sallie Stetson, 8-1-1868.
 Samuel—Sallie Stafford, 7-3-1868.
 Thomas J.—Adeline J. Lock, 12-31-1874.
 William—Emma Middleton, 8-3-1871.

Woodington, Joseph W.—Mary E. Davis, 8-26-1873.
Woodward, E. Stockton—Elvira Moore, 10-20-1875.
  Frank—Mary J. Snyder, 11-5-1872.
  Theodore F.—Eliza Wilkinson, 5-25-1872.
Woolston, Lemuel B., Plainfield—Mary R. Buckle, 5-28-1876.
Worrall, J. E., Mt. Holly—Martha Witcraft, Lumberton, 12-25-1875.
Worthington, Leslie Pierce, Summerton, Pa.— Elizabeth Harper Edwards, Bustleton, Pa., 7-3-1909.
Wozniak, Frank—Matadystana Stepanks, Philadelphia, 10-26-1897.
Wrifford, Charles H.—Loie Hammell, 8-16-1876.
Wright, Charles W.—Jane Cooper, 3-13-1877.
  George V.—Ellen Woodfall, Philadelphia, 5-14-1871.
  George W.—Elmira Chadwick, 8-27-1871.
  Harrison—Bennanner Suff, 4-13-1869.
  James—Margaret Quinn, 12-8-1868.
  John—Susan Hunt. 9-18-1872.
  William—Jane T. Thompson, 8-17-1873.
Wyatt, John E.—Lydia Ann Nuby, 3-12-1874.
Wynn, Benj. I., Jr.—Virginia Cheesman, 12-16-1875.
  E. S., M.D., Millville—Mary F. Kinsey, Bristol, Pa., 12-31-1872.
Yapp, Thomas—Alfreda Woolston, 8-9-1877.
Yates, George W.—Eliza B. Peak, 5-12-1872.
  Jonas—Rebecca Hawkins, 3-9-1873.
  Winfield—Maggie Ames, 5-8-1875.
Yearsley, Louis N.—Sallie A. Wilson, 4-25-1872.
Young, Albert F.—Clara V. Pate, both Philadelphia, 6-17-1871.
  Benjamin H.—Ammoline C. Gills, 1-20-1872.
  George R.—Virginia Stoy, 4-14-1875.
  John S.—Nancy Lovett, both Morrisville, Pa., 10-24-1876.
  Somers C.—Sallie J. Quick, both Cape May co., 5-5-1873.
  William G.—Susan M. Warrington, 3-19-1878.

CAMDEN COUNTY MARRIAGES—BOOK B 137

Zeigler, Jacob—Charlotte Rohrback, 6-15-1905.
Zeller, John W., North Wales, Pa.—Irene Redfield; license granted 10-14-1897.
Zimmerman, Franz—Josephine Felder, 9-3-1874.

———o———

MARRIAGES OMITTED IN THE FOREGOING

Bibble, Jeremiah—Susie A. Young, both Philadelphia, 2-5-1872.
Burtt, Robert Johnson, Trenton—Cynthia Goodyear Bateman, Gloucester co., 5-4-1853.
Champion, Lemuel—Mary Champion, 10-31-1875.
Craft, Norman, Philadelphia—Laura Virginia Davis, 7-16-1877.
Cuthbert, Joseph Ogden—Anna Browning, 6-2-1859.
Daniel, Josiah Robinson—Mary Shaffer (colored), 2-16-1854.
Davis, Sylvester—Rosanna Rogen, 10-11-1857.
Fletcher, Albert W., Philadelphia — Elizabeth Maguire, Freehold, 4-10-1866.
Henry, Thomas H.—Sarah Ann Butler (colored), 6-20-1872.
Howard, Samuel—Martha Harris, 3-27-1878.
Joseph, John—Hannah Bates, 8-24-1853.
Lloyd, David H.—Elizabeth Augustus, 3-31-1869.
Mills, Jacob, Marlton—Susanna H. Hunt, 2-9-1876.
Morton, Leonard—Hannah Ann Dill, 9-25-1869.
Trossell, J. Edward, Newark—Clara Jones, 10-24-1877.

INDEX TO BRIDES

Abbott—Abbie, 81; Margaretta, 27; Sarah Emma, 110.
Abeill—Ettie, 125.
Abrams—Emma, 103; Frances, 127.
Ackley—Sally Ann, 72.
Adams—Anna, 107; Augustine, 95; Clara, 111; Eliz, 129; Eliza Ann, 55; Elizabeth, 33, 41; Emma, 91; Hester Ann, 11; Isabella, 21; Mary, 7, 45, 127; Rebecca, 109; Sallie, 60; Susan, 69; Susanna, 75.
Adler—Emma, 97; Mary, 116.
Ageson—Nancy Ann, 29.
Aggerson—Mary Ann, 32.
Agnew—Sarah, 32.
Aides—Catherine, 9.
Albertson—Ablgail, 104; Anna, 71; Cornelia, 97; Emma, 111; Harriet, 81; Mary, 121; Mary Ann, 40; Sallie, 104; Sarah, 51, 52.
Aldsworth—Caroline, 40.
Alexander—Rachel, 55.
Algor—Emma, 66.
Alkire—Ann, 5.
Allen—Amy, 31; Hannah, 83; Lizzie, 110; Mary, 53; Mary Jane, 45.
Allgayer—Sophia, 114.
Alloway—Emma, 103; Georgia Anna, 125; Martha, 120.
Alston—Emoline, 118.
Alton—Carrie Maria, 65.
Ambruster—Adeline, 68; Mary, 58.
Ames—Amy, 60; Kate, 57; Maggie, 136.
Anderson—Eliza, 107; Frances Ann, 5; Malgaret, 33; Mary, 34, 107; Mary Ann, 46.

INDEX TO BRIDES

Andrews—Adelia, 21; Fannie, 95; Kate, 102; Martha, 10; Mary Ann, 12; Sallie, 27; Sarah, 40.
Angels—Barbara, 23.
Angeroth—Anna, 20.
Anneny—Mary, 4.
Annica—Georgean, 87.
Anthony—Catharine, 123.
Anthrem—Clara, 107.
Appel—Katie, 65.
Applegate—Elena, 85; Margaret, 112; Mary, 88.
Appleton—Pauline, 93.
Appley—Theodosia, 99.
Applin—Emma, 93.
Archer—Emily, 98.
Armstrong—Eleanor, 105; Eliz., 104; Julianna, 17; Rebecca, 73; Sarah Ann, 17.
Arnett—Cordelia, 11.
Arnold—Caroline 5; Mary, 61.
Arthur—Hannah, 125; Sadie, 82.
Asendorf—Emily Virginia, 73.
Ashley—Ida, 131; Isabel, 124.
Askins—Rachel, 26.
Asling—Amelia, 119.
Atkins, Elizabeth Lurressa, 110.
Augustus—Elizabeth, 137.
Austin—Mary, 60, 114.
Auts—Harriet, 122.
Auvach—Sarah, 135.
Ayres—Elizabeth, 22; Emma, 123, 125; Mary Eliz., 24.
Ayrton—Emma, 125.
Babcock—Sarah, 39.
Babnew—Kate, 135.
Bachelor—Mary, 9.
Bacon—Ann, 113; Martha, 75.
Bailey (Baily, Bailee)—Annie, 97; Elizabeth, 21; Margaret Ann, 54; Sarah, 28.
Bain—Villie, 91.

Bakeley (Bakley)—Clara, 121; Georgianna, 108; Lena, 132.
Baker—Aramella, 29; Arametta, 97; Emma, 86; Fannie, 125; Kate, 66; Margaret, 85; Mary, 87; Sallie, 77; Sarah, 70.
Ball—Anna, 66; Lizzie, 125; Martha, 128.
Baner—Anna, 50.
Banes—Elizabeth, .28
Banford—Anna, 36.
Banister—Abigail Ann, 27.
Bankhead—Martha, 44.
Banner—Maggie, 131.
Baraba—Elizabeth, 46.
Barber—Adeline, 16; Almeda, 135; Amelia, 122.
Barger—Cornelia, 116.
Barham—Eliza, 122.
Barker—Jane, 13.
Barkley—Mary, 73.
Barnes—Annie, 124; Ella, 63; Henrietta, 27. Mary, 11.
Barnett—Elizabeth, 5; Sarah, 31.
Barrett—Amy, 55; Catharine, 7, 13; Eliza, 15; Elizabeth, 11, 85; Maggie, 113; Phebe, 13; Rebecca, 124.
Barryman—Elizabeth, 20.
Bartholomew—Mary, 22.
Barton—Hephziba, 8; Mary Ann, 44.
Bartram—Mary, 135.
Basset—Zipporah, 65.
Batcheler—Hannah, 129.
Bateman—Cynthia, 137; Esther, 54; Harriet, 12; Mary, 53; Mazie, 81.
Bates (Bate)—Amanda, 19; Amy, 35; Ann, 5; Ann Phebe, 39; Charlotte, 23; Eliza, 52; Frances, 19; Hannah, 137; Jerusha, 24; Maggie Cecelia, 134; Martha, 35; Mary, 69; Sarah, 48.
Bath—Catharine, 135.
Bats (Batt)—Ellinor, 4; Whillie, 68.
Batten—Caroline, 40; Clara, 93; Elizabeth, 131; Keziah, 105; Louisa, 12; Margaret, 62; Martha, 13; Martie, 71; Priscilla, 43, 51; Rebecca, 65; Sarah Jane, 38.

Baylor—Mary, 92.
Bayron—Harriet, 49.
Beaber—Eva, 97.
Beadle—Emma, 91.
Beagary—Caroline, 42.
Beans—Eliza, 131.
Beariut—Esther, 114.
Beaston—Emily, 58.
Beatty—Anna, 81.
Bebrick—Ida, 71.
Beck—Sarah, 63.
Beckett (Becket)—Alice, 39; Elizabeth, 6; Fannie, 95; Hannah, 91; Lydia, 40; Mary, 75; Rachel, 52; Rebecca Ann, 35; Sarah, 98.
Becking—Elizabeth, 52.
Beckley—Elizabeth, 6; Marian, 135; Martha, 53.
Beckworth—Sarah, 26.
Bectel—Amelia, 95.
Bee—Sarah, 55.
Beebe—Carrie, 122; Mary, 111; Mary Ellen, 132.
Beecher—Julia, 117.
Beek—Deborah, 86.
Beely—Melisa, 71.
Beeny—Charlotte, 12.
Beetle—Louisa, 5; Mary Ann, 54; Sallie, 69.
Behsel—Duro, 46.
Beideman (Bideman)—Mary, 51; Wilimina, 134.
Bell—Abby, 120; Celinda, 18; Emily, 121; Esther, 20; Laura, 123; Mary, 36; Selinda, 18.
Beller—Ann, 118.
Belles—Ellen, 7.
Bellou—Lizzie, 26.
Bender—Charlotte, 102; Maria, 9.
Bendler, Catharine, 7; Elizabeth, 102; Priscilla Ann, 18.
Bennett (Bennet, Bennete)—Anna Maria, 30; Elizabeth, 61, Hetty, 61; Keziah, 6; Lidda Ann, 45; Lizzie, 81; Lucinda, 125; Mary, 85, 106; Mary Jane, 26; Priscilla, 109; Sarah, 8.

Bensing—Mary, 61.
Benson—Mary, 87.
Berenger—Ann Maria, 52.
Berner—Rosa, 45.
Berryman—Bella, 71; Eilzabeth, 20; Hessey, 33, Isabella, 62; Mary, 124.
Berrymont—Agnes, 93.
Bessee—Wilermina, 38.
Besser—Sarah, 4.
Betson—Rebecca, 67.
Beuhler—Clara, 74.
Biddle—Josephine, 112.
Bigelow—Sallie, 131.
Bilderback—Minnie, 57.
Bilhart—Kate, 99.
Bilson—Sarah Ann, 92.
Bird—Amanda, 80; Catharine, 57; Charlotte, 45; Hannah Elizabeth, 34; Margaret, 132.
Birdsall—Abbie, 94; Mary, 89; Sarah, 67.
Birmingham—Sallie, 132.
Bisby—Jane, 33.
Bishop—Anna Mary, 69; Joanna, 11; Mary, 20, 79; Phebe, 22; Sarah, 5, 7.
Bisnbaum—Kate, 111.
Biswick—Susan Ruth Ann, 3.
Bittle—Elizabeth, 39; Margaret, 131; Martha Ann, 64.
Black (Blacke)—Caroline, 62; Eliza, 42; Jane, 99; Mary, 36.
Blacscold—Marteine, 88.
Blair—Anna, 65; Elizabeth, 103; Jane, 32; Louisa, 26.
Blakeley—Rebecca Ann, 48.
Bland—Frances, 21; Mary, 106.
Blatherwick—Adda, 78.
Blelteman—Margaret, 48.
Blish—Lena, 70.
Bloom—Mary, 6.
Bloomer—Ann Jane, 133.
Blow—Catharine, 45.

Boardman—Sarah, 101.
Bodine—Amelia, 40; Emeline, 5;
Boen—Rebecca, 30.
Bofel—Jane, 38.
Boggs—Rachel, 54.
Bohm—Mary, 97.
Boileau—Mary Emma, 122.
Bond—Ann, 46.
Bonsal—Rebec, 18.
Bookhaumer—Eda, 131.
Boone—Emma, 18.
Booth—Emily, 108; Harriet, 43; Mary, 57.
Boots—Sarah, 97.
Booz—Emily, 35.
Borden—Rebecca, 134.
Born—Juliana, 76.
Borton — Elizabeth, 82; Lizzie, 64; Rachel, 64; Sarah Ann, 15.
Bosure—Susan, 51.
Boulton—Margaret, 131.
Bowen (Booen)—Adah, 39; Caroline, 81; Deborah, 46; Hannah, 49; Mary, 78; Rebecca, 36; Sarah, 60; Sarah Ann, 47.
Bowers—Anna, 86; Theodotia Ann, 27.
Bowker—Florence, 83.
Bowser—Sarah, 93.
Boyd—Sarah Jane, 107; Mary, 70; Susan, 52.
Boyer—Harriet, 42; Mary, 26.
Boyern—Juliann, 55.
Boyle—Julia, 26; Kate, 118; Sarah Ann, 21.
Bozorth (Bozarth, Bozerth)—Abigail, 6; Anna, 7; Elizabeth, 5; Hester Ann, 40; Leweasa, 50; Martha, 27 Mary, 62; Rebecca, 74.
Braddock—Mary, 90; Rachel, 52.
Bradley—Anna, 95; Caroline, 13.
Bradshaw—Annie, 72; Maggie, 68; Sarah; 68.
Braker—Laura, 72; Tabitha, 4.
Brannan (Brannin)—Marianna, 133; Mary Jane, 37.

Branson—Sarah, 20.
Brasington—Mary, 14.
Bray—Hannah, 96.
Brayman—Jane, 79.
Breen—Helen, 81.
Breffit—Elizabeth, 126.
Brenner—Mamie, 93.
Brewer—Emma, 47; Mary, 58, 125.
Brewin—Anna, 77.
Breyer—Harriet, 102; Margaret.
Brice—Elizabeth, 47.
Brickweil—Mary, 110.
Brindle—Anna, 81.
Bringhurst—Helen, 83.
Brinmer—Irene, 110.
Brinnisholtz—Sarah, 86.
Brisler—Matilda, 114.
Brister—Emma, 61.
Brittain (Britten)—Anna 116; Mary, 12.
Broadwater—Amelia, 4..
Brock—Amanda, 54; Sallie, 45.
Brooks—Amy, 25; Luanda, 93.
Broomfield—Ellen Eliza, 37.
Brothers—Maggie, 116.
Broughton—Ann, 53.
Brower—Esther, 62.

Brown—Anna, 100, 102; Amy, 82; Catharine, 64, 113 Deborah, 7; Elizabeth, 4, 90; Ellen, 60; Lotta, 109; Margaret 44; Martha, 30; Matilda, 50; Mary, 14, 23, 87, 113, 115; Mary Jane, 3; Rebecca, 3, 5, 81; Ruth Ann, 9; Sarah, 51, 54, 60 Sarah Jane, 43; Sarah Victoria, 4.

Browning—Anna, 137; Cecelia, 6; Hannah, 66; Josephine 76; Mattie, 120.

Bruden—Mary, 78.
Brunner—Emily, 67.
Bryan (Brian)—Elizabeth, 90, 123; Hannah Ann, 29; Maggie, 67.

INDEX TO BRIDES

Bryant (Briant)—Anna, 129; Elizabeth, 17; Lucy, 111; Sarah, 55, 94.
Buchanan—Mary, 60.
Buck—Sarah, 25.
Buckle—Mary, 136.
Buckley—Abigail, 38; Betty, 90.
Budd—Anna, 118; Eliza, 23; Elizabeth, 18; Luoy, 109; Louisa 23; Mahala, 46.
Budden—Elizabeth, 122.
Bulah—Elizabeth Ann, 55.
Bulson—Emily, 30.
Buner—Ann, 48.
Bunting—Annie, 51; Sarah, 73.
Burdean—Josephine, 68.
Burdick—Frances, 74.
Burdsall—Martha, 42; Sarah, 8.
Burey—Mary, 92.
Burgess—Addie, 93; Emma, 50.
Burket—Leonora, 104.
Burley—Adelia, 75.
Burnell—Lizzie, 66.
Burns—Elizabeth, 88; Mary, 126.
Burr—Ella, 78.
Burrough (Burroughs,, Burrows, Bonras)—Angeline, 45; Elizabeth, 19; Mary, 9, 37, 87, 89; Rachel, 15; Sarah, 50.
Burt—Edith, 95; Eva, 120.
Burton—Catharine, 127.
Butcher—Harriet, 75; Mary Elizabeth, 94.
Butler—Deborah Ann, 64; Mary, 108; Mary Ann, 124; Sarah Ann, 137.
Butterworth—Mary, 28, 34.
Butts—Katherine, 66.
Buzard—Maria, 60, 61.
Buzby—Ann, 52; Martha Ann, 41; Sarah, 98.
Byers—Lydia, 81.
Caddy—Eliza, 82.
Cade—Mary, 62; Rebecca, 14.

Cain—Elizabeth, 134. Mary, 67.
Cairoli—Emma, 25; Josephine, 130.
Cairote—Mary, 99.
Calhoun—Lettie, 92.
Callahan—Ann, 37.
Callery—Fannie 13.
Calloway—Rachel, 8.
Calvert—Charlotte, 67; Jane, 17.
Cambray—Ann, 25.
Cambridge—Sarah, 6.
Cameron—Ida, 71.
Camp—Margaret, 6; Mary, 120.
Campbell (Camal, Camel)—Adah, 102; Elizabeth, 76; Leonora, 53; Jane, 81; Louisa, 45; Maggie, 122; Mary, 23, 68, 95; Rebecca, 49; Sarah, 124.
Capewell—Cornelia, 135.
Carels—Amanda, 22; Mary, 121.
Carey—Anna, 80; Frances, 8; Louisa, 12; Sarah, 124.
Carl—Massa, 18.
Carlisle—Sarah, 71.
Carman (Carmen)—Ann, 35; Carrie, 126; Laura, 65; Lucy, 120; Mary, 81; Rachel, 19.
Carmany—Kate, 22.
Carnahan—Alice, 132.
Carney—Adeline, 44; Alice, 126.
Carpenter—Amanda, 36, 104.
Carr (Car)—Mary Ann, 55, 80; Nettie, 100.
Carson—Anna, 27; Grace, 25; Margaret, 93.
Carter—Eleanor, 68; Fannie, 114; Georgianna, 75; Mary, 64; Matilda, 34; Rachel, 118; Sallie, 100.
Case—Eliza Jane, 64.
Casperson—Hannah, 20; Ida Bell, 120; Sarah, 120.
Cassaday (Cassady)—Beulah, 14; Elizabeth, 4.
Castle (Castell)—Ann, 14; Catharine, 65; Sallie, 91.
Cathgard—Sarah Elizabeth, 71.
Cattell (Cattle)—Caroline, 112; Martha, 26.
Cavanaugh—Mary, 105; Saily, 85.

INDEX TO BRIDES

Caverly—Emma, 87.
Chadwick—Elmira, 136; Martha, 127;Mary Louina, 37.
Chamberlain—Debbie, 93.
Chambers—Adley, 41; Elizabeth, 94, 108; Sarah, 42; Susie, 116.
Champion—Mary, 55, 69, 137.
Channel (Channell)—Annie, 80; Hattie. 117.
Chapman—Lydia, 126; Margaret, 58; Matilda, 57.
Charles—Jennie, 78; Mariah, 20; Mary, 98, 132.
Chase—Sophia, 117.
Cheeseman (Cheesman)—Bathsheba, 93; Elila, 8; Elizabeth, 5, 19, 22; Hope Ann, 53; Mary Ann, 23; Rachel Ann, 130; Rebecca, 18; Sarah, 77; Virginia, 136.
Chew—Agnes, 9, 69; Annie, 107; Cornelia, 69; Elizabeth, 18, 38; Hannah Ann, 50; Harriet, 45; Isabella, 106; Mary, 78, 84; Rachel, 121; Rebecca, 115; Sarah Ann, 49; Sarah Elizabeth, 110; Susannah, 73.
Childs (Chiles)—Mary, 91; Sarah, 113.
Christian—Sarah, 42.
Christy—Mary, 6, 42, 62.
Church—Sarah, 22.
Churges—Sarah, 75.
Cithgart—Margaret, 18.
Clair—Annie, 96.
Clanagan—Louisa, 14.
Clark (Clarke)—Caroline, 8; Elizabeth, 88; Ella, 20, 106; Emma, 53; Estella, 58; Hannah, 12; Helen, 65, 90; Isabella, 31, 123; Jane, 135; Margaret, 72; Mary, 28, 110, 119; Mary Ann, 98; Rachel, 91; Sarah, 20, 135.
Clayton—Emily Alice, 95; Emma, 117; Sarah, 41; Susanna, 47.
Clement — Abigail, 16; Amelia, 116; Mary Ann, 43; Rachel, 20.
Clevenger—Mary Ann, 17.
Clewell—Catharine 12.
Clifford— Margaret, 45.
Clift—Mary, 89.

Clifton—Mary, 95.

Cline—Abigail, 112; Anna, 46, 123; Emeline, 43; Jennie, 19; Mary, 69, 130; Miriam, 59.

Clinger—Anna Amanda, 52.

Clinton—Dora, 58.

Cliver—Mary, 65.

Clohosey—Damaris, 113.

Cloud—Mary, 42.

Coates—Frances, 85; Mary. 48; Sarah Ann, 71.

Calahase—Rosa, 129.

Cobb—Mary, 7, 18, 82.

Colding—Julia, 112.

Cole — Adalaide, 80; Caroline, 35; Isabella, 28; Mary Matilda, 44.

Coleman—Catharine, 37; Elizabeth, 46; Hannah, 71.

Coley (Colley)—Anna, 127; Fanny, 100; Georgie, 133.

Collings—Anna, 64; Ella, 126; Martha Ann, 50; Rachel, 42.

Collins—Allice, 74; Annie, 89; Ella, 127; Elmina, 18; Emily, 67; Mary, 6, 124, 132; Sarah, 59.

Collyer—Victoria, 80.

Colson—Mary, 12, 70.

Columbus—Sarah, 105.

Combs—Phebe, 26.

Comden—Lydia, 100.

Comley—Cornelia, 89; Ella, 54.

Compton—Sallie, 124.

Conagam—Isabella, 10.

Conard—Mattie, 115.

Conley—Sarah, 130.

Conlin—Jane, 54.

Conover—Hester, 89; Rebecca, 16.

Conrad—Emma, 81.

Conway—Elizabeth, 112; Jean, 130.

Cook—Abbie, 10; Canam, 38; Catharine, 57; Clarissa, 91; Elizabeth, 75; Emeline, 39; Emma Jane, 117; Josephine, 115; Margaret, 10, 39, 40; Mary, 50; Mary Eliza, 83; Rebecca, 60.

Coolas, Lydia, 30.

INDEX TO BRIDES

Cooper—Ann, 44; Caroline Elizabeth, 43; Elizabeth, 48; Emily, 39; Hannah, 13; Helen, 46; Jane, 136; Josephine, 66; Martha, 86; Mary, 19; Minnie, 103; Sarah Ann, 55.

Cope—Florence, 101.
Corcoran—Mary, 46.
Cordery—Mary, 132.
Cordon—Mary, 7.
Core—Anna, 53.
Corels—Amanda, 105; Lidie, 48.
Cork—Lucind, 130.
Corletta—Anna, 91.
Cornish—Sarah Jane, 41.
Corson—Mary, 7, 94, 116; Ray, 78.
Cossaboon—Eliza, 40; Emma, 6; Isabel, 17; Mary, 133; Ruth, 14.
Cottington—Elizabeth, 35.
Cotton—Hannah, 106.
Couch—Lottie, 63.
Coulter—Jennie, 08.
Countryman—Emma, 121; Martha, 87.
Courier—Amelia, 101.
Courtenly—Emma, 100.
Courter—Mary, 72.
Cowan—Elizabeth, 15, 48.
Cowgill (Cogill)—Alice, 125; Louisa, 115.
Cowles—Mary Fidelia, 22.
Cowperthwaite—Emma, 82, 111; Harriet, 134; Mary, 8.
Cox—Eliza, 41; Jennie Eliza, 48; Emma, 22; Hannah, 38, 85; Hannah Ann, 15; Martha, 20; Mary, 87; Rachel, 3; Susan Ann, 4; Victoria, 130.
Coxen—Lydia, 62.
Coy—Mamie, 91.
Craft—Annie, 118.
Craig—Maria, 5; Mary, 46.
Cramer—Eliza Ann, 27; Fannie, 85; Isabella, 17.
Crammer—Martha, 122.
Crandal (Crandell, Crandoll)—Louisa, 100; Lucy, 120;

Maria, 75
  Crane (Crain)—Agnes, 49; Emma, 16; Frances, 14.
  Craver—Elizabeth, 13; Rebecca. 6.
  Crawford—Lizzie, 109; Matilda, 55.
  Cream—Bessie, 25.
  Creaty—Anna, 25.
  Creely—Ella, 114; Emma, 81
  Cresswell—Eleanor, 130.
  Crispin—Annie, 44; Elizabeth, 43; Emma, 109; Josephine, 92; Sarah, 70.
  Croadale, Lizzie, 63.
  Croak—Sarah, 134; Susan, 131.
  Crowley—Teressa, 60.
  Cronk—Mary, 70.
  Crosdale—Elizabeth, 108.
  Cross—Elizabeth, 94; Martha, 38.
  Crowley—Alice, 97.
  Cuff—Amanda, 67.
  Cugley—Mary Ann, 126.
  Culley—Mary, 60.
  Culp—Mary, 32, 59.
  Curing—Elizabeth, 81.
  Curtis—Elizabeth, 5; Leonora, 91; Lydia Ann, 32.
  Cuthburt—Mary, 117.
  Daim—Rebecca, 17.
  Daisey—Kate, 79.
  Dalbow—Emma, 116.
  Dale—Martha, 120.
  Dandinger—Mary, 111.
  Dare—Anna, 117; Catharine, 58; Martha, 124; Mary, 5, 81.
  Darnell—Mary Ella, 100; Sarah, 92.
  Daumler—Anna, 101.
  Davenport—Kade, 116; Sallie, 40.
  Daverty—Catharine, 34.
  Davidson—Ella, 60; Emma, 91; Henrietta, 55.
  Davis—Amanda, 18; Anna, 118; Caroline, 67; Eleanor, 24; Emma, 116; Harriet, 7; Ida, 107; Laura Virginia, 73; Lilah,

INDEX TO BRIDES 151

24; Lizzie, 74, 96, 106; Louisa, 67; Malgaret, 73; **Martha,** 76; Mary, 32, 38, 39, 55, 136; Mary Ann, 37; Mary Lizzie, 105; Rebecca, 117; Sarah, 25, 60, 125; Susan Ann, 49; Virginia, 101.

Davy—Mary, 38.
Dawson—Sarah, 24.
Day—Ann Eliza, 46; Mary, 117; Mary Jane, 36; Rachel, 25, 39.
Dayton—Alice, 125.
Deacon—Amanda, 94.
Decatur—Keziah, 50.
Deets—Atlantic, 121; Christiana, 70.
Dehart—Hannah, 24; Sallie, 37.
DeHaven, Ida May, 100.
DeLaconr—Sarah Jane, 34; 106.
De La Croix—Caroline, 63.
Delaferte—Elsie, 99.
Delamater—Kate, 98.
Delamore—Sophia Amelia, 19.
Denfer—Sarah, 15.
Dennis—Jane Maria, 87; Priscilla, 8.
Denny—Elizabeth, 5.
Deputy—Elizabeth, 38.
Dermott—Elizabeth, 13.
Derrickson—Arria, 118.
Detwiler—Ida, 75.
Devall—Matilda, 134.
DeVault—Anna, 79; Helen, 60.
Devine—Anna, 85.
Devinney—Emma, 69.
Devlin—Mary Ann, 81.
DeWolf—Lillian, 90.
Dexter—Melissa, 121.
Dialogue—Sarah, 3.
Dickson—Ann, 76.
Didifield—Rebecca, 28.
Dikalb—Christiana, 23.
Dilks—Abigail Ann, 24; Alice, 123; **Harriet,** 96; **Priscilla, 64.**

Dill—Elizabeth, 26; Ella, 66; Emma, 111; Hannah Ann, 137; Mary, 16.
Dingler—Maggie, 94.
Dinsdale—Barbara, 66;
Dirmitt—Emeline, 37.
Dixon (Dixson)—Jane, 48; Rebecca, 114; Sarah, 90.
Dobbins—Anna, 73, 123.
Dobleman—Malgaret, 18.
Dockerty—Elizabeth, 28.
Dodd—Anna Letitia, 99; Josephine, 99, 115.
Doerr—Caroline, 81.
Doherty—Adelia, 69.
Dolson—Hannah, 69.
Dolton—Catharine, 4.
Donald (Donalds Donnole) — Bella, 103; Elizabeth, 36; Mary Ann, 18.
Donback—Chataring, 85.
Donnelly—Ann Maria, 44; Ray, 61.
Donohugh—Sarah, 45.
Doran—Hannah, 103; Lucy, 104.
Dorsey—Caroline, 49; Mattie, 31.
Dotterer—Rebecca, 103.
Dougherty—Mary, 89.
Doughten (Dowton)—Betsey, 28; Sarah 39.
Foughty—Alice, 23; Mary, 31; Rosalie, 117.
Douglas (Douglass, Duglas) — Laura, 78; Marian; 32; Mary, 93.
Douthort—Elizabeth, 38.
Dow—Ellen, 78; Josephine, 111.
Down (Downs)—Adaline, 53; Catharine, 90; Lizzie, 78, 87, 112; Mary Jane, 91.
Downing—Ida Virginia, 131.
Doyle—Eliza, 123; Rebecca, 15.
Draper—Hannah, 9.
Drehr—Caroline, 33.
Driggits—Mary Jane, 81.
Duball (Dubell, Duble)—Annie, 74; Hannah, 30; Lizzie, 92.

DuBois—Margaret, 134; Rachel, 17.
Dudley—Anna, 112.
Duffield (Duffle)—Abbe, 102; Caroline, 12; Mary, 7.
Duffy—Catharine, 11.
Dugan, Annie, 89.
Dundas—Annie, 88, 127.
Dungan—Alice, 131.
Dunham (Donnem)—Anna, 104; Mary Jane, 81.
Durham—Ann, 54.
Dunn—Charlotte, 53; Cordelia Frances, 51; Elizabeth, 62; Harriet, 22; Margaret, 60; Mary, 124.
Dunning—Martha, 34.
Durr—Mary, 41.
Dutton—Mary, 92.
Duval—Amanda, 11.
Dych—Florence, 83.
Dyer—Catharine, 38; Keziah, 135.
Eacritt—J. L., 91.
Engen—Isabel, 111.
Earley—Emma, 105; Mary Ann, 40; Sallie, 31.
Earling—Emily, 73.
Edwards—Anna, 77; Charity, 36; Eliza, 116; Elizabeth, 136; Hannah, 133; Jane, 20; Martha, 67; Mary, 108; Rachel, 28; Sallie, 12.
Edgar—Kate, 72.
Eichel—Elizabeth, 100.
Eisele—Priscilla, 51.
Elder—Elizabeth, 28.
Eldridge—Catherine, 49; Elizabeth, 44; Louisa Caroline, 85; Sarah, 19.
Elliott—Prudence, 19.
Ellis—Anna, 112; Anne, 110; Annie, 86; Cornelia, 115; Eliz, 12; Elizabeth, 37; Hannah, 49; Josie, 109; Kata, 66; Mary, 117; Rebecca, 30; Susanna, 42.
Elwell—Adeline, 114; Elizabeth, 106; Mary, 10; Rachel, 93.
Ely—Reba, 96.
Emary—Ellen, 26.

Emley—Anna, 126; Henrietta, 130.
Emmet—Elizabeth, 14.
Emmon (Emons)—Edith, 55; Mary, 50.
Enders—Annie, 128.
Endslow—Sarah, 6.
Englebreak—Anna, 23.
English—Mary, 108.
Ennell—Sarah, 83.
Ensel—Caroline, 94.
Epley—Esther, 27; Mamie, 117.
Ernon—Mary, 133.
Erwin—Eliza, 133.
Escott—Ellen, 60.
Esher—Jane, 92.
Esleach—Ella, 61.
Esler—Rebecca, 79.
Estelow—Josephine, 12.
Estlack—Hannah, 99.
Etherington—Hannah, 112.
Ethridge—Isabella, 74.
Evans—Edith, 122; Eliza Ann, 39; Ella, 103; Ellender, 38; Jennie, 116; Lucinda, 16; Maggie, 107; Mary, 15, 113; Rachel, 92; Sarah, 45, 122.
Evaul—Lucinda, 79.
Everett—Anne, 20.
Ewing (Ewings)—Anna, 41; Catharine, 89.
Eyles—Sallie, 103.
Fairfield—Emma, 86.
Fagan—Delie, 23; Ella, 98.
Falkenburgh—Elizabeth, 10.
Farmer—Lizzie, 29.
Farmington—Elizabeth, 12.
Farnham (Farnum)—Caroline, 22; Sarah, 49.
Farr—Mary, 102.
Farrell—Anna, 123.
Faarow—Alice, 26; Emma, 80; Margaret, 25; Mary, 27; Sarah, 27.

Fayette—Harriet, 51.
Feeny—Mary, 12.
Felder—Josephine, 137.
Fellows—Emma, 81.
Fennemore (Fennimore)—Elizabeth, 48; Harriet, 47.
Fenner—Catharine, 19.
Fenton—Ella, 25; Mary, 17; Mary Ellen, 114; Sallie, 24.
Ferduson—Eliza, 102.
Ferris—Emma, 88.
Fetters—Eveline, 25.
Field—Ann, 76; Melvina, 116.
Fielding—Mary, 55.
Fieriglio—Maria Rosa, 80.
Fiering (Fireing)—Emma, 59; Mary, 119.
Finch—Eliza Jane, 81.
Fine—Johannah, 126.
Finigan—Marie Willet, 109.
Finney (Finny)—Emma, 28; Lucy, 85; Martha, 126; Sarah, 130.
First—Anna, 62.
Firth—Elizabeth, 129.
Fish—Arabell, 80; Emma, 109; Hannah Ann, 13; Joanna, 90; Mary Amanda, 8; Matilda Ann, 39; Rebecca, 48.
Fisher—Abigail Louis, 58; Elizabeth, 6, 49, 82; Florence, 129; Margaret, 83; Mary, 48, 52, 114, 117; Mary Ann, 134; Tamer, 38.
Fisler—Ella 41; Sarah, 88.
Fitch—Lydia, 83.
Fithian—Eliz., 69.
Fitzchew—Cordelia, 82.
Fltzer—Phebe, 127.
Flanigan—Florence, 107.
Flenard—Lizzie, 85.
Fletcher—Martha, 59; Mary Ann, 101.
Flick—Ann Eliza, 36; Margaret, 8.
Flocher—Louisa, 27.
Flowers—Anna, 29; Emily, 73.

Floyd—Anna, 23.
Focer—Hannah 126.
Fogg—Magdelain, 125; Mary, 96.
Folwell—Elizabeth, 61; Isabella, 112.
Forbes—Emma, 99; Hollis, 127.
Force—Celinda, 102; Patience, 74.
Ford—Adaline, 14; Anna, 29, 65; Maria, 27;Sarah, 17.
Forley—Abigail, 11.
Forrest—Henzy, 132.
Fort—Eliza Ann, 42.
Fortiner (Fortner)—Deborah, 132; Frances, 29, 66; Lora, 103; Matilda, 7.
Foster—Elizabeth 28; Jemima, 107; Joanna, 115; Maggie, 89; Mary, 98; Rachel, 38; Temperance, 20.
Fougeray—Emma, 58.
Foulke—Mary, 104.
Fountain—Mary, 101.
Fowler—Anna, 68; Amy, 78; Elizabeth, 19; Hannah, 65.
Fox—Ann, 32; Catherine, 129; Eatteth Ann, 19.
Fozzard—Anna, 81.
Fraenks—Amanda Bertha, 72.
Frambes—Annie, 55.
France—Emma, 32.
Francis—Hannah, 8; Sophia, 124.
Francisco—Sarah, 36.
Frank—Christeanna, 22.
Frankle—Annie, 107.
Frazier (Frazer)—Arabella, 119; Jane, 46; Mary, 58; Sophia, 117.
Fredericks—Cornelia, 108; Elizabeth, 56; Virginia, 131.
Freeman—Amelia, 42; Mary, 34, 106.
Freide—Catharine, 97.
French—Anna, 121; Emergine, 128; Maggie, 120; Sarah Josephine, 39.
Friell—Arabella, 29.
Fries—Rachel, 113.
Fullen—Anna, 104.

Fulton—Clara, 128; Elizabeth, 39.
Fults—Mary, 99.
Funk—Ella, 82.
Fusgan—Catharine, 70.
Gailand—Gertrude, 123.
Gainer—Amanda, 115.
Gaines—Elizabeth, 86.
Galbraith—Clara 68.
Gallagher—Jane, 127; Mary, 43.
Galloway—Emma, 100.
Ganges—Susanna, 54.
Gardiner (Gardner)—Harriet, 93; Mary Elizabeth, 45.
Garety—Mary, 4.
Garr—Hannah, 131.
Garren—Rachel, 30.
Garrigan—Nellie, 109.
Garrison—Lou, 87.
Garwood—Hannah, 35; Mary, 24, 80.
Gaskill—Lydia, 82; Mattie 48; Mary, 93.
Gates—Mary, 105; Susan, 132.
Gaul—Josephine, 130.
Gaunt (Gauntt, Gant) — Alice, 17; Angelina, 46; Anna Maria, 40; Caroline, 11; Emma, 19; Margaret, 92; Sarah, 14.
Gayner—Margaret, 106.
Gehris—Minerva, 117.
George—Emma, 104; Mary, 134.
Gerard—Anna, 100.
Gercke—Martha, 110.
Getsinger—Mary, 16.
Getz—Elizabeth, 114.
Gibbons—Sarah Ann, 51.
Gibbs—Elizabeth, 38; Lydia, 44; Sarah, 81.
Giberson—Beulah, 10; Elizabeth, 118; Mary, 49.
Gibson—Mary, 47, 76; Rebecca, 45; Sarah, 121.
Giddings—Frances, 39.
Giffins—Agnes, 14.
Gifford—Hannah, 54; Lizzie, 77; Rebecca, 46; Sarah, 46.

Gilbert—Clara, 119; Sarah, 12.
Gilfillian—Margaret, 51.
Gilkey—Caroline, 47.
Gill—Ammoline, 136; Rebecca, 125.
Gillard—Eunice, 11.
Gillen—Mary, 103, 121.
Gillette—Amelia, 108.
Gilmore—Annie, 123; Mary, 102; Sarah, 7.
Gindle—Sillia, 114.
Ginther—Josephine, 59.
Githens—Anna Louisa, 68; Kate, 102; Martha Ann, 52; Mary, 91; Sarah, 71.
Givens—Ann, 4.
Gleason—Emma, 68.
Glendora—Blanch, 65.
Glenn (Glin)—Elizabeth, 41; Margaret, 74; Sarah, 8.
Glover—Amelia, 90; Hope, 35.
Goddard—Mary, 22.
Godfrey—Rachel, 124; Sallie, 92; Susan, 87; Tabitha, 116.
Goernley—Hattie, 110.
Goff—Rachel, 15.
Goforth—Mary, 16.
Gohune—Christianna, 111.
Golback—Magdalena, 109.
Goldshall—Emma, 89.
Good—Annie, 130.
Goodenough—Maria, 60.
Goodway—Emma, 96.
Goodwin—Addie, 112; Sabina, 83.
Gordon—Jennie, 126; Lucinda, 65.
Gormley—Sarah, 91.
Goss—Elizabeth, 77.
Gosson—Marie, 109.
Goulblen—Elizabeth, 78;
Gowie—Laura, 91.
Grace—Ann, 104; Hannah, 6.
Grag—Ann, 3.

INDEX TO BRIDES 159

Graham—Elizabeth, 81; Lidie, 70.
Grain—Mary Ann, 51.
Grant—Bridget, 112.
Gratz—Anna Elizabeth, 29.
Graves—Mary Elizabeth, 52.
Gray—Maria 92; Mary, 93; Susannah, 46.
Green (Greene)—Avalinda, 122; Beulah, 45; Emma, 102; Hannah, 121; Lydia, 80; Kate, 126; Mary, 99; Sallie, 115;
Greenage—Annie, 93.
Greenley—Jennie, 94.
Greenman—Annie, 131.
Gregg—Rebecca, 32.
Gregory—Anna, 37, 123; Elizabeth, 6.
Greiker—Frederica, 122.
Greis—Anna, 93.
Griffee, (Griffy)—Elizabeth, 80; Margaret, 7; 125.
Griffin—Annie, 40; Elizabeth, 48; Maggie, 111; Rebecca, 73.
Griffith—Mary, 96.
Grinvault—Catharine Cecelia, 41.
Groff Groft)—Elizabeth, 38; Susanna, 57.
Gros (Grose, Gross)—Alice, 80; Barbarett, 46; Maria, 54.
Grupp—Elizabeth, 96.
Guice—Martha, 66.
Gulick—Catharine, 37.
Gull—Elizabeth, 34.
Gurn—Sarah, 83
Guy—Martha, 100.
Haas—Caroline, 4.
Hackett—Emeline, 94.
Hackney—Ann Eliza, 24.
Hadley—Anna, 91; Margaret, 103.
Hafner—Mary, 59.
Haforan—Bridges, 114.
Hagenback—Flossie, 85.
Hagerman—Ellen, 66.
Hagerty—Mary, 78.
Haines—Ann Eliza, 28; Catharine, 59; Clara, 77; **Hope**, 79;

Lidie, 112; Lydia Ann, 19; Mary, 65, 93, 118, 129; Rebecca, 10; Sarah, 17.

Hainstead—Virginia, 21.

Halaron—Maria Eliz., 21.

Hale—Josephine, 15; Ruth Ann, 97; Sarah Rebecca, 33.

Hall—Catherine, 45; Dora, 120; Sarah Ann, 73.

Hallowell—Olive, 76.

Halshart—Mina, 87.

Halzels—Maria, 14.

Hamilton—Cline, 13; Elizabeth, 27; Georgianna, 4; Mary, 48; Priscilla, 15.

Hammell—Loie, 136.

Hammond (Hamen, Hammon)—Anna, 132; Elizabeth, 49; Jennie, 68; Mary, 59; Sarah, 99.

Hampton—Fanny, 108; Ruth, 29.

Hancock—Mary, 44; Sarah, 38.

Hand—Louisa, 102; Rachel, 100, 134.

Haney—Mary, 113.

Hankerson—Mary, 42.

Hankins—Emma Margaret, 16; Hester, 73; Millisan, 46.

Hannah—Sarah, 11.

Hannold—Josephine, 48.

Hansel—Christiana, 67.

Hanson—Abby, 22.

Happera—Ella, 79.

Harden (Hardin)—Caroline, 128; Jane, 134.

Hardy—Levinia, 86.

Harker—Anna, 75; Ella, 133; Hannah, 61.

Harkins—Mary, 87.

Harley—Sarah, 82.

Harmer—Mary, 130.

Harned—Mary Ann, 79.

Harris—Alice, 35; Eliza, 59, 74; Elizabeth, 132; Ellie Elizabeth, 119; Harriet, 46; Jennie, 124; Kate, 132; Martha, 90, 137; Martina, 86; Mary, 27; Mary Ann, 78; Mary Jane, 28; Sallie, 85; Sarah, 47; Virginia, 122.

Harrison—Eliza, 11; Ella, 58; Eva, 72; Martha, 28; Sarah,

INDEX TO BRIDES 161

126; Tolitha, 47.
  Hart—Ann, 36; Ellen, 61; Lizzie, 122; Sarah, 87.
  Hartle—Bertha, 85; Lizzie, 117.
  Hartley—Amanda, 86.
  Hartman—Catharine, 15.
  Hartner—Kate Magdalene, 46.
  Harvey—Elizabeth Frances, 9; Emma, 65; Jane, 82; Mary 126; Mary Elizabeth, 4.
  Haslam—Louisa, 133.
  Hatch—Louisa, 81; Mary, 47.
  Hatfield—Amanda, 10.
  Hatton—Martha, 118.
  Haun—Clara, 120.
  Haus—Elsie, 97.
  Havengro—Catharine, 79.
  Hawk—Louisa, 102.
  Hawkins—Emma Margaret, 16; Rebecca, 136; Sarah, 103.
  Hay—Ann, 20; Hannah, 28.
  Hayden—Lizzie, 109.
  Hayes (Hays)— Anna, 113; Anne, 99; Julia, 122; Mary, 110.
  Hazleton—Elizabeth Jane, 53; Emma Rebecca, 33.
  Headley—Phebe, 17.
  Heaton—Eliza, 40; Ellie, 76.
  Heavylow—Mary, 109.
  Hedges—Mary, 129.
  Heesley—Christena, 23.
  Hefferman—Ellen, 102.
  Heill—Rebecca, 134.
  Hellermus—Lizzie, 128.
  Helms—Mary, 89
  Helmstadt—Josephine, 104.
  Hemmelwright—Mary, 41.
  Hemming—Martha, 10.
  Hempstead—Mary, 34.
  Henderson—Jessie, 35; Martie, 135; Mary, 60.
  Hendrickson—Deborah, 16; Elizabeth, 33; Henrietta, 21, 32; Mary, 112; Susan, 100.

Henry—Catharine, 59; Elizabeth, 23; Elizabeth Anna Bella, 9; Lizzie, 58; Martha, 34; Mary, 88; Mary Ann, 39; Mary Jane, 49; Sarah, 119.

Heppard—Mary, 70.

Hera (Herah)—Mary, 122; Sarah, 34.

Herbert—Elizabeth, 63.

Heritage—Amy, 47; Marrietta, 55.

Hess—Sarah, 96.

Hetrick—Bessie, 73.

Hetzell—Ella, 67.

Heusel—Elizabeth, 65.

Heusen—Mary, 129; Mary Ann, 132.

Heventhall—Tillie, 117.

Hewitt—Abigail, 76; Ann Eliza, 52; Caroline, 53; Elizabeth Ann, 6; Hannah, 27; Maggie, 81; Martha Ann, 6; Mary, 91.

Hewlings (Heulings)—Annie, 61; Elizabeth, 46; Hannah, 45; Ida, 111; Martha, 30.

Hews—Catharine, 58; Rachel, 35, 79.

Heyl—A. E., 34.

Hickey—Priscilla, 107.

Hickman—Beulah, 130; Elizabeth, 11; Mary Ann, 12; Parthena, 120; Sarah, 6.

Highgate—Matilda, 16.

Higbee—Mary, 112; Rebecca, 13.

Higginbotham—Elizabeth, 95.

Higgins—Bridget, 31; Mary Jane, 6.

Hilderman—Emma, 83.

Hill—Annie, 105; Caroline, 134; Catharine, 10; Emma, 23; Lizzie, 98; Jane, 34; Mary Ann, 54; Matilda, 125; Roselma, 72; Susan Ella, 113.

Hillman—Caroline, 119; Clara, 93; Hannah, 134; Martha, 123; Mary, 79; Mary Ann, 44; Theodocia Ann, 16;

Hinchman—Achseh, 123; Martha, Ann, 25; Mary, 47, 132; Sarah Ann, 24.

Hindle—Clare, 117.

Hinerdinger, Jane, 92.

Hines—Caroline, 49; Eleanor, 89.

Hinkle, Clara, 94.
Hires—Amanda. 44; Emma, 61; Georgie, 113.
Hix—Betsy Jane, 15.
Hoag—Jennie, 83.
Hoagland—Elizabeth, 19.
Hoare—Elizabeth, 43.
Hodges—Susanna, 101.
Hodgson—Ellen, 16.
Hoffinger—Elizabeth, 41.
Hoffle—Alzina, 117.
Hofflinger—Sarah, 120.
Hoffman—Caroline, 13; Georgian Cornelia, 47; Hannah, 55; Louisa, 80; Laura, 96; Mary, 83.
Hoffner—Maggie, 70.
Hogan—Anna, 115; Lydia, 27.
Hogson—Sarah, 32.
Hokum—Alice, 47.
Holcombe—Hester Ann, 8.
Holl—Louisa, 67.
Holland—Emma, 122; Susan Ann, 82.
Hollingshead—Abbie, 99.
Hollworth—Mary, 62.
Holmes—Abigail, 42; Abigail Emeline, 9; Amanda, 114; Laura, 7; Mary Jane, 10.
Holt—Mary, 122.
Holton—Sallie, 99.
Homan—Anna, 105; Sarah, 3.
Hommell—Mary, 66.
Hood—Mary, 113.
Hooper—Ann, 42; Lucy, 100; Margaret, 101; Sarah, 5.
Hope—Sarah, 89.
Hopkins—Angelina, 41; Isabella, 109; Josephine, 12; Sarah, 22
Horn (Horne)—Charlotte, 50; Ellen, 13; Johanna, 69; Rachel, 12.
Horneff—Elizabeth, 79.
Horner—Amanda, 79; Beulah, 57; Catharine, 43; Elizabeth

51; Emaline, 28; Emily, 106; Gertrude, 123; Hannah, 44; Hannah Ann, 9; Janett, 53; Laura, 68; Lizzie, 30; Louisa, 50; Margaret, 43; Mary, 76, 121; Mary Ann, 42; Rebecca, Ann, 40.

Houck—Elmira, 127.
Hough—Rachel, 87.
Howarth—Sarah, 29.
Howell—Anna, 99; Josephine, 128; Lizzie, 95; Mary, 61; Oceana, 106; Sarah Eliz., 68.
Hoxie—Mary Alice, 71.
Hoy—Adeline, 50.
Hubbs—Amelia, 94; Emeline, 18; Sallie, 98.
Hudson—Hannah, 51; Kate, 106; Margaret, 64; Maude, 107.
Huff—Mary Ann, 91.
Huffsey—Mary, 12.
Hufty—Anna, 92.
Hugg—Annie, 40; Mary, 73; Sarah Ann, 10; Theresa, 91.
Hughes (Hues)—Angeline, 50; Caroline, 122; Elizabeth, 128; Jane, 4, 129; Margaret, 93; Rachel, 26.
Hull—Kate, 87; Maria, 23.
Hulling (Hullings)—Elizabeth 28; Mary, 7.
Hults—Carrie, 68; Rebecca, 125.
Hummell, Emily, 126.
Humphries—Rachel, 118.
Hunt—Eliza, 118; Isabella, 26, 28, 38; Lizzie, 70; Mary Ellen, 68; Susan, 136; Susanna, 137.
Hunter—Elizabeth, 103; Ella, 120; Elva, 119; Josephine, 18; Sarah, 112, 120.
Huntington—Sarah, 75.
Hunsinger (Hunzinger)—Abigail, 51; Mary, 43.
Hurd—Maggie, 66.
Hurff—Deborah, 20; Mary, 62; Rebecca, 59; Tamson, 36.
Hurlburt—Emma, 53.
Hurley—Ella, 98; Mary, 34.
Hunlocke—Maria, 82.
Husted—Hannah, 73; Martha, 24; Melesa, 16.
Huston—Altha, 35; Charlotte, 32; Fanny, 101; Isabella, 32; Jennie, 116; Margaret, 75; Margaretta, 27; Rebecca, 120,

Snsan, 70.
  Hutchinson—Angie, 77; Lydia, 8.
  Hutton—Hannah, 3.
  Hyde—Annie, 71.
  Hyland—Phebe, 93.
  Illingsworth—Sarah, 67.
  Impson—Josephine, 19.
  Indicott—Sarah, 16.
  Ingersoll—Carrie, 118.
  Ingle—Lydia Ann, 45.
  Ingram (Ingraham)—Caroline, 25, 96; Ida Virginia, 130; Mary, 81.
  Iredell—Amanda, 129; Mary Folwell, 34.
  Irelan (Ireland)—Catharine, 34; Elizabeth, 9; Hannah, 3; Mary, 108; Mary Emma 30; Rachel, 51.
  Ireson—Margaret, 127.
  Ireton—Lydia, 22.
  Isese—Friderick, 79.
  Iszard (Izard)—Ann, 134; Mary, 31; Rosanna, 31, 47.
  Ivers—Emily, 33.
  Ivins—Elizabeth, 17; Charlotta, 122; Ellen, 20; Georgianna, 122; Hannah, 21; Mary Ann, 18.
  Jackson—Angeline, 79; Emma, 15; Kate, 126; Martha, 106. Mary, 77; Mattie, 112.
  Jacobs—Anna, 81; Martha, 58; Mary, 106; Sallie, 120.
  Jaggard—Ellen, 33; Susan, 52.
  Jaggers—Effie, 78; Hannah, 4; Keziah, 69.
  Jameison—Ann, 54.
  James—Lydia, 109; Margaret, 69; Sarah, 65.
  Jefferies (Jeffreis, Jeffries)—Ella, 97; Emma, 52; Mary, 95.
  Jellitt—Mary Jane, 79.
  Jennings—Elizabeth, 59; Ellen, 40; Hannah, 104; Mary Jane, 48.
  Jernis—Louise, 115.
  Jess—Emma, 7.
  Jessup—Ann, 47.
  Jester—Kate, 118.

Jewell—Elizabeth, 85.
Jinnett—Rebecca, 24.
Johns—Christiana Amelia, 50.
Johnson—Achsah, 76; Anna, 27, 37, 89; Cornelia, 28; Elizabeth, 57, 94, 96, 106; Elizabeth Ann, 110; Ella, 72; Emma, 79; Hannah, 49; Julia, 99; Ketura, 9; Letitia, 37; Maggie, 58; Margaret, 36; Margery, 119; Mary, 63, 68, 80, 107; Mattie, 97; Rebecca, 127; Sarah, 32, 51, 54.
Johnston (Johnstone)—Elizabeth, 49; Mary, 75; Rachel, 87.
Joline—Lacetta, 129.
Jones—Alice, 126; Ann Margaret, 133; Anne, 43; Caroline, 46; Clara, 137; Eliza, 3; Eliza Jane, 50; Elizabeth, 19, 30, 51; Ella, 97; Ellen, 7, 73; Hannah, 12; Harriet, 26; Henrietta, 132; Josephine, 118; Keziah, 23; Leonora, 77; Lewizer, 6; Louisa, 116; Lydia Ann, 12; Margaret, 23; Mariah, 14; Mary, 114; Mary Amanda, 29; Rachel, 27; Rebecca, 30, 57; Sarah Ann, 45; Susan, 18; Susanna Elmira 134.
Jordan— Caroline, 80.
Josline (Joslin)—Lydia, 37; Mary, 55; Sallie, 65.
Kaffer—Emma, 24.
Kahler—Georgie, 119.
Kain (Kane)—Jennie, 69; Lizzie, 60.
Kaiting—Mary, 95.
Kaltley—Elizabeth, 20.
Karge—Emma, 119.
Kates—Sallie, 8.
Kaufman—Lizzie, 109.
Kay—Emeline, 11.
Keeler—Elizabeth, 64.
Keen (Kean, Keene)—Annie, 105; Elizabeth, 22; Martha, 72; Mary, 11, 73; Mary Elizabeth, 129; Rachel, 118; Rosena, 38.
Kehan—Annie, 124.
Keighton—Laura, 59.
Keil—Barber, 119.
Kelley (Kelly)—Agnes, 103; Ann, 115, Anna, 58, 62; Caroline, 10; Josephine 114; Margaret, 35; Mary Ann, 89.

Kellogg—Emma, 61.
Kellum—Emeline, 7; Margaret, 87; Ruth, 67.
Kemble—Amanda, 73.
Kendell (Kendle, Kindel)—Amelia, 79; Catharine, 45; Sarah, 55.
Kennedy—Ella, 71; Emma Louisa, 19; Louisa, 81; Martha, 58; Sarah, 33.
Kenneman—Mary, 64.
Kerfis—Sue, 82.
Kesler (Kessler)—Amanda Jane, 27; Elizabeth, 53; Hattie, 103.
Ketterer—Mary, 98.
Key—Harriet, 40.
Keyser—Ella, 126; Emma, 54; Isalella, 104.
Kiehl—Caroline, 75.
Kier—Lydia, 72.
Kimberly, Maria, 122.
Kimble (Kimbal)—Almira, 123; Celesta, 133.
Kincade (Kincaid, Kinkade)—Isabella, 37; Margaret, 54; Mary, 103; Melissa, 114.
King—Anna, 32, Ellen, 82, 108; Laura, 69; Louisa, 86; Margaretta, 14; Mary, 105; Rachel, 103; Rebecca, 68; Sarah, 4, 20, 26.
Kinsey—Mary, 136.
Kinsil—Emma, 77.
Kinsley—Esther, 127.
Kirby—Melena, 20.
Kirchenbower—Sarah, 48.
Kirkbriee—Jane, 96; Susanna, 30.
Kirkwood—Maggie, 98.
Klein—Katharine Frederica, 25.
Kley—Mary, 135.
Kline—Elizabeth, 53; Lydia Ann, 68.
Knauf—Maria, 63.
Kni8ht—Etta, 101; Mary Ann, 5.
Knisel—Elizabeth, 48.
Kniser—Elizabeth, 82.

Knopp—Eliza, 68.
Knorr—Mary Alma, 54.
Knowles—Hannah, 96.
Knowlton—Matilda, 5.
Krattenmacher—Bertha, 87.
Kronk—Caroline, 51.
Kruse—Anna, 133.
Kugan—Catharine, 62.
Kulp—Emma, 31.
Kunitz—Hannah, 37.
Kurbow—Ruthanna, 31.
Kyle—Mamie, 59.
LaBlotier (LaBlothier)—Amelia, 31, 100.
Lackman—Elizabeth, 107.
Lacy—Sarah, 23.
LaDow—Theodosia, 99.
Lafferty—Annie, 91.
Lake—Lowanda, 131; Mary, 43; Susanna, 115.
Lalocker—Margaret, 111.
Lamar—Catherine, 26; Hetty, 53.
Lamb—Hannah Amanda, 76; Mary, 77; Sarah, 47.
Lane—Anna 31; Mary, 62.
Langcake—Sarah, 19.
Lanning—Mercy, 13.
Lansdown—Emma Frances, 126.
Larmouth—Lizzie, 81.
Larrance—Mary, 46.
Larzelere—Gertrude, 111.
Lashley—Mary, 4.
Laton—Mariah, 42.
Laughlin—Ann Elizabeth, 49; Mary, 76.
Lavery—Elizabeth, 127.
Laws—Anna, 74; Hannah, 67, 134; Harriet 87; Julia Ann, 65.
Lawless—Hattie, 68.
Leach—Alice, 124; Sadie, 99; Sarah Jane, 37.
Leadbester—Clara, 77.
Leady—Mary, 21.

Leake—Annie, 81.
Leaving—Hannah, 85.
LeConey—Carrie, 60; Lizzie, 110.
Lecroy—Mary, 21.
Ledden—Sallie, 101.
Lee—Annie, 58; Elizabeth, 132; Hannah, 41; Kate, 77; Margaret, 4; Mary, 81; Rachel, 68, 74.
Leeds—Mary, 36; Rebecca, 67; Susan, 19.
Lees (Leese)—Elizabeth, 12; Mary, 81.
Lefevour, Eliza Ann, 28.
Lehman—Anna, 83.
Leitenberger—Caroline, 70.
Lemisch—Ida, 122.
Lemons—Sarah Elizabeth, 4.
Lenard—Clara, 74; Priscilla, 18.
Lerenck—Mary, 73.
Lescher—Emily, 118.
Leslie—Eleanor, 83; Rebecca, 13.
Lester—Ella, 87.
Lewallen—Elizabeth, 12; Esther Ann, 20; Mary, 83, 135; Rebecca. 106; Sue, 120.
Lewis—Annie, 79; Caroline, 29; Charlotte, 129; Hannah 113; Ida, 108; Jennie, 25, 90; Louisa, 60; Martha, 11; Mary 66.
Levi (Levy)—Flora, 90; Mamie, 129.
Lezenby—Maggie, 91.
Libant—Sarah Jane, 14.
Lindale (Lindell)—Lizzie, 120; Sallie, 70.
Linden—Lizzie, 113.
Lindhurst—Mary, 101.
Lindmann—Barbara, 31.
Lindsey—Georgie, 107.
Ling—Laura, 66.
Lingerman—Blanche, 117.
Link—Elizabeth, 107.
Lippincott (Leppingcott)—Abigail, 51; Clara, 58; Clarissa, 43; Gertrude, 130; Hannah, 32; Harriet, 69; Lizzie, 57; Jane, 108; Mary, 23; Rebecca Jane, 39; Sallie, 63.

Lipsett—Adeline, 107.
Little (Lytle, Lyttle)—Anna, 65, 100; Margaretta, 49; Mary, 132.
Livermore—Adrienette, 98; Mary, 53.
Livezey—Anna, 97.
Lloyd—Clementina, 37; Jennetta, 42; Sarah, 18, 48.
Loane—Margaret, 99.
Lock (Locke)—Adaline, 135; Annie, Beulah, 35; Carrie, 132; Caroline, 58; Gertrude, 107; Hannah, 88; Kate, 113; Mary, 11, 38, 58; Matilda, 53; Priscilla, 4; Rejoinia, 32; Sallie, 60; Sarah, 103.
Lockman—Louisa, 132; Mary, 72.
Lockum—Sarah, 113.
Lockwood—Matilda, 128; Rachel, 127.
Lodge—Caroline, 8; Fannie, 105.
Logan—Mary Ann, 8.
Logue—Martha, 80.
Long—Abigail, 128; Blanche, 108; Emma, 71; Martha, 117; Phebe Ann, 51; Sarah, 128.
Longworth—Elizabeth, 55.
Loper—Catharine, 72; Sarah Jane, 127.
Lord—Rebecca Ann, 133.
Lore—Annie, 111.
Loring—Mattie, 93.
Lott—Kate, 111.
Loughlin—Adeline, 81.
Louis—Ella, 82.
Lovell—Elizabeth, 97.
Lovett—Nancy, 136; Rachel, 25.
Loving—Marietta, 7.
Lowe—Mary, 117.
Lucas—Addie, 88; Elizabeth, 36.
Ludavicy—Linda, 71.
Lukens—Jane, 13.
Lummis—Mary, 23.
Lyman—Carrie, 95.
Lynch—Margaret, 43.

INDEX TO BRIDES 171

Lynd—Catharine, 50.
Macauley—Mary, 63.
MacDonald—Mary Ellen, 124.
Mackey—Adaline, 17; Sarah Louisa, 82.
MacPherson, Louisa, 22.
Madenfort—Jennie, 99.
Madkiff (Madciff)—Rachel, 3; Jane, 5.
Magee—Rachel, 46; Rebecca, 123.
Magonigal—Anna, 45.
Magourly—Kate, 79.
Maguire—Elizabeth, 137.
Mahoney—Clara, 89.
Mall (Maul)—Sarah, 9; Tamson, 49.
Mallman—Eliza, 85.
Mandz—Harriet Ann, 86.
Mann—Ann, 19; Sarah, 4.
Mansfield—Anna, 134.
Manus—Hannah, 42.
Mapes—Caroline, 10; Mary Ann, 104; Roxanna, 11.
Marchant—Sarah, 36.
Marche—Catharine Maria, 45.
Marintyn—Jennie, 131.
Maris—Bessie, 112.
Marks—Eliza Jane, 8.
Marple—Emma, 23; Mary, 21.
Marshall—Abbie, 101; Elizabeth, 33, 47; Ella, 70; Jennie, 91; Mary, 60, 99; Matilda, 4; Sarah Ann, 9.
Martin—Annie, 20; Catherine, 4; Linda, 113; Sallie, 82; Sarah, 30; Sibilla, 67.
Mason—Jemima, 63; Rebecca, 134; Sarah, 59.
Mathers—Mary, 80.
Mathias—Mary, 94.
Mathis—Louisa, 124; Mary, 82.
Matlack (Matlock)—Eliza, 16; Elizabeth, 30, 121; Emma, 113; Hannah, 47; Josephine, 119; Maggie, 112; Mary, 119, 122; Rebecca, 87; Ruth Anna, 116; Sarah, 30; Susannah, 54.
Matthews—Mary, 102.

Maurice—Anna 106.
Mawhinney—Hannah, 74.
Mawrey—Leah, 56.
Maxwell—Ella, 78; Mary, 92.
May—Sarah, 58.
Mayberry—Ann Louise, 17.
Mayers—Amelia, 92.
Mayhew—Maggie, 133.
McAllister—Sophie, 111.
McBride—Sarah, 110.
McCain—Catharine, 133; Tillie, 91.
McCalla—Caroline, 36.
McCann—Ellen, 72; Isabell, 26; Margaret, 64.
McCartney—Anna, 105.
McCarty—Hannah, 40.
McClain—Mary, 67; Rebecca, 112; Ruth Maria, 39.
McClaskey—Lizzie, 126.
McClay—Annie, 44.
McClees—Anna, 121.
McCloud—Mary Elizabeth, 8.
McClure—Mary, 10.
McCollum—Henrietta, 70; Mary, 70; Miranda, 128.
McConley (McConnelly)—Ann, 51; Kate, 132.
McCormick—Annie, 7; Georgianna, 21; Lulu, 114; Lydia, 85.
McCown (McCowan)—Anna, 94; Jane, 6; Mary, 102.
McCreedy—Isabella, 33.
McCullay (McColey, McCulley, McCully) — Abigail, 80; Adeline, 115; Anna, 123; Deborah, 16; Hannah, 37; Kate, 127; Mary, 126.
McCurdy—Fannie, 17; Jane, 114.
McDonald (McDounell)—Almira, 114; Margaret, 33; Sadie, 119.
McDonongh, Sarah, 45.
McElroy—Ann, 31.
McEnany—Hannah, 39.
McEwen—Jane, 26.
McFarland—Eliza Jane, 32; Harriet, 24; Mary, 11; Sarah, 11.
McFee—Jane, 38.

McFerrill—Margaret, 41.
McFiners—Eliza, 22.
McGannon—Eliza, 68.
McGlindy—Elizabeth, 14.
McGuire—Ella, 121; Emma, 115.
McHugh—Catherine, 18.
McIlhone—Mary, 17.
McIlvee—Mary, 111.
McIlvaine—Hattie, 110; Rebecca, 50.
McIntire--Elizabeth, 73; Mary, 130.
McIsaac—Margaret, 96.
McKale—Delia, 124.
McKeen—Jane, 126.
McKeever—Annie, 102; Clara, 86; 124.
McKinley—Mary, 125.
McLain—Jennie, 103.
McMahon—Lizzie, 91; Mary Ann, 8.
McMann—Eliza, 93.
McManus—Maggie, 112; Sarah, 121.
MacNeal—Mary, 28.
McNelly—Martha, 28.
McNichols—Mary Ann, 46.
McPherson—Emma, 83.
McTay—Martha, 37.
McVery—Ann, 130.
McWhinney—Sarah, 79.
McWilliams—Mary, 88.
Mead—Martha, 89.
Meally—Margaret, 12.
Meckin—Lydia, 59.
Mecray—Hannah, 32.
Megonigle—Elizabeth, 118.
Meggs—Catharine, 76.
Melz—E., 133.
Merriel—Rebecca, 77.
Merrikew—Emma, 34.
Merrin—Elizabeth, 34.
Merritt (Merrott)—Elizabeth, 128; Phebe, 104.

Messick—Mary, 25.
Messner—Katie, 118.
Metz—Mary, 127.
Metzer—Sallie, 25.
Meyers (Meyer)—Anna Mary, 70; Jennie, 130; Virginia, 20.
Michener—Sallie, 114.
Mickle—Clara, 109; Rebecca, 88.
Middleton—Cecelia, 12; Charlotte, 14; Emma, 135; Elizabeth, 50, 55; Elizabeth Ann, 52; Fannie, 95; Hannah, 22; Harriet, 27; Jane, 33, 58; Priscilla, 24; Rebecca, 70.
Mike—Sophie, 126.
Miller—Abbie, 76; Alice, 127; Annie, 121, 131; Caroline, 20; Eliza, 63; Elizabeth, 61, 80; Ellen, 134; Emma, 115; Fanaie, 108; Louisa, 125; Maria, 96; Mary, 12, 122, 131; Olivia 109; Rachel, 37; Sallie, 8; Sarah, 129.
Mills—Hannah Ann, 23; Sarah, 85.
Mineo—Mary, 76.
Mines—Ida—119.
Minkler—Sarah Ann, 38.
Minnick—Miriam, 78.
Mintle—Mary, 30.
Miskelly—Hannah, 50.
Mitchell—Abbie, 89; Annie, 15, 128; Florence, 118.
Mitchler—Agnes, 96.
Moffit—Lizzie, 124.
Monell—Virginia, 127.
Monks—Catharine, 17.
Monroe (Munroe, Munrow)—Adie, 85; Cornelia, 129; Helen, 115; Maria, 32; Sallie, 27; Sarah, 36.
Montgomery—Susie, 81.
Moody—Rachel, 21; Sarah, 29.
Moon—Mary, 9.
Mooney—Ella, 125.
Moore—Anna, 44; Annie, 39; Beaula, 50; Clara, 32; Ella, 79, 98; Ellen, 33; Elvina, 136; Florence, 98; Hannah, 101, Jane, 4; Lydia, 34; Phebe Ann, 6; Rebecca, 40; Sarah, 13; Susan Ann, 52; Virginia, 79.
Morgan—Amanda, 116; Anna, 135; Caroline, 68; Drusilla,

127; Hannah, 101; Mary, 135; Sarah, 38; Susan, 104, 135.
Merrell (Morrill)—Frances, 122; Maria, 58.
Morris—Anne, 108; Elizabeth, 130; Isora, 86; Sarah; 10.
Morrison—Abbie, 59; Annie, 67.
Morrone—Felicetta, 68.
Morse—Mary, 110.
Morton—Margaret, 100.
Mosely—Louisa, 49.
Moss—Ann, 8; Jane, 13.
Moulton—Mary, 77.
Mounce—Mary, 128; Rachel, 45.
Mouton—Mary, 4.
Mowers—Amanda, 128; Mary, 50.
Mowry—Mulinda, 127.
Mudoon—Julia, 81.
Mulford—Emma, 8; Hannah, 10; Mary, 43; Martha, 127.
Mulhall—Matilda, 76.
Mullholland—Adelia, 42.
Mullen—Katy, 134.
Mullica, Anna, 35; Margaret, 38; Sarah, 15.
Mullin—Matilda, 14.
Muncey—Elizabeth, 43; Sarah, 11.
Munday (Mundy),Malinda 118; Netty, 116;
Munser—Amelia, 13.
Munshover—Martha Jane, 4.
Munyan—Annie, 75.
Murphy—Anna, 15; Catharine, 75; Harriet, 81; Laura, 79 Mary, 78; Sallie, 125; Sarah Ann, 47;
Murray(Murray Merry)—Amelia, 76; Emma, 100; Kate, 76. Lizzie, 119; Louisa, 110; Mary, 67, 135; Mrs. George, 120; Ruth, 135.
Myers (Myres)—Catharine, 39; Mattie, 78.
Myrase—Sarah, 19.
Myrose—Mary Ann, 110.
Nadine—Charlotte, 132.
Nagel—Lottie, 62.
Nail (Nale)—Elizabeth Jane, 31; Mattie, 58; Phebe, 29.
Nash—Josephine, 131.

Naylor—Martha, 88; Mary Caroline, 95; Ruth, 78; Susan 15.
Neal (Neale, Neill)—Bertha, 97; Eliza, 21; Mary, 73, 122; Sarah, 14.
Neald—Mary, 97.
Neiplin—Martha, 7.
Nelon—Anna, 88.
Nelson—Margaret, 50; Mary Ann, 94.
Nerld—Julia, 134.
Newbern—Sarah Ann, 72.
Newcomb—Keziah, 108.
Newkirk—Lizzie, 68; Lydia, 36; Matilda, 51; Sabilla, 77.
Newman—Clara, 103.
Newton—Anna, 72, 117; Jane, 86; Mary, 26, 48; Sallie, 83.
Nichols (Nickles, Nickols)—Anna, 30, 119; Annie, 127; Catharine, 15; Josephine, 76; Martha Jane, 30; Rebecca, 82; Sarah, 130.
Nicholson—Emma, 122; Lizzie, 77; Martha, 36.
Nidecker—Maria, 66.
Nofels—Sarah Jane, 110.
Noggel—Catharine, 53.
Norcross—Emma, 104; Martha, 24; Mary, 16; Sarah, 94; Susan, 52;
North—Abbey, 44; Ann, 44; Caroline, 78; Hannah, 76; Hattie, 81; Mary Ann, 45.
Northrope—Emily, 41.
Norton—Clara, 58.
Norwood—Mary Ann, 104.
Nuby—Lydia Ann, 130.
Nuller—Maggie, 125; Martha, 99.
Oakford—Mary Eliza, 21.
O'Conner - Catharine, 80.
Odling—Clow, 124.
O'Donnell—Josephine, 34; Laura, 78.
Officer—Jennie, 109.
Ogg—Emma, 105.
O'Hara (O'Hare)—Maggie, 109, 128.
Olden—Mary, 33.
Olive—Ida, 82.

INDEX TO BRIDES 177

Oliver—Sarah, 31.
Ollis—Elizabeth, 63.
Olmsted—Fannie Elizabeth, 89.
O'Neal—Ellen Sarah, 81.
Oney—Ella, 31; Ellen, 123; Mary, 89; Phebe, 64.
Opdyke, Louise, 116.
Orr—Mary Ann, 8.
Orund—Matilda, 119.
Osborn—Virginia, 115.
Osler (Ostler)—Carrie, 103; Hannah, 65; Lydia, 91; Katie, 130.
Oston—Elizabeth Alice, 105.
Outhout—Frances, 29.
Outwater—Maria, 93; Mary, 62.
Owen—Martha, 6; Mary, 125; Susan Ann, 23.
Packer—Susie, 124.
Paden—Sarah, 27.
Padlford—Cornelia, 102.
Paff—Elizabeth, 7.
Page—Adelaid, 63; Keziah, 50; Mary, 64.
Painter—Mary, 98, Susanna, 135.
Palmer—Annie, 74; Julia, 111; Mary, 42, Mary Afra, 33.
Pancoast—Keziah, 5; Lizzie, 65; Rhoda, 34.
Park (Parks)—Elizabeth, 131; Martha, 44; Rosanna, 105; Sallie, 135 Sarah, 120; Susan, 131.
Parker—Anna, 77; Ella, 70; Julia, 3; Kate, 4; Laura, 29; Martha, 105; Mary, 17; Sarah, 47, 120.
Parkhouse—Caroline, 29.
Parmer—Elizabeth, 118.
Parnell—Fannie, 48.
Parry—Sidney Mary, 7.
Partridge—Eliza Josephine, 75.
Parvin (Parvain)—Amelia, 19; Clara, 62; Lizzie, 100; Sarah, 94.
Paschall—Emma, 71.
Pascoe—Rebecca, 58.
Passeley—Henrietta, 128.
Pate—Clara, 136.

Patrick—Rachel, 83.

Patterson—Anna, 52; Catharine, 20; Emma, 108; Laura, 128; Margaret, 55; Mary Ann, 80; Matilda, 27; Rachel, 106.

Patton (Paton)—Lillie, 65; Maria, 67.

Paul—Anna, 108; Emma, 104; Lizzie, 72; Martha, 63; Mary, 94, 127.

Paullin—Sarah Jane, 124.

Payne—Clara, 110.

Peacock—Elizabeth, 22; Lydia, 114.

Peak (Peake)—Eliza, 136; Elizabeth, 25; Ella, 106; Sarah 16.

Pearce—Sarah, 119; Susanna 30.

Pearson—Martha, 81; Mary Ann, 16; Zebiah, 49.

Peas—Abigail, 23.

Peck—Caroline, 50.

Peckman—Lizzie, 24; Mary, 76.

Pedrick—Amy, 121; Ann, 30; Anna, 86; Rebecca, 90.

Pendergrass—Mary, 22.

Pengood—Mary Jane, 127.

Penn—Anna, 120.

Pennington—Laura, 125; Tessie, 61.

Penton—Ellen, 107.

Pepper—Alice, 23.

Perce—Deborah, 3.

Perkins—Adah, 121; Anna, 32, 111.

Permer—Elizabeth, 44.

Perry—Mary, 116.

Peters—Anna, 128; Emeline, 36; Mary, 14, 135; Phebe, 54; Susannah, 35.

Peterson—Georganna, 120; Mary, 94; Mary Eliza, 31.

Petit—Rebecca, 5.

Pew—Emma, 114.

Peyton—Jane, 89;

Phifer (Phiffer, Fifer)—Amanda, 102; Clara, 108; Emaline, 13; Hannah, 16; Manetta, 108; Martha, 77; Mary, 29, 78; Sarah, 15

Philips (Phillips)—Clara, 111; Eliza, 11; Joanna, 92; Louisa 133; Maria, 114; Sarah, 68; Susan Ann, 53.

Phinney—Saphronia, 38.

INDEX TO BRIDES 179

Pidgeon—Annie 106.
Pierce—Deborah, 34; Josephine, 46; Sarah, 37; Susan, 112.
Pierpont—Jane, 7.
Pierson—Harriet, 63; Mary, 109.
Pike—Beulah, 95;Elizabeth, 85; Ida, 72.
Pimlot (Pimlotte)—Adelaide, 97; Lizzie, 28.
Pine—Amy, 12; Anne, 49; Caroline,, 39; Elizabeth, 9; Emma, 80, 122; Lizzie, 134; Rachel, 53; Sarah Jane, 45.
Pinkert—Bertha, 86.
Piper—Hannah, 106.
Pitman—Mary, 73.
Platt—Clara—62; Emma, 104.
Pleasant—Hannah, 42.
Plimlott—Emma, 21.
Pluck—Hannah, 78.
Plum—Clara, 119, 131; Elizabeth, 47; Hannah Ann, 7; Linnie, 71.
Plummer—Pauline, 89.
Polk (Poke)—Edith, 37; Martha Ella, 94.
Pond—Margaret, 121.
Poole—Elizabeth, 76; Frances, 94.
Porce—Sarah, 25.
Porch—Amy, 21; Elizabeth, 14; Emma, 124; Millicent, 26; Sarah, 6, 11.
Porter—Agnes, 59.
Portler—Linda, 110.
Postley—Mary, 69.
Potter—Ella, 62.
Potts—Jennie, 72; Marian, 100.
Powell—Annie, 76; Anne Maria, 37; Bell Jane, 43; Harriet, 40, 45; Ida, 63; Louisa, 90; Margaret, 14; Phebe, 53; Priscilla, 88; Sarah, 8.
Powers—Alice, 19.
Pratt—Jane, 36.
Prescott—Ann. 17; Susannah, 25.
Price—Bernice, 106; Harriet, 103, 121; Lizzie, 125; Lottie, 64; Maggie, 104; Mary, 75; Mary Elizabeth, 21; Matilda, 58, 89.

Prickett—Elizabeth, 127; Lizzie, 134; Mary, 133; Sarah, 44.
Primrose—Hannah, 27.
Pritchett—Elizabeth, 104.
Prosser—Sarah, 92.
Pruitt—Martha, 130.
Purcell—Martha, 117.
Purnell—Lydia, 67; Mary, 81.
Pursglove—Miriam, 77.
Queen—Mary Ann, 44; Sarah, 6.
Quick -Rebecca, 73; Sallie, 136.
Quicksall (Quicksell)—Anna, 78; Charlotte, 11; Elizabeth, 33.
Quinn—Charlotte, 124; Eliza, 35; Margaret, 136.
Raddliffe—Kate, 7.
Rafine—Mary, 124.
Rainier—Alice, 115.
Rambo—Emmarantha, 101.
Ramseager—Elizabeth, 116.
Ramsey—Rebecca, 65.
Rankins—Sarah, 126.
Rapel—Nora Elmira, 51.
Rapp—Virginia, 97.
Ray—Jacobin, 13; Josephine, 36.
Redfield—Irene, 137.
Rediker—Eleanor, 51.
Reed—Annie, 111; Ella, 17; Lizzie, 68; Maria, 59; Martha, 60; Sallie, 10; Sarah, 70.
Reel—Lyde Ann, 10.
Reese—Anna, 86.
Reeves—Elizabeth, 10; Emma 104; Fannie, 47; Mary, 43, 63.
Rehig—Mary, 115.
Reidel—Ottilia, 88.
Remley—Elenor, 20.
Rendles—Mary Ann, 123.
Rennall—Mary Emily, 54.
Renny—Lizzie, 76.
Repman—Josephine, 59.
Repsher—Emma, 54; Sarah, Jane, 33.

Restine—Mary Ann, 50.
Reutykeing—Louisa, 6.
Rewbart—Sarah, 38.
Reynolds—Amanda, 92; Emma, 111; Lydia, 9; Mary, 95; Sallie, 107.
Rhoads (Rhodes, Roads)—Emma Jane, 115; Auguste Julianne, 113; Bathsheba, 27.
Richards—Beulah, 57; Eliza, 64; Elizabeth, 18, 103; Ellen, 106; Jane, 23; Mary, 94; Susannah, 116.
Richardson—Anna, 92; Sarah, 9.
Richie—Mary, 133.
Richman—Amanda, 4; Rose, 133; Sarah, 86.
Richmond—Anna, 106.
Ridge—Josephine, 134.
Ridgeway—Josephine, 133.
Riedel—Martha, 31.
Riggins—Sallie, 79.
Righter— Hannah, 42.
Rightly—Maggie, 135.
Riley (Reilley) — Fanny, 54; Maggie, 81; Mamie, 74 Sophie, 37.
Risley—Ann Eliza, 8; Anna, 69; Elizabeth, 5; Margaret, 5; Sarah, 6; Sarah Rebecca, 135.
Ritter—Elizabeth, 89.
Ritzel—Margaret, 96.
Rives—Sylvia, 127.
Rix—Caroline, 30.
Robb—Matilda, 53.
Robbins—Elizabeth, 51; Zippa, 104.
Roberson—Lydia, 29; Mary, 31;
Roberts—Ann, 97; Hannah, 77; Harriet, 116; Josephine, 71; Lizzie, 105.
Robertson—Jennie, 72; Jessie, 100; Julia, 109; Sarah Catharine, 12, 90; Tema, 130.
Robinson—Alwilda, 115; Ann, 54; Elizabeth, 43, 64; Louisa, 26; Martha, 69; Mary Jane, 39; Sarah, 89.
Rodman—Margaret Ann, 11.
Roe—Martha, 35; Rebecca, 35.

Rogen—Roxanna, 137.
Rogers (Rodgers)—Anna 125; Annie, 114; Elizabeth, 56; Fanny, 110; Gerusha, 13; Mary, 121; Sarah, 53.
Rohrback—Charlotte, 137.
Roller, Elizabeth, 3.
Rommelman—Emma Louise, 101.
Roop—Maria, 3.
Roork (Rorke)—Mary, 112; Rebecca, 81.
Rose—Catherine Ann, 46.
Roselle—Rebecca, 50.
Roseman—Sarah, 9.
Ross—Amelia—46; Anna; 91, 107; Maria, 47; Marion, 90 Mary, 27, 41; Mary Ann, 10; Patience, 25; Ruth, 22; Sarah, 14.
Rosten—Alice, 124.
Roth—Susanna, 31.
Roussel—Anna 18.
Rowan (Rowand, Rowans)—Caddie; 119; Emma, 112; Lizzie, 78; Mary, 23.
Rowley—Sarah, 19.
Rubart—Melissa, 131.
Rudden—Mary, 74.
Rudderow—Anna, 76; Caroline, 135; Eunice, 128; Sarah Ida, 97; Rachel, 43.
Rudraff—Susanna, 18.
Rue—Anna, 103.
Rully—Mary, 71.
Rulon—Margaret, 74.
Rulty—Mary Ann, 36.
Rumford—Ann, 81.
Rumsey—Georgianra, 105.
Rushton—Annie Lyle, 110.
Russell—Lydia Aun, 39; Mary, 129.
Rutter—Eliza, 35.
Ryan—Mary Ann, 121; Sarah, 80.
Sack—Annie, 57.
Sage—Lizzie, 70.
Sailor—Lydia, 110.
Sampson—Sarah, 15.

Sanderlin—Emaline, 100.
Sanders—Rebecca, 26.
Sanford—Catherine, 115.
Sanman—Lucy, 49.
Saphor—Louisa, 125.
Sapp (Sap)—Amanda, 64; Emma, 105; Margaret, 23.
Sarchet—Sarah, 24.
Satour—Mary, 113.
Saunders—Sarah, 103.
Saunderson—Hannah, 112.
Saurman—Emma Ada, 81.
Sautter—Mary Melvina, 80.
Savage—Georgianna, 79.
Sawyer—Emma, 74.
Sayre (Sayres)—Mary, 117; Sarah, 9; Serena, 126.
Shaeffer—Florence Ida, 75.
Schanck—Emma, 73;
Schell—Anna Mary, 86.
Scheperkotter—Annie, 71; Henrietta, 90.
Schick—Rosie, 97.
Schilling—Anna, 68.
Schlicter—Bertha, 61.
Schnellbacker—Mary, 66.
Schnetzler—Margaret, 63.
Schoentag—Emma, 114.
Schofield—Frances, 32; Marietta, 119.
Schrader—Mary, 73.
Schreen—Phebe, 119.
Schreger—Rebecca, 24.
Schuar—Mary, 28.
Schubert—Annie, 117; Mary, 88.
Schuster—Teresse, 128.
Schwaal—Mary Ann, 21.
Scott—Angie, 107; Anna, 100; Mary Elizabeth, 36; Hannah, 17; Joanna, 46; Lucinda, 132; Margaret, 8; Martha, 133; Susie, 100.
Scover—Louisa, 26.
Scroggy—Anna, 91.

Seager—Hepzibah, 59.
Sears—Theresa, 24.
Sedler—Lucy, 92.
Sedman—Sarah, 9.
Seeds—Susan, 7.
Seeley—Alice, 51; Emma, 64; Margaret, 67; Mary, 134.
Seitz—Catharine, 78.
Sell—Mary Elizabeth, 96.
Semm—Elizabeth, 39.
Senor (Senior)—Elizabeth, 54; Emma Matilda, 114.
Seran (Serrein)—Deborah, 39; Susan, 81.
Sermon—Mary, 49.
Serriel—Nellie, 109.
Serverson—Mary Ann, 15.
Settle—Emma, 133.
Severns (Saverns)—Amanda, 62; Ann, 25; Christeana, 10; Elizabeth, 39; Emma, 62; Hannah, 25; Ida, 87.
Seward—Mary Elizabeth, 52.
Shack—Bertha, 85.
Shackler—Elizabeth, 94.
Shaffer—Mary, 137.
Shall—Sarah, 123.
Shane—Belle, 126; Caroline, 14; Henrietta, 48; Mary, 58.
Shanklin—Margaretta, 65.
Sharp—Edith, 62, 113; Jane, 45; Laura, 62; Leonora, 43; Marietta, 131; Rebecca, 27, 67; Sarah, 29; Sarah Jane, 48. Tamson, 32.
Shaw—Augustine Alberta, 62; Gussie, 126; Hannah, 119; Harriet, 17; Lina, 71; Mary, 18, 50; Priscilla Ann, 21; Susanna, 26; Wilhelmina, 86.
Shealy—Ella, 50.
Shee—Keziah, 91.
Sheets (Sheetz)—Anna, 98; Chrissie, 135; Mary, 34.
Shields—Anna, 8.
Sheldon—Anna, 64; Maria, 42.
Shellhorn—Julia, 109.
Shenoskea—Margaret, 29.
Shep—Elizabeth, 18.

Sheppard (Shephard)—Anthor, 88; Kate, 94; Lydia, 9; Mary, 85; Sallie, 69.
Sheridan—Catharine, 59.
Sherman—Carrie, 71.
Shermer—Sarah, 41.
Shick—Eliza, 44; Mary 3.
Shields—Ella, 61; Mary, 35.
Shill—Ella, 125.
Shimp—Mary, 121; Sarah Ann, 25.
Shinn—Beulah, 38; Eliza, 48; Elizabeth, 8; Emma Jane, 74; Joanna, 130; Laura, 81; Mary Ellen, 13; Pamelia, 121, Rebecca, 74.
Shires—Hannah, 44.
Shivers—Anne, 78; Annie, 60; Elizabeth 41, 55.
Shocker—Agnes, 104.
Shoemaker—Mary, 35; Rhuma, 14.
Shone—Sarah Jane, 54
Short (Shorts)—Jane, 33; Sarah, 85.
Shourds—Mary, 32.
Showel—Jane, 80.
Shreve (Shreeve)—Anna, 3; Eveline, 49; Rebecca, 61.
Shuster—Annie, 117.
Shute—Abigail Ann, 21; Emma, 33; Hannah, 35; Kate, 92; Lydia, 47; Mary, 37, 54; Mary Ann, 21.
Sickler—Anna, 63; Keziah, 25, 53; Nellie, 15; Sarah, 15, 61; Susan, 15.
Sigars—Elmira, 74.
Silver—Anna, 5.
Simmerman—Sarah, 25.
Simmons—Anna, 41.
Simpers—Eliza, 42.
Simpkins—Hannah, 95; Josephine, 124.
Simpson—Ellen, 74; Sarah, 118.
Sinclair, Rachel, 116.
Sines (Siness)—Eliza, 36; Phebe, 54.
Sing—Sophie, 79.
Singer—Saddie, 111.
Skill—Sarah, 66.

Sloan—Anna, 101; Hannah, 70; Mary, 4; Roxanna, 38.
Smalley—Angeline, 111.
Smallwood—Sarah, 47.

Smith—Alice, 97; Amanda, 107; Ann, 56; Ann Eliza, 5; Anna, 104; Anna Josephine, 132; Bertha, 66; Carrie, 98; Catharine, 44, 45, 95, 118, 133; Clara, 69; Deborah, 60; Edith, 81; Eliza, 21, 47; Elizabeth, 21, 31, 48, 67; Ella, 88; Emily, 52; George Anna, 86; Harriet, 83; Huldah, 29; Isabella, 49; Jane Ann, 5; Josephine, 113; Judith, 44; Kate, 69; Laura, 127; Lena, 31; Lizzie, 93; Lydia, 70, 119; Lydia Ann, 101; Margaret, 3, 4, 8, 47; Martha Matilda, 48; Mary, 9, 30, 41, 64, 81, 86, 100, 107; Mary Ann, 43; Mary Elizabeth, 90; Matilda Ann, 10; Paulena, 59; Phebe, 42; Pinkie, 98; Prisclila, 41; Rebecca, 23, 70; Sallie, 128; Sarah, 25, 39, 118; S. V. A., 32; Teresa, 129.

Smyth—Caroline, 45.
Snow—Esther Ann, 36.
Snuffin—Ida, 72; Rebecca, 56; Sarah, 35.
Snyder—Anna, 130; Cecelia, 19; Hannah, 90; Mary, 37, 136; Mary Ann, 113.
Soder—Rebecca, 16.
Solly—Jeanette, 129.
Solomon—Sarah, 99; Susannah, 36.
Solter—Ann, 18.
Somers (Summers)—Eliza, 129; Judith, 33; Maggie, 132; Maria, 129; Millicent, 123; Sarah, 29; Susan, 14.
Sooy—Harriet, 15; Sarah, 17.
Sorver—Kate, 89.
Souders—Anna, 70; Eliza Jane, 86.
Southard—Barbury Ann, 28; Margaret, 26.
Southwood—Lillian, 59.
Sparks—Anna, 98; Lydia, 53; Martha, 46; Mary, 98; Mary Anne, 32.
Speas—Sarah, 41.
Spence—Mary 102.
Spencer—Arabella, 71; Hannah, 19; Mary Ann, 106.
Sperry—Ada Maria, 113.
Spidal—Catharine, 21.
Spiegle—Patience, 52.

Spooner—Mary, 118.
Springer—Sybella, 65.
Staar—Angeline, 52.
Stack—Mary Ellen, 31.
Stackhouse—Harriet, 22; Mary, 74.
Stafford—Hannah, 5; Mary, 44; Patience, 50; Sallie, 135.
Stanger—Elizabeth, 56; Jane, 24; Mary, 21.
Stanley—Sarah, 130.
Stansberry—Louisa, 67.
Stanton—Emilie, 81.
Stark—Ruth, 60.
Starkey—Mary, 53.
Starn—Deborah, 15; Ellen, 74; Louisa, 16.
Starr—Elizabeth, 133.
Statt—Rebecca, 37.
Steelman—Lydia, 126; Marietta, 128; Mary, 110, 125; Sarah, 30; Sarah Ann, 35.
Steen—Eleanor, 106; Eunice.
Stehr—Anna, 35; Bertha, 29.
Steidler—Abigail, 22.
Stepanka—Matadystana, 136.
Sterling—Jennie, 119; Sarah, 57.
Stetser (Stetzer)—Elizabeth, 38; Mariah, 40; Mary, 130; Ruth, 112; Sarah, 20, 40; Susan, 22;
Stetson—Ruth, 67; Sallie, 135.
Stetzell—Rebecca, 131.
Steubear—Wilhelmina, 6.
Stevens—Annie, 44; Elizabeth, 25; Lillian, 66; Rachel, 104.
Stevenson, Anna, 43, 107; Annie, 83; Mary, 100; Sarah, 76, 103.
Steward—Elen, 14; Sarah, 48.
Stewart—Carrie, 74; Isabella, 99; Lucy, 93; Margaret, 60; Mary Emma, 113; Rebecca, 74; Sarah, 40, 95; Sophia, 101.
Stibbs—Hannah, 20.
Stigale—Martha Louise, 79.
Stiles—Emma, 102; Amanda Lavinia, 34; Mary, 57; Sarah 35.
Stillwell—Mattie, 78; Nellie, 61.
Stine—Margaret, 44.

Stites—Elizabeth, 88; Mary, 57.
Stockton—Anna, 127; Coralie, 72; Laura, 90; Lucretia, 111.
Stocup—Elianer, 7.
Stokeley (Stokly)—Margaret, 20; Sarah, 10;
Stokes—Annie, 85; Laura, 133; Sarah, 96; Sarah Ann, 44.
Stone—Annie, 102; Mary, 47; Teenie, 61.
Stoops—Julia, 9.
Stoughten—Mary, 90.
Stout—Ellen, 131; Henrietta, 90.
Stow—Ann, 64; Beulah, 46; Esther Ann, 52; Mary, 4, 86; Mary Ann, 33, 37.
Stoy—Virginia, 136.
Strang—Annie, 53.
Stratton—Charity, 101; Evelena, 86; Sarah, 4.
Streeper—Edith Viola, 70.
Street—Sarah, 120.
Stretch—Lydia, 97.
Stretcher—Bella, 81.
Strickland—Angeline, 21; Henrietta, 82.
Striker—Mary, 98.
String—Elizabeth, 12.
Strock—Amelia, 40; Anna, 51.
Stroop—Helen, 35.
Strovel—Mary, 100.
Stultz—Mary, 92.
Sturges (Sturgis)—Martha, 27; Mary, 24.
Sturr—Helena, 109.
Suster—Rebecca, 23.
Suff—Bennanner, 136.
Sullivan—Angelina, 71; Charlotta, 35; Emeline, 75; Hannah, 128; Mary, 44.
Suters—Anna. 25.
Suran—Charity, 36.
Surdam—Mary Martha, 91.
Sutten (Sutton) — Bridget, 96; Emma, 75; Mary, 55; Phebe, 29.
Sutts—Lydia, 101.
Swain—Rachel, 44.

Swartly—Catharine, 52.
Sweeten—Clara, 83; Ida Emily, 135; Mary, 98.
Swing—Celestia, 128; Ella, 115; Kate, 112; Louisa, 89.
Swope—Martha, 7.
Tarpine—Abigail, 49.
Tash—Emma, 109.
Tate (Tait)—Rachel, 38; Theressa, 5.
Tatem—Mehitable, 70.
Taylor—Amanda, 80; Anna, 115; Annie, 11; Belinda, 66; Elizabeth, 28, 96; Ellie, 59; Eveline, 95; Hannah, 52; Lizzie, 103, 104; Louisa, 69; Lydia, 55; Martha, 41; Mary, 76, 78.
Teagg—Caroline, 87.
Tebbett—Rosa, 85.
Templeton—M. E., 131.
Tenbner—Ollie, 81.
Tenner—Meminia, 24.
Tenney—Kate 124.
Terry—Elizabeth, 129.
Test—Fanny, 73.
Thackara (Thackery) — Elizabeth, 62; Mary, 52, 107; Rebecca, 71.
Thatcher—Elizabeth, 101; Jennie, 72.
Thomas—Amelia, 115; Anna, 63; Annie Eliza, 62; Elizabeth, 30; Eunice, 29; Hannah, 23, 48; Jennie, 113; Louis, 116; Lydia Ann, 15; Rebecca, 54, 128; Sarah, 121.
Thompson (Tompson)—Anna, 77; Bessie, 72; Elizabeth, 94; Elvira, 83; Emma, 101; Jane, 136; Margaret, 127; Maria, 59; Mary, 47, 72, 113, 118; Mary Ella, 62; Minerva, 92; Rebecca, 87; Sarah, 36, 49, 55, 77, 121.
Thorn—Beulah, 94; Catharine Ann, 15; Elizabeth, 3; Laura, 86; Sophia, 28.
Thornly—Sarah, 17.
Throckmorton—Lydia, 114.
Tice—Ann, 11; Anna, 17; Charlena, 83; Eliza, 65; Ellen Amelia, 17; Sophia, 6.
Till—Annie, 95.
Tillman—Ann, 62; Edith, 113; Susannah, 41.
Tilton—Isabella, 9.

Todd—Anna, 41, 118; Elizabeth, 112.
Tomlin—Caroline, 128; Lydian, 30.
Tomlinson—Barbara, 14; Mattie, 64.
Torman—Frances, 69.
Torp—Jane, 35.
Tourtelol—Henrietta, 104.
Townsend—Mary, 85,
Toy—Ann, 5; Elizabeth Ann, 11.
Tracey—Clara, 119.
Trafford—Lucy, 69.
Travis—Julia, 118.
Trays—Mary Ann, 27.
Treadway—Rebecca, 111; Roseanna, 96.
Treen—Sarah, 40.
Tribbitt—Susanna, 126.
Trimble—Jennie, 80; Maggie, 95.
Tripler—Elizabeth, 87.
Triplett—Maggie, 66.
Troth—Anna, 93; Laura, 49.
Trotter—Anne, 78; Susanna 120.
Trout—Adeline, 83.
Truxton—Sallie, 86.
Tucker—Acsah, 50; Amy, 5; Bathsheba, 13; Carrie, 114; Catharine, 64; Mary, 22.
Tuckert—Sarah, 120.
Tull—Emma, 101.
Tunnelin—Ruth, 123.
Turkington—Ellen, 11.
Turner—Abbie, 134; Abigail, 29; Ann, 7; Annie, 133; Catharine, 72; Elizabeth, 88; Lizzie, 98; Mary, 39; Sophia, 26; Susannah, 88.
Tweed—Ann, 34; Mary Jane 88.
Tyler—Helen, 122; Sarah Lillian, 125.
Tyman—Mary Isabel, 117.
Ulmer—Annie, 32.
Unpleby—Melvina, 58.
Upham—Lucy, 40; Mary Augusta, 88.
Urbar—Sallie, 88.

INDEX TO BRIDES 191

Urven—Rebecca, 14.
Valentine—Anna, 81; Ida, 72.
Vance—Sarah, 133.
Vandegrift (Vandergrift) — Maria, 32; Mehitable, 105; Susan, 105; Susanna, 73.
Vanderbilt—Sarah, 23.
Vanderslice—Anna, 128; Mary Ann, 15.
Vandeveer—Sarah, 50.
Vandyke—Phalina, 132.
Vanhart—Amanda, 24.
VanHorn—Elizabeth, 10, 124.
Vanicomb—Rebecca, 18.
Vanleer—Mira, 126.
VanMeter—Theresa, 90.
Vansant—Jemima, 86; Rebecca, 21.
VanSciver—Jane, 36; Lydia, 116; Mary, 10, 75; Minnie, 68; Sallie, 76.
Vanstavens—Louisa, 72.
VanWiggin—Bridget, 5.
Vare—Elizabeth, 33.
Venable—Abigail, 47; Anna, 95; Eliza, 79; Rachel Ann, 16.
Venel—Lydia Ann, 49.
Vernon—Laura, 112.
Vickers—Margaret, 112.
Vincent—Amelia, 130.
Vliet—Anna, 63.
Vogel—Pauline, 115..
Vogt—Willamina, 107.
Voigt—Augusta, 108.
Voll—Anna, 70.
Voorhees—Mary, 78.
Voutier—Elizabeth, 48; Susanna, 120.
Wagner—Ernestine, 62; Maggie, 119.
Waithman—Eleanor, 87; Josephine, 23.
Walker—Ann, 87; Belle, 70; Elizabeth, 52, 75, 101; Emily, 74; Hope Anna, 116; Jane, 15; Lizzie, 119; Maria, 134; Mary, 82; Sallie, 101; Sarah, 94.
Wall—Kate, 59; Lizzie, 81; Lucinda, 110; Mary 71.

Wallace—Carrie, 61; Julia, 92; Marian, 24.
Wallen (Wallin)—Catharine, 113; Hannah, 86.
Waller—Rebecca, 62.
Walsh—Catharine, 10.
Walthall—Evelyn, 98.
Walton—Louisa, 63.
Wannan—Jennie, 68; Rachel, 96.
Wany—Mary, 48.
Ward—Annie, 65.
Warden—Elizabeth, 90; Mary Jane, 37.
Wardle—Sarah, 90.
Ware—Clarinda, 121; Emeline, 28; Gertrude, 74; Harriet, 61.
Warfield—Elizabeth, 38.
Warner—Abigail, 52; Ann, 5; Mary, 134.
Warnock—Lydia, 63.
Warren—Anna, 58; Mary, 83.
Warrick—Mary, 70; Roxanna, 49; Theodosia, 93.
Warrington—Anna, 75; Deborah, 34; Elizabeth, 88; Kesiah, 43; Mary Emma, 106; Nancy, 21; Susan, 136.
Waters—Emma; 81; Leanna, 91.
Watkins—Sallie, 92.
Watson—Anna, 107; Barbary, 40; Catharine, 62; Eliza Ann, 13; Helen Rebecca, 81; Martha 52; Nancy, 112; Naomi, 10; Patience, 82; Rachel, 4, 112; Susan, 19.
Watts—Elizabeth, 13.
Way—Matilda, 132.
Weatherby—Anna, 68; Ruth, 63.
Weaver—Emma, 108; Mary Ann, 109.
Webb—Ann, 5; Georgianna, 127; Hannah, 11; Rebecca, 118.
Weber—Annie, 121.
Weeart—Emma, 75.
Weeks—Kate, 130; Margaret Sarah, 94 Rachel, 94; Sarah, 71, 117; Sarah Jane, 52.
Weintz—Harrietta, 85.
Weiser—Susan, 92.
Weiss—Sadie, 131.
Welden—Jane, 45.
Weldie—Elizabeth, 76.

INDEX TO BRIDES 193

Wells—Anna, 104, 132; Annie, 73; Annie Eliza, 26; Charlotte, 46; Martha, 33; Martha Ann, 18; Mary Ann, 112; Rebecca, 6; Sallie, 107.
Wensley—Caroline, 36.
Wentworth—Mary, 24.
Wentzel—Sarah, 41.
West—Elizabeth, 27; Rachel, 95.
Westcott (Westcoat)—Christina, 123; Elizabeth, 22; Elmira, 18; Mary, 66.
Westle—Jennie, 87.
Westsall—Elizabeth, 16.
Wetherell—Mary, 132.
Weymer—Nellie, 95.
Wheaton—Maria, 83; Mary, 26.
Whilldin—Mary, 87.
White—Dora, 66; Elizabeth, 49; Josephine, 78; Margaret, 31; Mary, 100; Mary Ann, 11; Sallie, 88; Virginia, 105.
Whitecar (Whiteker, Whitaker)—Elizabeth, 31; Harriet, 64; Mary, 31, 122; Sarah, 103.
Whitehead—Lucretia, 13.
Whitelock (Whitlock)—Eliza, 89; Mary, 117.
Whiteside—Elizabeth, 5.
Whitmore—Jennie, 45.
Whittington—Cordelia, 55.
Whittle—Martha Matilda, 42.
Wiatt—Mary, 110.
Wible—Henrietta, 53.
Wicks—Emma, 6.
Widdows—Ann, 97.
Wieland—Clara, 72.
Wier—Ellen, 93.
Wigo—Carrie, 65.
Wiley—Rebecca, 33.
Wilke—Susette, 34.
Wilkins—Caroline, 97; Emily, 129; Josephine, 92, 78; Mary, 80; Mary Ann, 9; Sallie, 3; Sarah, 38, 60.
Wilkinson—Annie, 119; Eliza, 136; Emma, 79.
Willard—Mary Josephine, 85.

Williams—Ann Eliza, 76; Ane Elizabeth, 5; Charlotte, 25; Deborah, 7; Elizabeth, 25, 66; Emily, 67; Emma, 63; Georgianna, 66; Hannah, 39; Jane, 131; J. F., 95; Josephine, 71; Louisa, 22; Margaret, 13, 31; Mary, 6, 19, 27, 102, 109, 129; Mary Josephine, 13; Mercy Ann, 16; Rachel, 57; Rebecca, 8, 16; Ruth, 31; Sallie, 40; Sarah, 3, 41; Stella Melissa, 75.

Williamson—Rachel, 8.

Willie (Willy)—Anna, 108; Cecelia, 85.

Willis—Ann, 13; Mary Ann, 82; Susan, 82.

Willitts (Willatts, Willets)—Almeda, 98; Eliza, 59; Francis 109; Mary, 63.

Wills—Abigail, 91; Clara, 74; Martha, 103; Priscilla, 105; Sarah, 21.

Wilmerton—Jeannie, 61.

Wilmot—Ann, 58; Rebecca 41.

Wilsey (Wiltse Wiltsey)—Annie, 81; Deborah, 31; Elizabeth, 94; Hannah, 29; Rachel, 66.

Wilson—Anna, 85, 124; Eliza Ann, 5; Emma, 27; Hannah, 35; Hanna Mary, 131; Harriet, 27, 105; Hester, 76; Jane, 10; Julia, 65; Julia Ann, 16; Lizzie, 81; Lydia Ann, 39; Mary, 74, 97, 99, 133; Mary Ann, 54; Mary Rebecca, 15; Millie, 116; Phebe, 43; Rachel, 83; Rebecca, 51; Sallie, 136; Sarah, 3; Violet, 36.

Wiltshire—Kate, 102.

Wincheater—Lydia, 121.

Winner—Ann Eliza Lavinia, 13; Mary, 82; Rebecca, 28.

Wise—Mary, 131.

Wiser—Mary, 40.

Witcraft—Martha, 136.

Witheat—Susan, 5.

Witten—Susan, 62.

Wolf (Wolfe)—Addie, 116; Maggie, 135; Mary, 123; Rebecca, 115.

Wolfsen—Annie, 81.

Wolohon—Helen, 78.

Wolverton—Rebecca, 64.

Wood (Woods)—Amelia, 94; Ann, 123; Anne, 72; Charlotte 29; Emma, 24, 75; Lizzie, 115; Laura, 62; Mary, 10, 55, 102,

INDEX TO BRIDES

123, 125; Rebecca, 10, 40, 69; Ruth, 115; Sarah, 60, 75; Victoria, 130.
  Woodfall—Ellen, 136; Mary, 129.
  Woodington—Mary Ann, 7.
  Woodland—Sarah, 16.
  Woodrow (Woodroe)—Emily, 83; Sallie, 126.
  Woodruff—Hannah, 37.
  Woodward—Frances, 76; Maggie, 126.
  Woolford—Harriet, 66; Sarah, 94.
  Woolmer—Catharine, 105.
  Woolston—Elfleda, 136.
  Wooster—Sallie, 98.
  Worley—Georgiana, 88.
  Worth—Nancy, 108.
  Worthy—Elizabeth, 70.
  Wreistner—Mary. 115.
  Wrifford—Mary, 79.
  Wriggins—Ella, 73; Lydia, 63.
  Wright—Dorcas, 42; Hannah, 80; Harriet, 124; Kate, 127; Laura, 61; Lydia, 125; Mariah 100; Mary, 93, 106; Rebecca, 52; Sarah, 30, 62.
  Wykand—Alena, 135.
  Wynkoop—Lizzie, 77.
  Wynocker—Caroline, 37.
  Yeager—Mary, 113; Minnie, 59.
  Yehner—Emeline, 85.
  Yohe—Caroline, 16.
  Yonker—Mary, 89.
  Yost—Anna, 77.
  Young—Alice, 88; Hannah Maria, 10; Lilas, 48; Mary, 80, 97; Phebe, 30; Sarah, 124; Susie, 137.
  Zepselum—Mary, 56.
  Zimborman—Anna, 116.
  Zimmerman—Barbara, 73, 81; Elizabeth, 42; Hannah, 113.

www.ingramcontent.com/pod-product-compliance
Lightning Source LLC
Chambersburg PA
CBHW020650300426
44112CB00007B/324